VOLUME 1: COMPREHENSIVE GUIDE TO PHARMACEUTICAL REGULATORY AFFAIRS

PRINCIPLES AND PRACTICES

MURALIDHAR RAO AKKALADEVI, VEERAREDDY PRABHAKAR REDDY

Contents

Volume 1: Comprehensive Guide To Pharmaceutical Regulatory Affairs

Principles and Practices

EDITED BY

Dr. Muralidhar Rao Akkaladevi

Principal,

St. Mary's College of Pharmacy,

Secunderabad, Telangana, India

Dr. Prabhakar Reddy Veerareddy

Head,

University College of Pharmaceutical Sciences,

Palamuru University,

Mahabubnagar, Telangana, India

Published by Notion Press

Notion Press, Inc.

800, West El Camino Real #180,

California, USA 94040

Notion Press Media Pvt Ltd

#7, Red Cross Road,

Egmore, Chennai, Tamil Nadu 600008

Email ID: publish@notionpress.com

Phone Number: +91 44 46315631

Preface

The pharmaceutical industry plays a crucial role in ensuring public health by developing, manufacturing, and regulating medications and healthcare products. This comprehensive guide aims to provide an in-depth understanding of pharmaceutical regulatory affairs, offering valuable insights for professionals, researchers, and students involved in this dynamic field.

The field of pharmaceutical regulatory affairs encompasses a wide range of activities, from the initial stages of drug development to post-marketing surveillance. Ensuring the safety, efficacy, and quality of pharmaceutical products is paramount, and regulatory practices are guided by stringent laws, regulations, guidelines, and standards. This book is designed to serve as a reliable reference for understanding these complex processes, providing practical knowledge and strategies for navigating the regulatory landscape.

We have meticulously compiled and organized the content to cover all essential aspects of pharmaceutical regulatory affairs. Our aim is to present the information in a clear and accessible manner, using simple Indian English to ensure that readers from diverse backgrounds can grasp the concepts without difficulty. Each chapter delves into specific regulatory practices, providing detailed explanations, case studies, and real-world applications to enhance understanding.

This guide is the result of extensive research and practical experience in the field. We have endeavored to make the material as error-free and comprehensive as possible, with the hope that it will serve as a valuable resource for both academic and professional pursuits. We believe that a solid understanding of regulatory practices is essential for ensuring the development of safe and effective pharmaceutical products, ultimately contributing to the betterment of global health.

We would like to express our gratitude to all those who have supported and contributed to the creation of this book. We hope that it will not only educate but also inspire readers to continue advancing their knowledge and expertise in pharmaceutical regulatory affairs.

Muralidhar Rao Akkaladevi
Prabhakar Reddy Veerareddy

CHAPTER ONE

Good Regulatory Practices

1.1 Introduction to Regulatory Practices

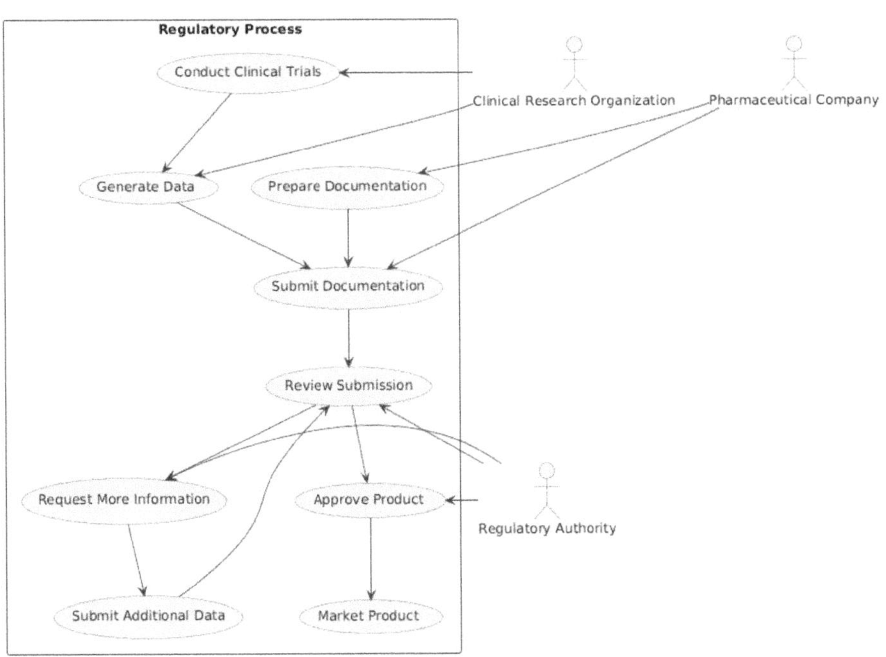

Regulatory Submissions and Approval Process

Regulatory practices in the pharmaceutical industry are essential for ensuring the safety, efficacy, and quality of drugs, medical devices, and other healthcare products. These practices encompass a wide range of activities, from the initial stages of drug development to post-marketing surveillance. Regulatory practices are guided by laws, regulations, guidelines, and standards set by regulatory authorities, which vary from country to country but share common goals of protecting public health and ensuring that products meet stringent safety and quality requirements.

Regulatory authorities, such as the **US Food and Drug Administration (FDA)**, the **European Medicines Agency (EMA)**, and the **Central Drugs Standard Control Organization (CDSCO)** in India, play crucial roles in overseeing and enforcing regulatory practices. These bodies establish guidelines and standards that manufacturers must follow throughout the product lifecycle. This lifecycle includes research and development, clinical trials, manufacturing, labeling, marketing, and post-marketing activities.

Good Regulatory Practices (GRP) are a set of principles that ensure the regulatory process is transparent, consistent, and efficient. These practices involve the development of regulatory frameworks, guidelines, and procedures that help streamline the approval process and maintain high standards for product safety and quality. GRP includes **Good Manufacturing Practices (GMP)**, **Good Laboratory Practices (GLP)**, and **Good Clinical Practices (GCP)**, each focusing on different aspects of the product lifecycle.

Good Manufacturing Practices (GMP)

GMP guidelines ensure that products are consistently produced and controlled according to quality standards. This includes proper design, monitoring, and control of manufacturing processes and facilities. Key aspects of GMP include the use of validated processes, stringent quality control measures, and thorough documentation. Compliance with GMP helps prevent contamination, mix-ups, and errors, ensuring that products are safe and effective.

Good Laboratory Practices (GLP)

GLP focuses on the quality and integrity of non-clinical laboratory studies. These practices ensure that studies are planned, performed, monitored, recorded, reported, and archived in a manner that allows for accurate and reliable results. GLP compliance involves detailed documentation of study protocols, standard operating procedures (SOPs), and the roles and responsibilities of personnel. This ensures that non-clinical studies provide valid data that can support regulatory submissions.

Good Clinical Practices (GCP)

GCP guidelines govern the conduct of clinical trials, ensuring the protection of human subjects and the integrity of data collected. GCP encompasses ethical and scientific quality standards for designing, conducting, recording, and reporting clinical trials. It includes the responsibilities of investigators, sponsors, and ethics committees, as well as requirements for informed consent, study protocols, and documentation. Adherence to GCP ensures that the rights, safety, and well-being of trial participants are safeguarded and that the data generated is credible.

Methodology and Procedures in Regulatory Practices

Regulatory practices involve a systematic approach to ensuring compliance with established guidelines and standards. This begins with a thorough understanding of the regulatory requirements relevant to the product and market in question. Companies must develop comprehensive regulatory strategies that outline the steps necessary to achieve compliance, from initial product development through to post-marketing surveillance.

1. **Regulatory Strategy Development:** This involves identifying applicable regulations and guidelines, assessing the regulatory environment, and defining a clear path to market. It includes planning for clinical trials, manufacturing, quality control, and post-marketing activities.
2. **Documentation and Submission:** Accurate and complete documentation is critical for regulatory compliance. This includes preparing regulatory submissions such as Investigational New Drug (IND) applications, New Drug Applications (NDA), and Abbreviated New Drug Applications (ANDA). Each submission must include detailed information on the product's safety, efficacy, and quality.
3. **Regulatory Review and Approval:** Regulatory authorities review submissions to ensure that products meet all necessary requirements. This involves evaluating data from clinical trials, manufacturing processes, and quality control measures. Authorities may request additional information or clarification before granting approval.

4. **Post-Marketing Surveillance:** After a product is approved and marketed, regulatory practices continue to ensure ongoing safety and efficacy. This includes monitoring adverse events, conducting post-marketing studies, and implementing risk management plans. Regulatory authorities may also conduct inspections and audits to ensure continued compliance with GMP, GLP, and GCP.

Importance of Regulatory Practices

Regulatory practices are vital for maintaining public trust in the pharmaceutical industry. They ensure that products are safe, effective, and of high quality, which is essential for protecting public health. By adhering to regulatory guidelines, companies can avoid costly recalls, legal issues, and damage to their reputation. Moreover, regulatory compliance facilitates international trade, allowing companies to market their products globally.

1.2 US Current Good Manufacturing Practices (cGMP)

Introduction

The **Current Good Manufacturing Practices (cGMP)** established by the United States Food and Drug Administration (FDA) are essential regulations that ensure the quality of pharmaceutical products. These practices are designed to ensure that products are consistently produced and controlled according to quality standards, minimizing the risks involved in pharmaceutical production. The cGMP regulations are detailed in **Title 21 of the Code of Federal Regulations (CFR), Parts 210 and 211**. These parts outline the minimum requirements for the methods, facilities, and controls used in the manufacturing, processing, and packing of drug products.

Key Principles of cGMP

The cGMP regulations encompass a broad range of activities and controls, focusing on several key areas:

1. **Quality Management System:** Companies must establish a robust quality management system (QMS) that includes detailed standard

operating procedures (SOPs) and quality control measures. The QMS ensures that all processes are controlled, and deviations are properly documented and investigated.

2. **Personnel Qualifications and Training**: Personnel involved in the manufacturing process must have appropriate education, training, and experience. Regular training programs are required to ensure that employees are updated on current practices and procedures.

3. **Facility and Equipment**: Manufacturing facilities must be designed and maintained to prevent contamination and mix-ups. Equipment used in production must be appropriately designed, cleaned, maintained, and calibrated to ensure consistent performance.

4. **Production and Process Controls**: Detailed written procedures must be established for production and process controls to ensure that products have the identity, strength, quality, and purity they are supposed to have. This includes validating critical steps in the manufacturing process to ensure they produce the desired outcome.

5. **Packaging and Labeling Controls**: Packaging operations must be designed to prevent mix-ups and ensure that labels accurately reflect the product's identity and other essential information. This includes the use of barcode systems and other technology to reduce errors.

6. **Laboratory Controls**: Adequate laboratory facilities must be available for testing and approval of components, containers, in-process materials, and finished products. This includes the establishment of specifications, standards, sampling plans, and test procedures.

7. **Records and Reports**: Detailed records must be maintained for all aspects of the manufacturing process. This includes batch production records, equipment cleaning and use logs, and records of all laboratory tests performed. These records must be retained for at least one year after the expiration date of the batch.

8. **Returned and Salvaged Products**: Procedures must be in place to handle returned and salvaged products. This includes examining returned products for possible defects and ensuring that salvaged products meet all required quality standards before being reintroduced into the market.

Implementation and Compliance

Implementing cGMP requires a systematic approach to ensure that every aspect of the manufacturing process is controlled. Companies must conduct regular internal audits to verify compliance with cGMP standards and identify areas for improvement. Additionally, the FDA conducts inspections of manufacturing facilities to ensure compliance with cGMP regulations.

Quality Risk Management

A critical component of cGMP is quality risk management, which involves identifying and controlling potential risks to product quality. This includes performing risk assessments to evaluate the potential impact of deviations and implementing control measures to mitigate identified risks. Risk management helps ensure that processes remain in control and that products consistently meet quality standards.

Continuous Improvement

Continuous improvement is a key principle of cGMP. Companies are encouraged to regularly review and update their processes, procedures, and technologies to enhance product quality and manufacturing efficiency. This involves analyzing data from quality control tests, production records, and customer feedback to identify opportunities for improvement.

Challenges and Solutions

Implementing cGMP can be challenging due to the complexity of pharmaceutical manufacturing processes and the need for rigorous documentation and control. Common challenges include maintaining consistent training programs, ensuring proper equipment maintenance, and managing extensive documentation requirements. Solutions to these challenges include investing in automated systems to streamline documentation, implementing robust training programs, and using advanced technologies to monitor and control manufacturing processes.

1.3 EC Principles of GMP (Directive 91/356/EEC)

Introduction

The **European Community (EC) Principles of Good Manufacturing Practices (GMP)** are established under **Directive 91/356/EEC**. This directive sets the legal framework for GMP in the manufacture of medicinal products for human use within the European Union (EU). The principles outlined in this directive are designed to ensure that products are consistently produced and controlled to the quality standards appropriate to their intended use. This includes the requirements for manufacturing, processing, packaging, and storage of medicinal products.

Key Principles of EC GMP

The EC Principles of GMP focus on several critical areas to ensure the quality and safety of medicinal products. These principles are detailed in Articles 6 to 14 of Directive 91/356/EEC.

Article 6: Quality Assurance

Quality assurance is the overarching principle of GMP. It ensures that medicinal products are designed and developed in a way that meets the requirements for quality and safety. This includes establishing a comprehensive quality management system (QMS) that covers all aspects of production, from the initial development stages to the final release of the product. The QMS should ensure that:

- All manufacturing processes are clearly defined and controlled.
- Necessary resources, including adequately trained personnel, are available.
- Adequate records are maintained to demonstrate that all steps required by the defined procedures have been followed.
- Any deviations from the standard procedures are documented and investigated.

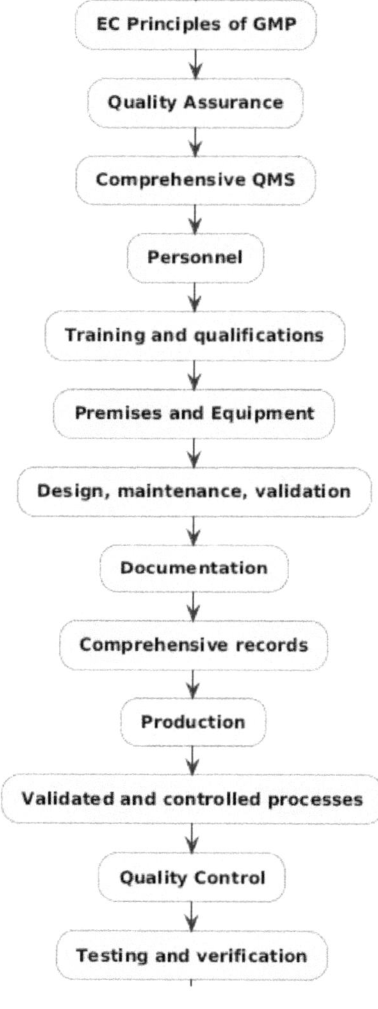

EC Principles of GMP

Article 7: Personnel

Personnel involved in the manufacture of medicinal products must have the appropriate qualifications and experience. Training programs should be in place to ensure that all employees are adequately trained in GMP principles and procedures. Key responsibilities include:

- Ensuring that personnel at all levels are aware of the critical aspects of GMP.
- Providing continuous training to keep personnel updated with the latest GMP standards.
- Clearly defining the roles and responsibilities of all personnel involved in the manufacturing process.

Article 8: Premises and Equipment

Manufacturing premises and equipment must be designed, located, and maintained to suit the intended operations. Key requirements include:

- Designing premises to minimize the risk of errors and contamination.
- Ensuring that equipment is properly maintained, cleaned, and calibrated.
- Implementing procedures for the validation and qualification of equipment and premises.

Article 9: Documentation

Comprehensive documentation is a cornerstone of GMP. Proper documentation ensures traceability and accountability throughout the manufacturing process. Essential documents include:

- Standard Operating Procedures (SOPs) for all manufacturing processes.
- Batch records for each stage of production.
- Specifications and test methods for raw materials, intermediates, and finished products.
- Records of equipment maintenance, cleaning, and calibration.

Article 10: Production

Production operations must follow clearly defined procedures to ensure consistency and control. This includes:

- Validating critical production processes to ensure they achieve the desired outcomes.
- Monitoring process parameters and product attributes to maintain control.
- Implementing in-process controls to detect and correct deviations in real-time.

Article 11: Quality Control

Quality control involves testing and verifying that products meet predefined quality standards. This includes:

- Establishing specifications for raw materials, in-process materials, and finished products.
- Conducting thorough testing at various stages of production.
- Investigating and documenting any deviations or out-of-specification results.

Article 12: Contract Manufacture and Analysis

When part of the manufacturing process is contracted out, the principles of GMP must be maintained. This requires:

- Clearly defining the responsibilities of both the contract giver and contract acceptor.
- Ensuring that the contract acceptor complies with GMP standards.
- Implementing appropriate quality agreements and regular audits of the contract acceptor.

Article 13: Complaints and Product Recalls

A robust system for handling complaints and product recalls is essential to ensure product safety. This includes:

- Implementing procedures for the prompt investigation of complaints.
- Maintaining records of complaints and the actions taken.
- Establishing a system for the timely recall of defective products.

Article 14: Self-Inspection

Regular self-inspections are critical for ensuring ongoing compliance with GMP. This involves:

- Conducting regular internal audits to assess compliance with GMP standards.
- Documenting the findings of these audits and taking corrective actions where necessary.
- Reviewing the effectiveness of corrective actions to ensure continuous improvement.

Implementation and Compliance

Implementing the EC Principles of GMP requires a comprehensive approach that integrates quality management, risk management, and continuous improvement. Companies must establish robust quality management systems that include detailed procedures, thorough documentation, and continuous training. Regular audits, both internal and external, are essential to ensure compliance and identify areas for improvement.

1.4 WHO cGMP Guidelines

Introduction

The **World Health Organization (WHO) Current Good Manufacturing Practices (cGMP) Guidelines** are a set of international standards that ensure the quality, safety, and efficacy of pharmaceutical products. These guidelines are critical for countries that may not have their own comprehensive regulatory frameworks and serve as a benchmark for manufacturing practices worldwide. The WHO cGMP guidelines are designed to be flexible enough to be applicable to a wide range of settings, from small-scale manufacturers to large, complex operations.

Key Principles of WHO cGMP Guidelines

The WHO cGMP guidelines cover all aspects of pharmaceutical production, emphasizing quality management, personnel, facilities and equipment, documentation, production, quality control, contract manufacturing, complaints, and self-inspection. These guidelines ensure that pharmaceutical products are consistently produced and controlled to meet the quality standards appropriate to their intended use.

Quality Management

The foundation of WHO cGMP is a robust **quality management system (QMS)**. This system ensures that pharmaceutical products are of the required quality for their intended use. The key elements of a QMS include:

- **Quality Assurance (QA):** Ensures that products are consistently produced and controlled according to quality standards.
- **Quality Control (QC):** Involves the testing of raw materials, in-process materials, and finished products to ensure they meet specified standards.
- **Good Manufacturing Practices (GMP):** Provides guidelines for the systematic production and quality control of pharmaceutical products.

Personnel

Qualified and adequately trained personnel are crucial for maintaining cGMP standards. The guidelines emphasize:

- **Training:** Regular and comprehensive training programs to keep employees updated on cGMP standards and procedures.
- **Qualifications:** Personnel must have the appropriate education, training, and experience for their roles.
- **Hygiene:** Strict hygiene practices to prevent contamination and ensure the safety of pharmaceutical products.

Facilities and Equipment

The design, location, and maintenance of facilities and equipment are vital to ensure the quality of pharmaceutical products. Key aspects include:

- **Design and Layout:** Facilities should be designed to minimize risks of errors and contamination. This includes appropriate air handling systems to control air quality.
- **Maintenance:** Regular maintenance and calibration of equipment to ensure consistent performance.
- **Validation:** Validation of critical processes and equipment to ensure they produce consistent and reliable results.

Documentation

Accurate and complete documentation is a cornerstone of WHO cGMP. Documentation ensures traceability and accountability throughout the manufacturing process. Essential documents include:

- **Standard Operating Procedures (SOPs):** Detailed instructions on how to perform tasks and processes.
- **Batch Records:** Documentation of all activities and controls related to the production of each batch of product.

- **Specifications:** Detailed criteria for raw materials, in-process materials, and finished products.
- **Logbooks:** Records of equipment usage, maintenance, and cleaning.

Production

Production processes must be clearly defined, controlled, and monitored to ensure consistency and quality. This includes:

- **Process Validation:** Validating critical steps in the production process to ensure they consistently produce the desired outcome.
- **In-Process Controls:** Monitoring production processes in real-time to detect and correct deviations.
- **Contamination Control:** Implementing measures to prevent contamination and cross-contamination of products.

Quality Control

Quality control involves testing and verifying that products meet predefined quality standards. This includes:

- **Sampling and Testing:** Conducting tests on raw materials, in-process materials, and finished products to ensure they meet specifications.
- **Stability Testing:** Ensuring that products maintain their quality, safety, and efficacy throughout their shelf life.
- **Release Procedures:** Only releasing products for sale or distribution after they have been tested and found to comply with all quality standards.

Contract Manufacture and Analysis

When part of the manufacturing process is contracted out, the WHO cGMP guidelines ensure that the principles of GMP are maintained. This includes:

- **Quality Agreements:** Clearly defining the responsibilities of the contract giver and contract acceptor.
- **Audits:** Regularly auditing contract facilities to ensure they comply with cGMP standards.
- **Documentation:** Ensuring that all contracted activities are properly documented and traceable.

Complaints and Product Recalls

A robust system for handling complaints and product recalls is essential to ensure product safety. This includes:

- **Complaint Handling:** Implementing procedures for the prompt investigation and resolution of complaints.
- **Recall Procedures:** Establishing a system for the timely recall of defective products to protect public health.
- **Root Cause Analysis:** Investigating the root causes of complaints and recalls to prevent recurrence.

Self-Inspection

Regular self-inspections are critical for ensuring ongoing compliance with cGMP. This involves:

- **Internal Audits:** Conducting regular internal audits to assess compliance with cGMP standards.
- **Corrective Actions:** Implementing corrective actions to address any deficiencies identified during audits.
- **Continuous Improvement:** Continuously reviewing and improving processes and procedures to enhance quality and compliance.

Implementation and Compliance

Implementing WHO cGMP requires a systematic approach that integrates quality management, risk management, and continuous improvement.

Companies must establish robust quality management systems, conduct regular training, and maintain thorough documentation. Regular internal and external audits are essential to ensure compliance and identify areas for improvement.

Challenges and Solutions

Implementing WHO cGMP guidelines can be challenging, particularly for smaller manufacturers or those in resource-limited settings. Common challenges include maintaining consistent training programs, ensuring proper equipment maintenance, and managing extensive documentation requirements. Solutions to these challenges include investing in automated systems to streamline documentation, implementing robust training programs, and using advanced technologies to monitor and control manufacturing processes.

1.5 Good Automated Manufacturing Practice (GAMP-5)

Introduction

The **Good Automated Manufacturing Practice (GAMP-5)** is a set of guidelines designed to ensure that automated systems used in pharmaceutical manufacturing are reliable and fit for their intended purpose. Developed by the International Society for Pharmaceutical Engineering (ISPE), GAMP-5 provides a risk-based approach to the validation of automated systems, emphasizing product quality, data integrity, and patient safety. The guidelines help manufacturers implement, validate, and maintain computerized systems efficiently and effectively.

Key Principles of GAMP-5

GAMP-5 is built around several core principles, which focus on a life cycle approach to computerized systems, emphasizing risk management and quality by design. These principles ensure that systems are designed, tested, and maintained to meet regulatory requirements and industry standards.

Quality by Design

Quality by Design (QbD) is a fundamental principle of GAMP-5. It involves designing automated systems with quality built into every stage of development. This proactive approach helps identify and mitigate risks early in the system's life cycle, ensuring that the final product meets all quality and regulatory standards.

Life Cycle Approach

The GAMP-5 guidelines advocate a life cycle approach to the development and management of computerized systems. This involves several phases:

- **Concept and Planning:** Define the system requirements, scope, and objectives. Conduct a preliminary risk assessment to identify potential issues.
- **Specification:** Develop detailed specifications for the system, including functional, operational, and performance requirements. This phase also includes the development of user requirements specifications (URS) and functional specifications (FS).
- **Design and Configuration:** Design the system architecture and configure software and hardware components to meet the specified requirements.
- **Verification and Testing:** Conduct thorough testing to verify that the system meets all specified requirements. This includes installation qualification (IQ), operational qualification (OQ), and performance qualification (PQ).
- **Implementation:** Implement the system in the operational environment, ensuring that all procedures and controls are in place.
- **Operation and Maintenance:** Operate and maintain the system, conducting regular reviews and updates to ensure continued compliance and performance.
- **Decommissioning:** When the system is no longer needed, decommission it in a controlled manner, ensuring that all data is securely archived and the system is properly disposed of.

Risk Management

Risk management is a critical component of GAMP-5. The guidelines emphasize a risk-based approach to system validation, focusing resources on areas that impact product quality and patient safety. Key steps in the risk management process include:

- **Risk Assessment:** Identify and assess potential risks associated with the automated system. This involves evaluating the likelihood and impact of each risk.
- **Risk Mitigation:** Implement controls and measures to mitigate identified risks. This may include design changes, additional testing, or enhanced monitoring.
- **Risk Review:** Regularly review and update the risk assessment to account for changes in the system or its environment.

Scalable Approach

GAMP-5 promotes a scalable approach to validation, allowing manufacturers to tailor their efforts based on the complexity and risk associated with the system. This ensures that resources are used efficiently, focusing on critical areas that impact product quality and compliance.

Implementation of GAMP-5

Implementing GAMP-5 involves several key steps, each contributing to the overall goal of ensuring that automated systems are reliable and compliant.

Defining System Requirements

The first step in implementing GAMP-5 is to clearly define the system requirements. This includes developing a detailed user requirements specification (URS) that outlines what the system needs to do. The URS should be comprehensive, covering all functional, operational, and performance requirements.

Developing Specifications

Once the system requirements are defined, the next step is to develop detailed specifications. This includes functional specifications (FS), which describe how the system will meet the user requirements, and design specifications (DS), which detail the system architecture and configuration.

System Design and Configuration

The system design and configuration phase involves designing the system architecture and configuring the software and hardware components to meet the specified requirements. This phase also includes developing and documenting procedures for system operation, maintenance, and security.

Verification and Testing

Verification and testing are critical to ensuring that the system meets all specified requirements. This involves conducting installation qualification (IQ), operational qualification (OQ), and performance qualification (PQ) tests. Each of these tests serves a specific purpose:

- **Installation Qualification (IQ):** Verifies that the system components are installed correctly and according to specifications.
- **Operational Qualification (OQ):** Tests the system's functionality to ensure it operates as intended under various conditions.
- **Performance Qualification (PQ):** Confirms that the system performs consistently and reliably in the operational environment.

Documentation

Documentation is a key aspect of GAMP-5 implementation. Comprehensive documentation ensures traceability and accountability throughout the system's life cycle. Essential documents include:

- **Validation Plan:** Outlines the overall validation strategy, including scope, objectives, and responsibilities.

- **Test Plans and Reports:** Document the procedures and results of IQ, OQ, and PQ tests.
- **Standard Operating Procedures (SOPs):** Provide detailed instructions for system operation, maintenance, and security.
- **Change Control Records:** Track changes to the system and ensure they are properly reviewed and approved.

Operation and Maintenance

Once the system is implemented, it must be operated and maintained according to established procedures. This includes regular monitoring, maintenance, and updates to ensure continued compliance and performance. Periodic reviews and audits help identify areas for improvement and ensure that the system remains aligned with regulatory requirements.

Decommissioning

When the system is no longer needed, it must be decommissioned in a controlled manner. This involves securely archiving all relevant data, removing the system from operation, and properly disposing of hardware and software components. Decommissioning should be documented and conducted in accordance with established procedures to ensure traceability and compliance.

1.6 Medical Device and IVDs Global Harmonization Task Force (GHTF) Guidance Documents

Introduction

The **Global Harmonization Task Force (GHTF)** was established in 1992 as a partnership between regulatory authorities and industry representatives from Europe, the United States, Canada, Japan, and Australia. Its primary aim was to harmonize the regulatory requirements for medical devices and in vitro diagnostics (IVDs) across different regions. The GHTF has since been succeeded by the **International Medical Device Regulators Forum**

(IMDRF), but its guidance documents remain influential in shaping global regulatory practices. These documents provide a comprehensive framework to ensure the safety, efficacy, and quality of medical devices and IVDs.

Key Principles of GHTF Guidance Documents

The GHTF guidance documents cover various aspects of medical device regulation, focusing on harmonizing standards to facilitate international trade and ensure consistent product quality and safety. The key principles include:

Regulatory Framework

The GHTF guidance documents outline a regulatory framework that includes the classification of medical devices and IVDs based on risk, requirements for conformity assessment, and post-market surveillance. This framework helps ensure that devices meet safety and performance standards appropriate to their intended use.

Device Classification

Medical devices and IVDs are classified into different categories based on the level of risk they pose to patients and users. The classification system typically includes four classes:

- **Class I:** Low risk (e.g., surgical instruments, examination gloves)
- **Class II:** Medium risk (e.g., infusion pumps, diagnostic ultrasound)
- **Class III:** High risk (e.g., pacemakers, heart valves)
- **Class IV:** Very high risk (e.g., implantable defibrillators, complex IVDs)

Class	Risk Level	Examples
Class I	Low	Surgical instruments, examination gloves
Class II	Medium	Infusion pumps, diagnostic ultrasound
Class III	High	Pacemakers, heart valves
Class IV	Very High	Implantable defibrillators, complex IVDs

Fig: Regulatory Submissions and Approval Process

Conformity Assessment

Conformity assessment involves evaluating whether a medical device or IVD meets the regulatory requirements for safety and performance. The GHTF guidance documents recommend a risk-based approach, where higher-risk devices undergo more rigorous assessment processes. Key elements include:

- **Quality Management System (QMS):** Implementing a QMS that complies with ISO 13485 standards to ensure consistent product quality.
- **Design and Manufacturing Controls:** Ensuring that devices are designed and manufactured to meet specified requirements.
- **Clinical Evaluation:** Conducting clinical trials and evaluations to demonstrate the safety and efficacy of the device.
- **Documentation:** Maintaining comprehensive documentation to support the conformity assessment process.

Post-Market Surveillance

Post-market surveillance is crucial for monitoring the performance of medical devices and IVDs after they have been released to the market. The GHTF guidance documents emphasize the importance of:

- **Adverse Event Reporting:** Implementing systems for reporting and investigating adverse events and incidents involving medical devices.
- **Periodic Safety Update Reports (PSUR):** Regularly submitting reports on the safety and performance of devices.
- **Field Safety Corrective Actions (FSCA):** Taking corrective actions when necessary to address safety issues, such as product recalls or updates.

Regulatory Compliance and Harmonization

The GHTF guidance documents promote harmonization of regulatory requirements across different regions to facilitate international trade and reduce regulatory burdens. This includes:

- **Common Submission Dossier Template (CSDT):** A standardized format for regulatory submissions to streamline the approval process.
- **Summary Technical Documentation (STED):** A comprehensive document that summarizes the technical information and evidence supporting the safety and performance of a device.

Implementation of GHTF Guidance Documents

Implementing GHTF guidance documents requires manufacturers to adopt a systematic approach to compliance, ensuring that all aspects of the device lifecycle are controlled and documented.

Establishing a Quality Management System

A key step in implementing GHTF guidelines is establishing a Quality Management System (QMS) that complies with ISO 13485 standards. The QMS should cover all aspects of design, manufacturing, and post-market activities, ensuring consistent product quality and regulatory compliance.

Device Classification and Risk Assessment

Manufacturers must classify their devices based on the level of risk and conduct a thorough risk assessment. This involves evaluating potential hazards associated with the device and implementing controls to mitigate these risks. The risk assessment should be documented and regularly reviewed to ensure it remains current.

Conformity Assessment Procedures

Depending on the classification and risk level of the device, manufacturers must follow appropriate conformity assessment procedures. This includes:

- **Design Verification and Validation:** Ensuring that the device design meets all specified requirements and performs as intended.
- **Clinical Evaluation:** Conducting clinical trials and evaluations to demonstrate the device's safety and efficacy.
- **Regulatory Submissions:** Preparing and submitting the Common Submission Dossier Template (CSDT) and Summary Technical Documentation (STED) to regulatory authorities.

Post-Market Surveillance and Vigilance

Implementing robust post-market surveillance systems is essential for monitoring the performance of medical devices and IVDs. This includes:

- **Adverse Event Reporting Systems:** Establishing procedures for detecting, reporting, and investigating adverse events.
- **Field Safety Corrective Actions (FSCA):** Implementing corrective actions, such as product recalls or updates, to address safety issues.
- **Periodic Safety Update Reports (PSUR):** Regularly submitting reports on the safety and performance of devices to regulatory authorities.

Challenges and Solutions

Implementing GHTF guidance documents can be challenging, particularly for small manufacturers or those operating in multiple regions with different regulatory requirements. Common challenges include maintaining consistent quality standards, ensuring comprehensive documentation, and managing regulatory submissions. Solutions to these challenges include:

- **Investing in Training:** Providing regular training for personnel on GHTF guidelines and regulatory requirements.

- **Using Advanced Technologies:** Implementing automated systems for documentation, risk management, and post-market surveillance.
- **Collaborating with Regulatory Experts:** Engaging regulatory consultants or experts to ensure compliance with GHTF guidelines and streamline the approval process.

Overview of Good Manufacturing Practices (GMP) Key Activities and Interactions

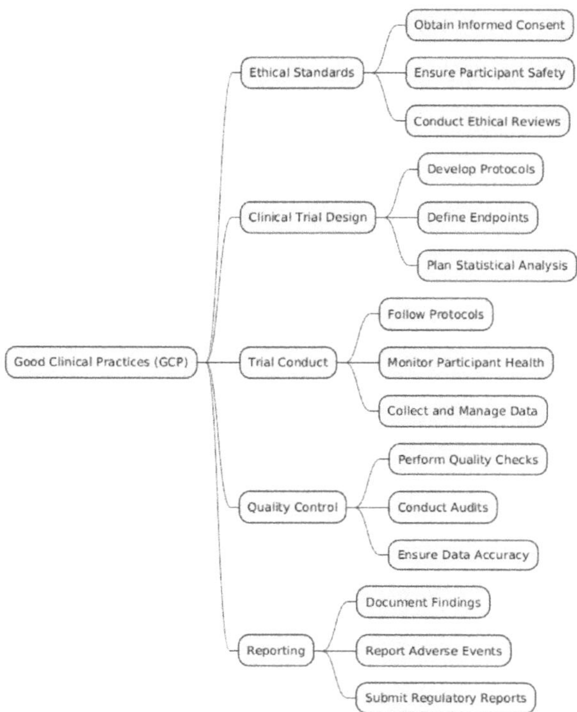

Overview of Good Clinical Practices (GCP) Key Activities and Interactions

CHAPTER TWO

Good Laboratory Practices

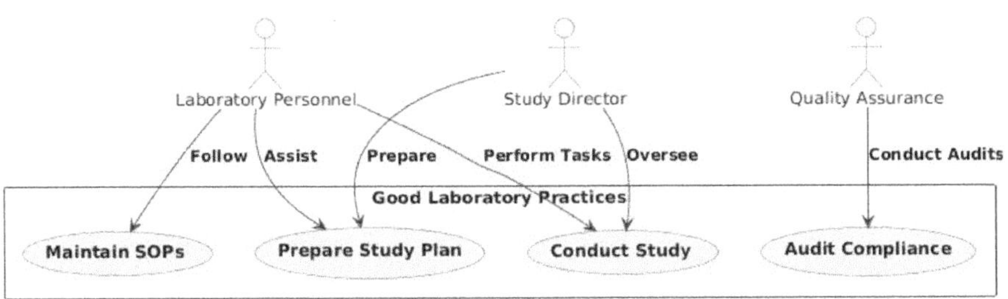

Fig: Good Laboratory Practices

2.1 INTRODUCTION TO GOOD LABORATORY PRACTICES

Good Laboratory Practices (GLP) are a set of principles intended to ensure the quality and integrity of non-clinical laboratory studies. These principles were first established by the Organisation for Economic Co-operation and Development (OECD) in 1979. The main goal of GLP is to ensure that the data generated in laboratories are reliable, reproducible, and can be used to support research, regulatory submissions, and risk assessments. GLP encompasses various aspects of laboratory management and operations, including study planning, performance, monitoring, recording, reporting, and archiving. It is essential for ensuring that laboratories operate to the highest standards, thereby providing confidence in the safety and efficacy of the products being tested.

Study Planning and Design

A fundamental aspect of GLP is the meticulous planning and design of studies. This includes the preparation of a detailed study plan or protocol, which outlines the objectives, methodology, data collection methods, and statistical analysis procedures. The study plan must be approved by the study director, who is responsible for the overall conduct of the study. Key elements in the study design include defining the test and control substances, specifying the test system (e.g., animals, cells, or biochemical systems), and detailing the experimental procedures. Adhering to the study plan ensures that the study is conducted in a systematic and reproducible manner.

Personnel and Training

The quality of a laboratory's work is heavily dependent on the competence and training of its personnel. Under GLP, it is mandatory that all staff involved in the study are adequately qualified and trained for their specific roles. Training records must be maintained, and personnel should receive continuous training to stay updated with the latest techniques and regulations. The study director, as the key individual responsible for the study, must possess the necessary scientific expertise and experience to oversee the study effectively.

Standard Operating Procedures (SOPs)

Standard Operating Procedures (SOPs) are detailed, written instructions designed to achieve uniformity in the performance of specific functions. SOPs are a critical component of GLP, providing a framework for conducting all routine operations within the laboratory. These include procedures for handling test and control substances, operating equipment, performing tests, and managing data. Adherence to SOPs ensures that each aspect of the laboratory's work is performed consistently and accurately, thereby minimizing variability and enhancing the reliability of the results.

Test Systems and Environment

The test systems used in GLP studies must be carefully selected and managed. Whether using animal models, cell cultures, or biochemical assays, it is crucial to ensure that the test systems are appropriate for the study objectives and are maintained under optimal conditions. Environmental controls, such as temperature, humidity, and light cycles, must be monitored and recorded to prevent any adverse effects on the test systems. Proper housing, care, and handling of animal subjects are also paramount, adhering to ethical standards and minimizing stress to the animals.

Equipment Calibration and Maintenance

The reliability of laboratory data is highly dependent on the proper functioning of laboratory equipment. GLP requires that all equipment used in the study be calibrated and maintained regularly. Calibration ensures that the equipment provides accurate and precise measurements, while maintenance prevents breakdowns and ensures the equipment operates at optimal performance. Detailed records of calibration and maintenance activities must be kept, and any deviations or malfunctions must be promptly addressed and documented.

Data Management and Integrity

One of the core principles of GLP is ensuring the integrity of the data generated during the study. Data management includes the accurate recording, verification, storage, and retrieval of study data. All raw data, including observations, measurements, and calculations, must be recorded promptly, accurately, and legibly. Any changes or corrections to the data must be clearly documented, including the reason for the change, the date, and the identity of the person making the change. This transparency ensures that the data is reliable and can be independently verified.

Quality Assurance

Quality assurance (QA) plays a pivotal role in GLP by providing an independent assessment of the study's conduct and the data generated. QA personnel are responsible for auditing the study processes and ensuring compliance with GLP regulations. They review study plans, SOPs, and data records, conduct facility inspections, and verify that all procedures are followed correctly. QA audits help identify and rectify any issues that could compromise the integrity of the study, thereby ensuring the validity of the study outcomes.

Reporting and Archiving

The final stage of a GLP-compliant study involves the preparation of a comprehensive study report. The report must include all relevant data, methodologies, results, and conclusions, as well as any deviations from the study plan or SOPs. The study director is responsible for the accuracy and completeness of the report, which must be reviewed and approved by QA personnel. After the study is completed, all records, including raw data, study plans, SOPs, and reports, must be archived in a secure and accessible manner. Proper archiving ensures that the study data can be retrieved and reviewed if needed for regulatory submissions or future reference.

2.2 USFDA GLP REGULATIONS (SUBPART A TO SUBPART K)

The US Food and Drug Administration (USFDA) has established comprehensive Good Laboratory Practice (GLP) regulations to ensure the quality and integrity of non-clinical laboratory studies. These regulations are outlined in Title 21, Code of Federal Regulations (CFR), Part 58, and are divided into several subparts, from Subpart A to Subpart K. Each subpart addresses specific aspects of laboratory practices and procedures, aiming to create a framework for consistent and reliable study conduct.

Subpart A - General Provisions

Subpart A outlines the **scope** and applicability of GLP regulations. It defines key terms such as "study director," "quality assurance unit," and "test system." This subpart sets the foundational principles, stating that the regulations apply to all non-clinical laboratory studies intended to support applications for research or marketing permits for products regulated by the FDA, including drugs, biological products, and medical devices. The objective is to ensure that these studies are conducted in a manner that guarantees data reliability.

Subpart B - Organization and Personnel

Subpart B focuses on the **organization and personnel** involved in laboratory studies. It mandates that each testing facility must have a clearly defined organizational structure with designated roles and responsibilities. The **study director** is identified as the single point of control for the study, responsible for its overall conduct and interpretation of results. Personnel involved in the study must be adequately trained and qualified for their roles, and **training records** must be maintained. This subpart emphasizes the importance of proper staffing and management to ensure the integrity of the study.

Subpart C - Facilities

Subpart C addresses the **facilities** used for conducting studies. It requires that testing facilities be of suitable size, construction, and location to meet the requirements of the study. The design and construction of the facilities must minimize any potential for cross-contamination or environmental influences that could affect the study. This includes provisions for proper housing of **test systems**, control of environmental conditions, and separation of activities to prevent **cross-contamination**. The facilities must be equipped with adequate resources to support the study's needs.

Subpart D - Equipment

Subpart D specifies requirements for **equipment** used in laboratory studies. All equipment must be of appropriate design and capacity, and it must be suitably located for its intended use. Equipment must be regularly **calibrated, maintained, and inspected** to ensure accuracy and reliability. Records of all maintenance, calibration, and inspection activities must be kept, and any equipment found to be defective must be promptly repaired or replaced. This subpart ensures that all instruments and devices function correctly to generate reliable data.

Subpart E - Testing Facilities Operation

Subpart E pertains to the **operation** of testing facilities. It requires that standard operating procedures (SOPs) be established and followed for all aspects of study conduct. SOPs must cover procedures for the handling, storage, and use of test and control substances, as well as the operation and calibration of equipment. Deviations from SOPs must be documented and justified. This subpart also mandates that all data generated during the study be recorded promptly, accurately, and in accordance with the SOPs, ensuring **data integrity**.

Subpart F - Test and Control Articles

Subpart F deals with **test and control articles** used in the studies. It mandates that the identity, strength, purity, and composition of these articles be adequately characterized. This includes proper storage, handling, and documentation of all test and control articles to prevent **contamination** or deterioration. Records must be maintained to track the receipt, use, and disposal of these substances, ensuring that they are used correctly and consistently throughout the study.

Subpart G - Protocol for and Conduct of a Nonclinical Laboratory Study

Subpart G outlines the requirements for the **protocol and conduct** of non-clinical laboratory studies. Each study must have a written protocol that specifies the study's objectives, design, methods, and statistical analysis. The protocol must be approved by the study director and any amendments must be documented. This subpart also details the responsibilities of the study director in ensuring that the study is conducted in accordance with the protocol and GLP regulations. This includes overseeing all aspects of the study and ensuring compliance with regulatory requirements.

Subpart H - Records and Reports

Subpart H focuses on the management of **records and reports**. All raw data, documentation, protocols, final reports, and specimens must be retained and archived in a manner that allows for accurate and complete retrieval. The final report must include a description of the study methods, results, and conclusions, and it must be signed by the study director. Quality assurance personnel must review the final report to ensure compliance with GLP standards. This subpart ensures that all study documentation is properly managed and accessible for review and verification.

Subpart I - Disqualification of Testing Facilities

Subpart I provides the criteria and procedures for the **disqualification** of testing facilities that fail to comply with GLP regulations. The FDA may disqualify a facility if it finds significant deviations from GLP standards that impact the integrity of the study data. Disqualification can result in the rejection of study data submitted in support of regulatory applications. This subpart serves as a deterrent against non-compliance and underscores the importance of adhering to GLP standards.

Subpart J - Miscellaneous Provisions

Subpart J includes **miscellaneous provisions** related to GLP compliance. This section addresses issues such as the availability of study records for FDA inspection and the responsibilities of management in ensuring GLP compliance. It reinforces the need for cooperation between the testing facility and regulatory authorities, ensuring that all relevant information is available for inspection and review.

Subpart K - Retention of Records

Subpart K specifies the requirements for the **retention of records**. It mandates that all records pertaining to the conduct of a non-clinical laboratory study, including raw data, protocols, final reports, and any other supporting documentation, be retained for a specified period. This retention period is typically at least five years following the submission of the study data to the FDA or two years after the approval of a regulatory application. Proper retention ensures that study data can be accessed for future reference, verification, or regulatory review.

2.3 CONTROLLING THE GLP INSPECTION PROCESS

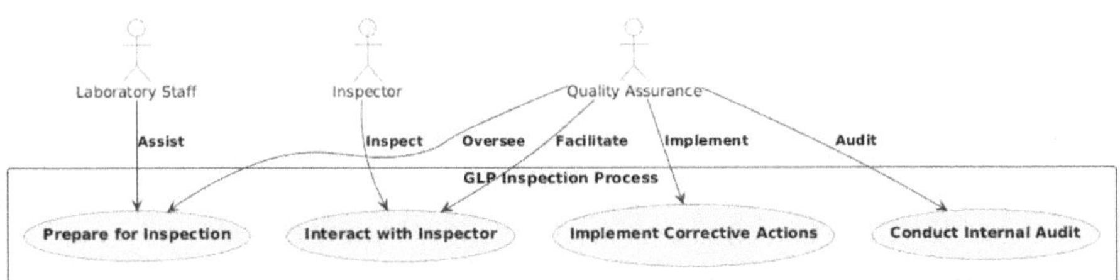

Fig: GLP Inspection Process

Good Laboratory Practice (GLP) inspections are critical for ensuring that laboratories adhere to regulatory standards and produce reliable and high-quality data. Controlling the GLP inspection process involves systematic preparation, proactive management, and continuous improvement of laboratory practices. The goal is to ensure that the laboratory is always ready for an inspection, thereby minimizing disruptions and ensuring compliance with GLP regulations. Below is an in-depth look at the key elements involved in controlling the GLP inspection process.

Preparation for Inspection

Effective preparation is fundamental to controlling the GLP inspection process. Laboratories should maintain a state of continuous readiness by adhering to GLP principles in all operations. This involves regular training of personnel, updating standard operating procedures (SOPs), and conducting internal audits to identify and address any gaps in compliance. Key documents, such as SOPs, study plans, raw data, and quality assurance records, should be organized and readily accessible. Preparing a checklist of essential documents and procedures can help ensure that nothing is overlooked.

Internal Audits and Mock Inspections

Conducting internal audits and mock inspections is a proactive approach to identifying and correcting potential compliance issues before an official inspection. Internal audits should be performed by quality assurance (QA) personnel or external consultants who are knowledgeable about GLP requirements. These audits involve a thorough review of all aspects of laboratory operations, including documentation, equipment calibration, personnel training, and study conduct. Mock inspections simulate the actual inspection process, helping staff become familiar with the procedures and expectations. Findings from internal audits and mock inspections should be documented, and corrective actions should be implemented promptly.

Document Management

Proper document management is crucial for demonstrating compliance with GLP regulations during an inspection. All documents related to GLP studies, including study plans, SOPs, raw data, and final reports, should be accurately maintained and easily retrievable. Implementing an electronic document management system (EDMS) can streamline document control, ensure version control, and facilitate quick access to required documents. Regular audits of document management practices can help identify and rectify any inconsistencies or gaps.

Personnel Training and Awareness

Ensuring that all personnel are adequately trained and aware of GLP requirements is essential for controlling the inspection process. Training programs should cover GLP principles, the importance of compliance, and specific roles and responsibilities within the laboratory. Regular refresher courses and updates on regulatory changes should be provided. Personnel should also be trained on how to interact with inspectors, including how to present documents, answer questions, and demonstrate procedures. Maintaining detailed training records is important for demonstrating compliance during an inspection.

Facility and Equipment Readiness

The physical condition of the laboratory and the readiness of equipment play a significant role in GLP inspections. Laboratories should be well-maintained, clean, and organized. Equipment used in GLP studies must be regularly calibrated, maintained, and inspected to ensure proper functioning. Calibration and maintenance records should be up-to-date and readily available. Any equipment that is out of service or in need of repair should be clearly labeled and documented. Regular checks of the facility and equipment can help ensure that everything is in compliance with GLP standards.

Quality Assurance Oversight

The quality assurance (QA) unit is integral to maintaining GLP compliance and controlling the inspection process. QA personnel are responsible for conducting regular audits, reviewing study plans and reports, and ensuring adherence to SOPs. They provide an independent assessment of the laboratory's compliance status and identify areas for improvement. QA oversight helps ensure that any deviations from GLP standards are promptly addressed and that corrective actions are implemented. Regular communication between QA personnel and laboratory staff is essential for maintaining a culture of quality and compliance.

Interaction with Inspectors

Effective communication and interaction with inspectors are critical during a GLP inspection. Laboratory personnel should be prepared to provide clear, concise, and accurate information about their operations and compliance with GLP regulations. It is important to establish a positive and cooperative relationship with the inspectors. Designating a knowledgeable and experienced point of contact, such as the study director or a senior QA representative, can help facilitate smooth communication. During the inspection, personnel should be prepared to demonstrate procedures, present documents, and answer questions confidently and accurately.

Handling Inspection Findings

Post-inspection, laboratories may receive findings or observations from the inspectors. It is crucial to handle these findings promptly and effectively. A thorough review of the inspection report should be conducted, and a detailed response plan should be developed. This plan should address each finding, outlining the corrective actions to be taken, the timeline for implementation, and the personnel responsible. Documentation of all corrective actions and follow-up activities is essential for demonstrating compliance. Continuous monitoring and improvement based on inspection findings help strengthen the laboratory's overall GLP compliance.

Continuous Improvement

Controlling the GLP inspection process is not a one-time effort but an ongoing commitment to continuous improvement. Laboratories should regularly review and update their practices, procedures, and training programs to align with evolving GLP standards and regulatory expectations. Implementing a robust quality management system (QMS) can facilitate continuous improvement by providing a structured approach to identifying, addressing, and preventing compliance issues. Engaging in regular benchmarking and sharing best practices with other laboratories can also help enhance compliance and readiness for inspections.

2.4 DOCUMENTATION AND AUDITS IN GLP

Documentation and audits are critical components of Good Laboratory Practices (GLP). They ensure that all aspects of non-clinical laboratory studies are conducted with integrity, reliability, and traceability. Effective documentation provides a detailed and accurate record of all study activities, while audits serve as a verification mechanism to ensure compliance with GLP standards. Together, they form the backbone of a robust quality assurance system, essential for generating data that is credible and acceptable for regulatory submissions.

Importance of Documentation

Documentation in GLP is fundamental to maintaining the quality and integrity of laboratory studies. It serves several key purposes:

1. **Traceability**: Documentation ensures that all aspects of the study can be traced back to their origin. This includes records of study protocols, raw data, test system handling, equipment calibration, and maintenance activities. Traceability is essential for verifying the authenticity of data and identifying the sources of any deviations or errors.
2. **Transparency**: Comprehensive documentation provides transparency in study conduct, allowing independent reviewers to understand the methodologies and processes used. This is crucial for the reproducibility of results and for building confidence in the study findings.
3. **Accountability**: By documenting all procedures and activities, laboratories can establish accountability among personnel. It clearly defines roles and responsibilities, ensuring that each individual involved in the study is aware of their duties and is held responsible for their actions.
4. **Regulatory Compliance**: Documentation is a regulatory requirement under GLP standards. It demonstrates that the study has been conducted according to the prescribed protocols and regulations, making the data acceptable for regulatory review and approval.

Types of Documentation

Several types of documentation are essential for GLP compliance:

1. **Standard Operating Procedures (SOPs)**: SOPs are detailed, written instructions that describe how specific tasks and procedures should be performed. They ensure consistency and uniformity in laboratory operations. Each SOP must be reviewed, approved, and periodically updated to reflect any changes in procedures or regulations.
2. **Study Protocols**: The study protocol outlines the objectives, design, methodology, data collection methods, and statistical analysis plan for the study. It must be approved by the study director and any amendments must be documented and justified.
3. **Raw Data**: Raw data includes all original observations, measurements, and calculations generated during the study. It must be recorded promptly, accurately, and legibly. Any changes or corrections to raw data must be clearly documented, including the reason for the change and the identity of the person making the change.
4. **Study Reports**: The final study report summarizes the study findings, including methodologies, results, discussions, and conclusions. It must be reviewed and signed by the study director and quality assurance personnel to confirm its accuracy and compliance with GLP standards.
5. **Training Records**: Training records document the qualifications and training of personnel involved in the study. They provide evidence that staff members are adequately trained and competent to perform their assigned tasks.
6. **Equipment Records**: These records include calibration, maintenance, and inspection logs for all equipment used in the study. They ensure that the equipment is functioning correctly and producing accurate and reliable data.

Role of Audits in GLP

Audits are systematic, independent examinations of all aspects of a laboratory's operations and studies to ensure compliance with GLP regulations. They serve several crucial functions:

1. **Verification**: Audits verify that the laboratory is adhering to GLP standards and that all procedures are being followed as documented in the SOPs and study protocols. This helps identify any deviations or non-compliance issues that could compromise the integrity of the study.
2. **Continuous Improvement**: Audits provide an opportunity for continuous improvement by identifying areas where practices can be enhanced. Recommendations from audits can lead to the development of better procedures and more efficient workflows.
3. **Regulatory Assurance**: Audits provide assurance to regulatory authorities that the laboratory operates in compliance with GLP standards. This is essential for the acceptance of study data in regulatory submissions.

Types of Audits

There are several types of audits conducted in GLP:

1. **Internal Audits**: Internal audits are conducted by the laboratory's own quality assurance (QA) personnel. They involve a thorough review of the laboratory's operations, including documentation, equipment, and study conduct. Internal audits help identify and address compliance issues before an external inspection.
2. **External Audits**: External audits are conducted by regulatory authorities or third-party auditors. These audits provide an independent assessment of the laboratory's compliance with GLP standards. External audits are often more rigorous and can result in significant findings if non-compliance is detected.
3. **Study Audits**: Study audits focus on specific studies to ensure that they are conducted according to the approved protocols and GLP regulations. These audits review all aspects of the study, from protocol development to data collection and reporting.

Audit Process

The audit process typically involves several steps:

1. **Planning**: The audit process begins with planning, where the scope, objectives, and criteria for the audit are defined. An audit plan is developed, detailing the areas to be audited, the audit schedule, and the resources required.
2. **Execution**: During the execution phase, auditors review documentation, observe procedures, and interview personnel to gather evidence of compliance. They may also inspect facilities and equipment to ensure they meet GLP standards.
3. **Reporting**: After the audit, the auditors compile their findings into an audit report. The report details any non-compliance issues, deviations from GLP standards, and areas for improvement. It may also include recommendations for corrective actions.
4. **Follow-Up**: The final step involves follow-up activities to ensure that the findings from the audit are addressed. Corrective actions are implemented, and the effectiveness of these actions is verified. Follow-up audits may be conducted to ensure sustained compliance.

2.5 LABORATORY QUALITY AUDIT GOALS AND TOOLS

Laboratory quality audits are essential for ensuring compliance with Good Laboratory Practices (GLP) and maintaining the highest standards of data integrity and reliability. The goals of these audits are multifaceted, aiming to verify adherence to regulatory standards, identify areas for improvement, and ensure the overall quality of laboratory operations. To achieve these goals, various tools and techniques are employed during the audit process. This section will explore the primary goals of laboratory quality audits and the tools used to conduct them effectively.

Goals of Laboratory Quality Audits

1. **Compliance Verification**: One of the primary goals of laboratory quality audits is to verify that the laboratory adheres to GLP standards and regulatory requirements. This involves a thorough review of all aspects of laboratory operations, including documentation, procedures, equipment, and personnel qualifications. Compliance verification ensures that the data generated is reliable and acceptable for regulatory submissions.

2. **Data Integrity Assurance**: Ensuring the integrity of the data is crucial for the credibility of laboratory studies. Audits aim to confirm that data is accurately recorded, stored, and reported, with appropriate traceability and accountability. This includes checking for proper documentation of raw data, ensuring that any changes or corrections are appropriately justified and recorded, and verifying that data handling procedures minimize the risk of errors or fraud.

3. **Identification of Non-Compliance and Gaps**: Audits help identify any deviations from GLP standards or gaps in the laboratory's quality management system. This includes detecting any procedural inconsistencies, equipment malfunctions, or documentation errors that could impact the quality of the study. By identifying these issues, audits provide an opportunity for corrective actions to be implemented, thereby enhancing overall compliance and quality.

4. **Continuous Improvement**: A key goal of quality audits is to promote continuous improvement within the laboratory. Audits provide valuable insights into the effectiveness of existing procedures and practices, highlighting areas where improvements can be made. This proactive approach helps laboratories stay updated with the latest regulatory standards and industry best practices, fostering a culture of quality and excellence.

5. **Risk Management**: Audits play a critical role in identifying and managing risks associated with laboratory operations. By evaluating potential risks to data integrity, personnel safety, and regulatory compliance, audits help laboratories implement effective risk mitigation strategies. This ensures that potential issues are addressed before they can escalate into significant problems.

6. **Enhancement of Credibility and Trust**: Regular and thorough quality audits enhance the credibility and trustworthiness of the laboratory. They demonstrate a commitment to maintaining high standards of quality and compliance, which is essential for gaining the confidence of regulatory authorities, clients, and other stakeholders. This, in turn, can lead to increased opportunities for collaboration and business growth.

Tools and Techniques for Laboratory Quality Audits

1. **Checklists and Audit Plans**: Checklists are fundamental tools for conducting systematic and comprehensive audits. They help auditors ensure that all critical aspects of the laboratory's operations are reviewed. Audit plans outline the scope, objectives, and schedule of the audit, providing a clear roadmap for the audit process.

2. **Standard Operating Procedures (SOPs)**: SOPs provide detailed guidelines for conducting various laboratory procedures and activities. During an audit, SOPs are reviewed to ensure they are up-to-date, accurately followed, and properly documented. Compliance with SOPs is crucial for maintaining consistency and reliability in laboratory operations.

3. **Documentation Review**: Reviewing documentation is a core component of the audit process. This includes examining study protocols, raw data, final reports, equipment calibration records, and training records.

Documentation review helps verify that all activities are properly recorded and compliant with GLP standards.

4. **Interviews and Observations**: Interviews with laboratory personnel and direct observations of laboratory procedures provide valuable insights into the actual practices followed. These techniques help auditors assess the understanding and adherence to GLP principles among staff members and identify any deviations from documented procedures.

5. **Traceability and Data Integrity Tools**: Tools that ensure traceability and data integrity, such as electronic laboratory notebooks (ELNs) and laboratory information management systems (LIMS), are essential for modern laboratory audits. These systems facilitate accurate and secure data recording, storage, and retrieval, enhancing overall data management.

6. **Calibration and Maintenance Records**: Reviewing calibration and maintenance records of laboratory equipment ensures that all instruments are functioning correctly and providing accurate measurements. This includes checking calibration schedules, maintenance logs, and any corrective actions taken for faulty equipment.

7. **Risk Assessment Tools**: Risk assessment tools, such as Failure Mode and Effects Analysis (FMEA) and Hazard Analysis and Critical Control Points (HACCP), help identify and evaluate potential risks in laboratory operations. These tools enable auditors to prioritize areas for improvement based on the level of risk they pose to data integrity and compliance.

8. **Internal and External Audit Reports**: Reviewing previous internal and external audit reports provides insights into recurring issues and the effectiveness of corrective actions implemented. This helps auditors focus on areas that require further attention and ensures that past findings have been adequately addressed.

9. **Corrective and Preventive Actions (CAPA) Records**: CAPA records document the actions taken to correct identified issues and prevent their recurrence. Auditors review these records to ensure that effective corrective actions have been implemented and that there is a continuous improvement process in place.

10. **Training and Competency Records**: Ensuring that personnel are adequately trained and competent is essential for GLP compliance. Auditors review training records to verify that staff members have received the necessary training and possess the required qualifications. f

2.6 FUTURE OF GLP REGULATIONS

The landscape of Good Laboratory Practices (GLP) is continually evolving to keep pace with advancements in science, technology, and regulatory expectations. As we look to the future, several trends and developments are poised to shape the direction of GLP regulations. These changes aim to enhance the quality, integrity, and efficiency of laboratory studies, ensuring they meet the demands of modern research and regulatory scrutiny.

Technological Advancements

Digital Transformation: The adoption of digital technologies is transforming laboratory operations. Electronic Laboratory Notebooks (ELNs), Laboratory Information Management Systems (LIMS), and other digital tools are becoming integral to data management. Future GLP regulations are likely to emphasize the use of these technologies to enhance data accuracy, traceability, and accessibility. Digital tools facilitate real-time data capture, automated workflows, and improved compliance monitoring, reducing the likelihood of human error and ensuring robust data integrity.

Automation and Robotics: Automation and robotics are increasingly being integrated into laboratory processes. Automated systems for sample handling, testing, and data analysis can significantly improve efficiency and consistency. Future GLP regulations may provide specific guidelines on the validation, calibration, and maintenance of automated equipment. These regulations will ensure that automated systems are reliable and produce high-quality data.

Artificial Intelligence (AI) and Machine Learning (ML): AI and ML have the potential to revolutionize data analysis in GLP studies. These technologies can identify patterns, predict outcomes, and optimize study designs. Future regulations may include provisions for the use of AI and ML in data analysis, focusing on algorithm validation, transparency, and ethical considerations. The goal will be to harness the power of these technologies while ensuring the reliability and reproducibility of results.

Regulatory Harmonization

Global Standards: As scientific research becomes increasingly global, there is a growing need for harmonization of GLP regulations across different regions. Future developments may include efforts to align GLP standards internationally, facilitating cross-border collaboration and data acceptance. Harmonized regulations would reduce the burden on laboratories operating in multiple jurisdictions and promote the global exchange of scientific data.

Collaborative Efforts: International organizations such as the Organisation for Economic Co-operation and Development (OECD) and the International Council for Harmonisation (ICH) are likely to play a pivotal role in harmonizing GLP regulations. Collaborative efforts among regulatory bodies, industry stakeholders, and academic institutions will drive the development of consistent and comprehensive GLP standards. This collaboration will ensure that regulations are globally applicable and reflect the latest scientific advancements.

Enhanced Data Integrity and Transparency

Blockchain Technology: Blockchain technology offers a secure and transparent way to manage and verify data. Its application in GLP studies could enhance data integrity by providing an immutable record of all study-related transactions. Future GLP regulations may explore the use of blockchain for data recording, tracking, and verification, ensuring that all data is traceable and tamper-proof.

Open Data Initiatives: There is a growing trend towards open data and increased transparency in scientific research. Future GLP regulations may encourage or mandate the sharing of raw data, study protocols, and results in publicly accessible databases. This transparency would enable independent verification of data, promote reproducibility, and foster scientific collaboration.

Focus on Ethics and Sustainability

Ethical Considerations: As research methodologies evolve, ethical considerations will remain a central focus of GLP regulations. Future guidelines may place greater emphasis on the ethical treatment of test systems, including animals and human-derived materials. Enhanced protocols for ensuring animal welfare, informed consent, and the ethical use of biological samples will be integral to GLP compliance.

Sustainability Practices: Environmental sustainability is becoming increasingly important in laboratory operations. Future GLP regulations may incorporate guidelines for sustainable practices, such as reducing waste, conserving resources, and minimizing the environmental impact of laboratory activities. This focus on sustainability aligns with broader societal goals and promotes responsible scientific research.

Integration of New Scientific Methods

Advanced Analytical Techniques: The adoption of advanced analytical techniques, such as genomics, proteomics, and metabolomics, is expanding the scope of GLP studies. Future regulations may include specific provisions for the validation and application of these techniques, ensuring they are used appropriately and generate reliable data. Guidelines for integrating these advanced methods into study designs will enhance the comprehensiveness of GLP studies.

Personalized Medicine and Biotechnology: The rise of personalized medicine and biotechnological innovations presents new challenges and opportunities for GLP. Future regulations may address the unique aspects of these fields, including the validation of personalized therapies, the use of genetically modified organisms, and the application of gene

2.7 RELEVANT ISO AND QUALITY COUNCIL OF INDIA (QCI) STANDARDS

The integration of international standards, such as those from the International Organization for Standardization (ISO) and the Quality Council of India (QCI), is crucial for maintaining high-quality laboratory practices. These standards provide comprehensive guidelines and frameworks that help laboratories achieve excellence in their operations, ensuring reliability, reproducibility, and compliance with regulatory requirements. This section will explore the key ISO and QCI standards relevant to Good Laboratory Practices (GLP) and their impact on laboratory quality management.

ISO Standards

ISO/IEC 17025: General Requirements for the Competence of Testing and Calibration Laboratories

ISO/IEC 17025 is the primary international standard for testing and calibration laboratories. It specifies the general requirements for the competence, impartiality, and consistent operation of laboratories. Key aspects of ISO/IEC 17025 include:

- **Management Requirements**: These include the laboratory's organizational structure, management system, and documentation. The standard emphasizes the need for a robust quality management system (QMS) that ensures consistent delivery of reliable results.
- **Technical Requirements**: These cover factors such as personnel competence, equipment calibration, testing methods, and result validation. The standard requires laboratories to demonstrate technical proficiency and maintain accurate records of all testing and calibration activities.

ISO 9001: Quality Management Systems – Requirements

ISO 9001 outlines the criteria for a quality management system and is applicable to any organization, regardless of size or field. For laboratories, it provides a framework to ensure consistent quality in their operations and services. Key components include:

- **Customer Focus**: Ensuring that customer requirements are understood and met.
- **Leadership**: Establishing strong leadership to guide the laboratory's quality objectives and policies.
- **Process Approach**: Managing activities as interconnected processes to achieve more efficient results.
- **Continuous Improvement**: Committing to ongoing improvement in all aspects of the laboratory's operations.

ISO 15189: Medical Laboratories – Requirements for Quality and Competence

ISO 15189 is specific to medical laboratories and combines the requirements of ISO/IEC 17025 and ISO 9001. It focuses on the quality and competence of medical laboratories and includes provisions for:

- **Quality Management**: Implementing a QMS that ensures the quality of laboratory services.
- **Technical Competence**: Ensuring that laboratory personnel are adequately trained and qualified, and that equipment and procedures are appropriately validated and maintained.
- **Patient Safety**: Emphasizing the importance of patient safety and confidentiality in medical testing and reporting.

Quality Council of India (QCI) Standards

National Accreditation Board for Testing and Calibration Laboratories (NABL) Accreditation

NABL is a constituent board of the QCI, responsible for the accreditation of testing and calibration laboratories in India. The NABL accreditation is based on ISO/IEC 17025 and ISO 15189 standards. Key aspects of NABL accreditation include:

- **Accreditation Criteria**: Laboratories must meet the criteria for competence, quality management, and technical proficiency as outlined in ISO standards.
- **Assessment Process**: NABL conducts thorough assessments and audits to evaluate a laboratory's compliance with the accreditation criteria. This includes on-site evaluations, proficiency testing, and review of documentation and procedures.
- **Continuous Monitoring**: Accredited laboratories are subject to periodic surveillance and reassessments to ensure ongoing compliance with NABL standards.

Indian Pharmacopoeia Commission (IPC) Guidelines

The IPC provides guidelines for laboratories involved in pharmaceutical testing and analysis. These guidelines align with international standards and emphasize the importance of quality assurance in the pharmaceutical sector. Key components include:

- **Quality Control**: Implementing rigorous quality control measures to ensure the accuracy and reliability of test results.
- **Good Laboratory Practices (GLP)**: Adhering to GLP principles to maintain data integrity and regulatory compliance.
- **Standard Operating Procedures (SOPs)**: Developing and following SOPs for all laboratory processes to ensure consistency and reproducibility.

Bureau of Indian Standards (BIS)

BIS develops and publishes standards for various sectors, including laboratory practices. Relevant BIS standards include:

- **IS/ISO 17025: General Requirements for the Competence of Testing and Calibration Laboratories**: Aligns with the international ISO/IEC 17025 standard, providing guidelines for laboratory competence and quality management.

- **IS 15489: Information and Documentation – Records Management**: Provides guidelines for the management of records, ensuring that laboratory documentation is accurate, accessible, and securely stored.

Integration of ISO and QCI Standards in GLP

The integration of ISO and QCI standards into GLP practices ensures that laboratories operate at the highest levels of quality and compliance. By adhering to these standards, laboratories can achieve the following benefits:

- **Enhanced Credibility**: Accreditation and certification under ISO and QCI standards enhance the credibility of laboratory operations, making them more trustworthy to regulatory authorities, clients, and stakeholders.
- **Improved Quality Management**: Implementing a robust QMS based on ISO and QCI standards ensures that all laboratory processes are well-documented, controlled, and continuously improved.
- **Increased Competence**: Adhering to these standards ensures that laboratory personnel are well-trained, equipment is properly maintained, and testing methods are validated, leading to more reliable and accurate results.
- **Regulatory Compliance**: ISO and QCI standards provide a framework for meeting national and international regulatory requirements, facilitating the acceptance of laboratory data in regulatory submissions.
- **Operational Efficiency**: Standardized processes and continuous improvement initiatives enhance operational efficiency, reducing errors and increasing productivity.

Overview of Good Laboratory Practices (GLP) Key Activities and Interactions

CHAPTER THREE

Good Automated Laboratory Practices

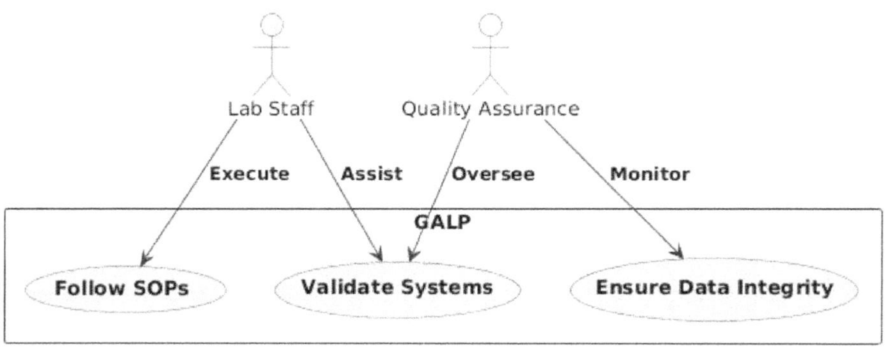

Good Automated Laboratory Practices (GALP)

3.1 Introduction to GALP

GALP, or **Good Automated Laboratory Practice,** refers to a set of guidelines and standards designed to ensure the accuracy, reliability, and consistency of data generated by automated laboratory systems. In the modern pharmaceutical and biotechnological industries, the automation of laboratory processes has become essential due to the need for high-throughput screening, precision, and reproducibility. GALP encompasses a comprehensive framework that covers the design, operation, and maintenance of automated systems to ensure that they perform optimally and generate valid results.

One of the key aspects of GALP is the **validation of automated systems**. This process involves a series of tests and procedures that confirm that the system is operating correctly and producing accurate results. Validation includes the **qualification of equipment** (installation, operational, and performance qualification), **software validation**, and the **calibration of instruments**. For instance, in the calibration process, instruments are tested against known standards to ensure their readings are accurate. Regular calibration helps in identifying any deviations from expected performance and correcting them promptly.

Another critical component of GALP is the **standardization of procedures**. Standard operating procedures (SOPs) are developed to provide detailed instructions on the operation and maintenance of automated systems. These SOPs ensure that all personnel follow the same steps, which minimizes variability in results. For example, an SOP for an automated liquid handling system might include steps for preparing the system, loading samples, running the program, and cleaning the equipment afterward. This standardization is crucial for maintaining consistency across different batches of experiments.

Data integrity is a fundamental principle of GALP. Ensuring data integrity involves implementing measures to prevent unauthorized access or modifications to data. This includes using secure data storage systems, maintaining audit trails, and conducting regular data reviews. For example, an audit trail might log every action taken on a dataset, such as when data was entered, modified, or deleted, along with the identity of the person performing the action. This transparency helps in tracing any errors or discrepancies back to their source.

Training and competency of personnel is also emphasized in GALP. Personnel involved in operating automated systems must be adequately trained and qualified. Regular training sessions and assessments help ensure that they are familiar with the systems and procedures. This not only improves the efficiency of operations but also reduces the likelihood of errors. For example, training programs might include hands-on sessions where operators practice using the equipment under supervision, followed by assessments to evaluate their competency.

In addition to these aspects, **maintenance and troubleshooting** of automated systems are integral to GALP. Preventive maintenance schedules are established to keep systems in good working condition and prevent unexpected breakdowns. Troubleshooting guidelines are also provided to help personnel quickly identify and resolve issues. For instance, a maintenance schedule for an automated spectrophotometer might include regular cleaning of optical components, checking and replacing filters, and running diagnostic tests to ensure the system's accuracy.

Furthermore, GALP involves the **continuous improvement** of automated systems and processes. This is achieved through regular reviews and updates of procedures, incorporating feedback from users, and staying abreast of technological advancements. For example, feedback from laboratory personnel might reveal that a particular step in an SOP is prone to errors, leading to a revision of the procedure to make it more foolproof. Additionally, advancements in automation technology might introduce new features that enhance the performance or capabilities of existing systems.

Regulatory compliance is another crucial aspect of GALP. Automated systems used in pharmaceutical and biotechnological laboratories must comply with relevant regulations and standards, such as those set by the FDA, EMA, and ISO. Compliance ensures that the data generated is acceptable for regulatory submissions and that the systems meet the required quality standards. For instance, the FDA's 21 CFR Part 11 outlines requirements for electronic records and signatures, and automated systems must be designed to meet these requirements to ensure data integrity and security.

3.2 Principles and Requirements of GALP

Good Automated Laboratory Practice (GALP) is underpinned by a set of principles and requirements designed to ensure the reliable and consistent performance of automated laboratory systems. These principles provide a framework for laboratories to achieve high standards of accuracy, reproducibility, and compliance. Below are the key principles and requirements of GALP.

Principles of GALP

1. Accuracy and Precision: One of the core principles of GALP is to ensure that automated systems produce accurate and precise results. Accuracy refers to the closeness of a measured value to a standard or true value, while precision indicates the repeatability or consistency of measurements. For example, an automated pipetting system must dispense exact volumes of liquid with minimal variation to ensure experimental consistency.

2. Validation: Validation is essential in GALP to confirm that automated systems perform as intended. This includes the validation of software, hardware, and processes. Validation involves rigorous testing and documentation to demonstrate that systems can consistently produce valid results. For instance, during software validation, each function of the laboratory information management system (LIMS) is tested to ensure it meets the specified requirements.

3. Standardization: Establishing and following standard operating procedures (SOPs) is critical in GALP. SOPs provide detailed instructions for operating and maintaining automated systems, ensuring consistency in laboratory practices. For example, an SOP for using an automated liquid handler would include steps for system setup, sample loading, and cleaning protocols.

4. Data Integrity: Ensuring the integrity of data generated by automated systems is a fundamental principle of GALP. This involves protecting data from unauthorized access, alteration, or deletion. Implementing secure data storage solutions, maintaining audit trails, and conducting regular data reviews are essential practices. An example is the use of electronic signatures and access controls to prevent unauthorized modifications to data.

5. Training and Competency: Personnel operating automated systems must be adequately trained and qualified. Continuous training programs and competency assessments are necessary to ensure that operators are proficient in using the equipment and following SOPs. For instance, training sessions for an automated analyzer might include hands-on practice and theoretical knowledge assessments.

6. Maintenance and Troubleshooting: Regular maintenance and prompt troubleshooting of automated systems are crucial to their optimal performance. Preventive maintenance schedules help prevent system failures, while troubleshooting guidelines assist in quickly resolving issues. For example, regular calibration and cleaning of an automated spectrophotometer ensure its accurate performance.

7. Continuous Improvement: GALP encourages continuous improvement of systems and processes. This involves regularly reviewing and updating procedures, incorporating feedback from users, and adopting new technologies. For example, feedback from laboratory staff might lead to the refinement of an SOP to reduce errors and improve efficiency.

8. Regulatory Compliance: Automated systems must comply with relevant regulatory standards and guidelines. Compliance ensures that the data generated is acceptable for regulatory submissions and that systems meet the required quality standards. For instance, adherence to FDA regulations such as 21 CFR Part 11 ensures the reliability and security of electronic records.

Requirements of GALP

1. System Design and Selection: Automated systems should be carefully selected and designed to meet the specific needs of the laboratory. Factors such as the type of analysis, sample throughput, and compatibility with existing systems must be considered. For example, choosing an automated DNA sequencer involves evaluating its sequencing capacity, accuracy, and integration with data analysis software.

2. Documentation: Comprehensive documentation is a requirement of GALP. This includes detailed records of system validation, calibration, maintenance, SOPs, and training activities. Proper documentation ensures traceability and accountability. For instance, maintaining logs of calibration activities for an automated balance ensures that its performance can be tracked over time.

3. Calibration and Validation: Regular calibration and validation of automated systems are essential to ensure their accurate performance. Calibration involves comparing the system's output against known standards, while validation confirms that the system meets specified requirements. For example, calibrating an automated titrator involves using standard solutions to verify its accuracy in measuring concentrations.

4. Quality Control: Implementing quality control measures helps maintain the reliability of automated systems. This includes running control samples, conducting performance checks, and monitoring system outputs. For instance, running control samples on an automated immunoassay analyzer helps ensure that it produces accurate and consistent results.

5. Risk Management: Identifying and managing risks associated with automated systems is crucial in GALP. This involves conducting risk assessments, implementing mitigation strategies, and regularly reviewing risks. For example, a risk assessment for an automated liquid handler might identify potential issues such as pipetting errors or contamination, leading to the implementation of additional quality checks.

6. Change Management: Any changes to automated systems or procedures must be managed carefully to ensure continued compliance and performance. This includes documenting changes, assessing their impact, and validating the updated system or process. For example, updating the software of an automated data analysis tool requires thorough testing to ensure it continues to function correctly.

7. Audits and Inspections: Regular audits and inspections help ensure compliance with GALP standards. Internal audits, as well as external inspections by regulatory bodies, provide an objective assessment of the laboratory's practices. For instance, an internal audit might review the laboratory's adherence to SOPs and identify areas for improvement.

8. Incident Reporting: A robust incident reporting system is essential for identifying and addressing issues with automated systems. This involves documenting incidents, investigating their causes, and implementing corrective actions. For example, if an automated cell counter malfunctions, documenting the incident and investigating its cause helps prevent future occurrences.

3.3 Standard Operating Procedures (SOPs) for GALP

Standard Operating Procedures (SOPs) are a fundamental component of **Good Automated Laboratory Practice (GALP)**, providing detailed, written instructions to ensure that automated laboratory systems are used consistently and correctly. SOPs help maintain the accuracy, reliability, and reproducibility of data by standardizing operations and minimizing variability. Here, we delve into the principles, structure, and essential elements of SOPs for GALP.

Principles of SOPs

1. Consistency and Uniformity: SOPs are designed to ensure that all personnel follow the same procedures, thereby reducing variability and ensuring consistency in the results. This uniformity is crucial in maintaining the integrity of laboratory data.

2. Compliance: SOPs help laboratories comply with regulatory requirements and industry standards. Adhering to these procedures ensures that laboratory practices meet the necessary legal and quality standards.

3. Training and Competency: SOPs serve as a training tool for new personnel and provide a reference for experienced staff. They ensure that all personnel have a clear understanding of how to operate and maintain automated systems correctly.

4. Efficiency: By providing clear instructions, SOPs streamline laboratory processes, reducing the time and effort required to perform tasks. This efficiency leads to increased productivity and reduces the likelihood of errors.

Structure of SOPs

SOPs typically follow a structured format to ensure clarity and comprehensiveness. The standard sections of an SOP include:

1. Title and Purpose: The title clearly identifies the procedure, and the purpose explains why the SOP is necessary and what it aims to achieve.

2. Scope: This section defines the boundaries of the SOP, specifying what activities are covered and who should follow the procedures.

3. Responsibilities: The responsibilities section outlines the roles and duties of personnel involved in the procedure. It specifies who is responsible for performing, supervising, and reviewing the procedure.

4. Definitions: Key terms and abbreviations used in the SOP are defined in this section to ensure that all personnel have a common understanding of the terminology.

5. Materials and Equipment: This section lists the materials, equipment, and software required to perform the procedure. It ensures that all necessary resources are available before starting the procedure.

6. Procedure: The procedure section provides step-by-step instructions for performing the task. It includes detailed descriptions of each step, along with any precautions that need to be taken. Diagrams, flowcharts, and photographs may be included to enhance clarity.

7. Quality Control and Assurance: This section describes the measures taken to ensure the quality and accuracy of the procedure. It may include guidelines for performing quality control checks and documenting results.

8. Documentation and Records: The documentation section specifies what records need to be kept, how they should be maintained, and where they should be stored. This ensures traceability and accountability.

9. References: Any relevant references, such as regulatory guidelines, industry standards, or related SOPs, are listed in this section.

10. Revision History: The revision history tracks changes made to the SOP over time, including the date of each revision and a summary of the changes.

Essential Elements of SOPs for GALP

1. System Operation:

- **Start-Up Procedures:** Detailed instructions for starting up the automated system, including any preliminary checks and settings adjustments.
- **Routine Operation:** Step-by-step guidance on how to operate the system during normal use, including sample loading, running protocols, and monitoring performance.

- **Shut-Down Procedures:** Instructions for safely shutting down the system, including any cleaning or maintenance tasks that need to be performed.

2. Maintenance and Calibration:

- **Regular Maintenance:** A schedule and description of routine maintenance tasks, such as cleaning, lubrication, and part replacements. For example, an SOP for an automated liquid handler might include weekly cleaning of the dispensing nozzles and monthly calibration of the pipetting volumes.
- **Calibration Procedures:** Detailed steps for calibrating the system to ensure accurate performance. This might include using standard solutions, running calibration protocols, and documenting the results.

3. Troubleshooting and Error Handling:

- **Common Issues:** A list of common problems that may arise during system operation, along with their possible causes and solutions. For example, an SOP might describe how to address a blockage in a liquid handling system or an error message on an automated analyzer.
- **Emergency Procedures:** Guidelines for handling emergencies, such as system failures, power outages, or safety hazards. This ensures that personnel know how to respond quickly and effectively to minimize disruptions and risks.

4. Data Management:

- **Data Entry:** Instructions for entering data into the laboratory information management system (LIMS) or other data storage systems. This includes guidelines for data formatting, labeling, and organization.

- **Data Review:** Procedures for reviewing and verifying data to ensure its accuracy and completeness. This might include cross-checking data entries, performing statistical analyses, and conducting peer reviews.
- **Data Storage:** Guidelines for securely storing data, including backup procedures and access controls. This ensures that data is protected from loss, corruption, and unauthorized access.

5. Compliance and Documentation:

- **Regulatory Requirements:** Specific instructions for complying with relevant regulations, such as FDA guidelines or ISO standards. This ensures that laboratory practices meet legal and quality requirements.
- **Record Keeping:** Detailed guidance on maintaining accurate and complete records of all activities, including system operation, maintenance, calibration, and data management. This ensures traceability and accountability.

Example SOP for an Automated Liquid Handling System

Title: Operation and Maintenance of Automated Liquid Handling System

Purpose: To ensure the accurate and consistent operation of the automated liquid handling system.

Scope: This SOP applies to all personnel operating the automated liquid handling system in the laboratory.

Responsibilities:

- Operators are responsible for following the procedures outlined in this SOP.
- The laboratory manager is responsible for ensuring compliance with this SOP and for conducting regular reviews.

Definitions:

- Pipetting Volume: The volume of liquid dispensed by the system.
- Calibration: The process of adjusting the system to ensure accurate pipetting volumes.

Materials and Equipment:

- Automated liquid handling system
- Standard solutions for calibration
- Cleaning agents

Procedure:

Start-Up Procedures:

1. Ensure the system is connected to a power source.
2. Turn on the system and wait for it to complete the initialization process.
3. Check that all necessary reagents and consumables are loaded correctly.

Routine Operation:

1. Load the samples into the appropriate positions.
2. Select the desired protocol from the system's software.
3. Run the protocol and monitor the system for any errors or alerts.

Shut-Down Procedures:

1. Remove any remaining samples and reagents.
2. Clean the dispensing nozzles using the recommended cleaning agents.
3. Turn off the system and perform any required maintenance tasks.

Maintenance and Calibration:

Regular Maintenance:

1. Weekly: Clean the dispensing nozzles using the recommended cleaning agents.
2. Monthly: Check and replace any worn or damaged parts.

Calibration Procedures:

1. Prepare standard solutions of known concentrations.
2. Run the calibration protocol using the standard solutions.
3. Document the results and adjust the system settings as necessary.

Troubleshooting and Error Handling:

Common Issues:

1. Blockage in the dispensing nozzles: Clean the nozzles using the recommended cleaning agents.
2. Error message on the display: Refer to the user manual for specific error codes and solutions.

Emergency Procedures:

1. Power outage: Safely shut down the system and restart once power is restored.
2. System failure: Contact the manufacturer's technical support for assistance.

Data Management:

Data Entry:

1. Enter data into the LIMS according to the specified format.
2. Label data entries with the date, time, and operator's initials.

Data Review:

1. Review data entries for accuracy and completeness.
2. Perform statistical analyses as required to verify data integrity.

Data Storage:

1. Back up data regularly to a secure location.
2. Implement access controls to protect data from unauthorized access.

Compliance and Documentation:

Regulatory Requirements:

1. Follow FDA guidelines for electronic records and signatures.
2. Ensure compliance with ISO standards for laboratory practices.

Record Keeping:

1. Maintain logs of all system operations, maintenance, and calibration activities.
2. Store records securely and make them available for audits and inspections.

• 67 •

References:

- FDA 21 CFR Part 11
- ISO 9001:2015

Revision History:

- Version 1.0: Initial release (Date)
- Version 1.1: Updated calibration procedures (Date)

3.4 Training Documentation for GALP

Training Documentation is a critical element of **Good Automated Laboratory Practice (GALP).** Effective training ensures that all personnel operating automated laboratory systems are competent, knowledgeable, and capable of following Standard Operating Procedures (SOPs) correctly. Comprehensive training documentation serves as a reference for staff, provides a record of training activities, and ensures compliance with regulatory requirements. Below, we discuss the principles, structure, and key elements of training documentation for GALP.

Principles of Training Documentation

1. Comprehensive Coverage: Training documentation should cover all aspects of automated system operation, including start-up, routine use, maintenance, troubleshooting, and data management. It should provide detailed information on each procedure to ensure personnel understand every step.

2. Consistency: Training materials should be standardized to ensure that all personnel receive the same information and instructions. Consistent training helps maintain uniformity in laboratory practices and reduces variability in results.

3. Clarity and Simplicity: Training documentation should be written in clear, simple language to ensure it is easily understood by all personnel. Complex technical jargon should be avoided, or if necessary, clearly defined.

4. Continuous Improvement: Training programs should be regularly reviewed and updated to incorporate new technologies, procedures, and feedback from personnel. Continuous improvement ensures that training remains relevant and effective.

Structure of Training Documentation

Training documentation typically includes the following sections:

1. Introduction: This section provides an overview of the training program, including its objectives, scope, and the importance of training in the context of GALP.

2. Training Modules: The training content is divided into modules, each focusing on a specific aspect of automated system operation. Modules are designed to be comprehensive and self-contained.

3. Learning Objectives: Each module includes specific learning objectives that outline what personnel should know or be able to do after completing the module.

4. Training Materials: This section lists all materials required for the training, including manuals, SOPs, videos, presentations, and any hands-on equipment needed for practical training.

5. Training Procedures: Detailed instructions on how the training will be conducted, including the format (e.g., classroom training, hands-on practice, e-learning), duration, and assessment methods.

6. Assessments and Evaluations: This section describes the methods used to assess the trainees' understanding and competency, such as quizzes, practical tests, and performance reviews.

7. Records and Documentation: Guidelines for documenting training activities, including attendance records, assessment results, and training certificates.

8. Feedback and Improvement: Procedures for collecting feedback from trainees and using it to improve the training program.

Key Elements of Training Documentation for GALP

1. System Overview:

- **Introduction to the System:** An overview of the automated system, including its purpose, components, and how it integrates into laboratory workflows. For example, an introduction to an automated liquid handling system might cover its various modules, such as the liquid handler, control software, and accessories.
- **System Capabilities and Limitations:** A detailed description of what the system can and cannot do, helping users understand its strengths and limitations.

2. Operation and Maintenance:

- **Start-Up Procedures:** Step-by-step instructions for starting the system, including any preliminary checks and system initialization steps.
- **Routine Operation:** Detailed guidelines for the routine use of the system, including loading samples, running protocols, and monitoring system performance.

- **Shut-Down Procedures:** Instructions for safely shutting down the system, including cleaning and maintenance tasks.

3. Troubleshooting and Error Handling:

- **Common Issues:** A list of common problems that may arise during system operation, along with their possible causes and solutions. For example, a training module for troubleshooting might include scenarios like a pipetting error in an automated liquid handler and how to resolve it.
- **Emergency Procedures:** Guidelines for handling emergencies, such as system failures, power outages, or safety hazards.

4. Data Management:

- **Data Entry and Storage:** Instructions for entering and storing data generated by the system, including guidelines for data formatting, labeling, and backup procedures.
- **Data Review and Integrity:** Procedures for reviewing and verifying data to ensure its accuracy and completeness. This might include methods for cross-checking data entries and conducting regular audits.

5. Compliance and Documentation:

- **Regulatory Requirements:** Training on relevant regulatory standards and guidelines, such as FDA regulations or ISO standards. This ensures that personnel understand the legal and quality requirements for operating automated systems.
- **Record Keeping:** Guidelines for maintaining accurate and complete records of all activities, including system operation, maintenance, and training activities.

Example Training Module for an Automated Liquid Handling System

Title: Training Module for Automated Liquid Handling System Operation

Introduction: This training module provides comprehensive instructions for the operation of the automated liquid handling system. It aims to ensure that personnel are competent in using the system, following SOPs, and maintaining data integrity.

Learning Objectives:

- Understand the components and functions of the automated liquid handling system.
- Perform start-up, routine operation, and shut-down procedures correctly.
- Troubleshoot common issues and handle emergencies.
- Manage data accurately and maintain compliance with regulatory standards.

Training Materials:

- User manual for the automated liquid handling system
- SOPs for system operation, maintenance, and troubleshooting
- Video tutorials on system setup and operation
- Practical training sessions with hands-on practice

Training Procedures:
Start-Up Procedures:

1. Ensure the system is connected to a power source and turned on.
2. Perform preliminary checks, such as verifying reagent levels and ensuring no blockages in the dispensing nozzles.
3. Initialize the system by following the steps outlined in the user manual.

Routine Operation:

1. Load the samples into the designated positions on the sample tray.
2. Select and run the desired protocol using the system's control software.
3. Monitor the system during operation and address any alerts or error messages promptly.

Shut-Down Procedures:

1. Remove any remaining samples and reagents.
2. Clean the dispensing nozzles and other components using the recommended cleaning agents.
3. Safely shut down the system following the steps outlined in the SOP.

Assessments and Evaluations:

- **Quizzes:** Short quizzes to test understanding of the theoretical aspects of the system operation.
- **Practical Tests:** Hands-on assessments where trainees perform start-up, routine operation, and shut-down procedures under supervision.
- **Performance Reviews:** Regular reviews to assess the competency and performance of personnel over time.

Records and Documentation:

- **Attendance Records:** Documenting who attended the training sessions.
- **Assessment Results:** Recording the results of quizzes and practical tests.
- **Training Certificates:** Issuing certificates to personnel who successfully complete the training program.

Feedback and Improvement:

- **Feedback Forms:** Collecting feedback from trainees about the training program's effectiveness and areas for improvement.
- **Regular Updates:** Using feedback to update and improve training materials and procedures.

3.5 21 CFR Part 11 Overview

21 CFR Part 11 is a regulation established by the United States Food and Drug Administration (FDA) that sets forth the criteria under which electronic records and electronic signatures are considered trustworthy, reliable, and equivalent to paper records and handwritten signatures. This regulation is essential for industries such as pharmaceuticals, biotechnology, and medical devices, where data integrity and security are paramount. Below is an overview of the key aspects, principles, and requirements of 21 CFR Part 11.

Key Aspects of 21 CFR Part 11

1. Scope and Applicability: 21 CFR Part 11 applies to electronic records that are created, modified, maintained, archived, retrieved, or transmitted under any records requirements set forth by the FDA. It also covers electronic signatures that are intended to be the equivalent of handwritten signatures.

2. General Requirements: The regulation outlines the general requirements for electronic records and electronic signatures to ensure their integrity and reliability. This includes controls for closed systems (where system access is controlled by the persons responsible for the content) and open systems (where system access is not controlled by persons responsible for the content).

3. Electronic Records: Part 11 specifies the requirements for electronic records, including validation, audit trails, record retention, and the use of secure, computer-generated, time-stamped audit trails to track the creation, modification, and deletion of records. These audit trails must be maintained and readily available for FDA inspection.

4. Electronic Signatures: The regulation defines the requirements for electronic signatures, ensuring that they are unique to the individual and used only by the intended person. It requires proper identity verification and controls to ensure the authenticity and integrity of electronic signatures.

5. System Validation: Organizations must validate their electronic systems to ensure accuracy, reliability, consistent intended performance, and the ability to discern invalid or altered records. Validation documentation must be maintained and available for FDA review.

Principles of 21 CFR Part 11

1. Data Integrity: Data integrity is the foundation of 21 CFR Part 11. The regulation ensures that electronic records are accurate, complete, and protected from unauthorized access or alterations. This involves implementing measures such as access controls, audit trails, and data encryption.

2. Security: Security measures are essential to protect electronic records from unauthorized access, modification, or deletion. This includes physical and logical access controls, user authentication, and regular security assessments to identify and mitigate vulnerabilities.

3. Accountability: Part 11 requires clear accountability for electronic records and signatures. This involves ensuring that each electronic signature is unique to one individual and that there are procedures in place to prevent the unauthorized use of electronic signatures.

4. Traceability: The regulation mandates the use of audit trails to provide a traceable history of record creation, modification, and deletion. These audit trails must be secure, time-stamped, and available for review to ensure transparency and traceability.

5. Compliance: Compliance with 21 CFR Part 11 involves adhering to all the requirements outlined in the regulation. This includes system validation, maintaining documentation, and implementing standard operating procedures (SOPs) to ensure that electronic records and signatures meet the FDA's criteria.

Requirements of 21 CFR Part 11

1. System Validation:

- **Validation Plans:** Organizations must develop and maintain detailed validation plans that outline the validation process, including objectives, scope, responsibilities, and methodologies.
- **Validation Documentation:** Comprehensive documentation of the validation process, including protocols, test scripts, results, and reports, must be maintained.

2. Audit Trails:

- **Audit Trail Implementation:** Secure, computer-generated, time-stamped audit trails must be implemented to record the creation, modification, and deletion of electronic records.
- **Audit Trail Review:** Audit trails must be regularly reviewed to ensure compliance and identify any unauthorized changes to records.

3. Record Retention:

- **Retention Policies:** Organizations must establish and maintain record retention policies that comply with FDA requirements. Electronic records must be retained for the duration specified by applicable regulations.
- **Archiving Procedures:** Procedures for the secure archiving and retrieval of electronic records must be in place to ensure their integrity over time.

4. Security Controls:

- **Access Controls:** Physical and logical access controls must be implemented to prevent unauthorized access to electronic systems and records.
- **User Authentication:** Robust user authentication mechanisms, such as passwords, biometrics, or two-factor authentication, must be used to verify the identity of users accessing electronic systems.

5. Electronic Signatures:

- **Unique Signatures:** Electronic signatures must be unique to the individual and not reused by others. They must include the signer's name, the date and time of signing, and the meaning associated with the signature (e.g., approval, review).
- **Signature Authentication:** Procedures must be in place to verify the identity of individuals using electronic signatures. This includes initial identity verification and periodic re-verification.

6. Training and Documentation:

- **Training Programs:** Comprehensive training programs must be implemented to ensure that personnel understand the requirements of 21 CFR Part 11 and how to comply with them.
- **SOPs:** Standard operating procedures must be developed and maintained to outline the processes for system validation, audit trail management, record retention, security controls, and the use of electronic signatures.

Example of 21 CFR Part 11 Compliance in Practice

Title: Compliance with 21 CFR Part 11 for Electronic Laboratory Records

Scope: This document outlines the procedures for ensuring compliance with 21 CFR Part 11 for electronic laboratory records in a pharmaceutical research laboratory.

Responsibilities:

- The Quality Assurance (QA) Manager is responsible for overseeing compliance with 21 CFR Part 11.
- The IT Department is responsible for implementing and maintaining secure electronic systems.
- Laboratory personnel are responsible for following SOPs related to electronic records and signatures.

Procedure:
System Validation:

1. Develop a validation plan outlining the scope, objectives, and methodology for system validation.
2. Perform validation testing according to the plan, including installation qualification (IQ), operational qualification (OQ), and performance qualification (PQ).
3. Document all validation activities and maintain records for review.

Audit Trails:

1. Implement audit trails to track all changes to electronic records, including the creation, modification, and deletion of data.
2. Ensure audit trails are secure, time-stamped, and cannot be altered.

3. Review audit trails regularly to ensure compliance and detect any unauthorized changes.

Record Retention:

1. Establish record retention policies that comply with FDA requirements.
2. Archive electronic records securely and ensure they are retrievable for the specified retention period.
3. Regularly review retention policies and update as necessary.

Security Controls:

1. Implement physical and logical access controls to secure electronic systems.
2. Use robust user authentication mechanisms to verify the identity of users.
3. Conduct regular security assessments to identify and mitigate vulnerabilities.

Electronic Signatures:

1. Ensure that electronic signatures are unique to each individual and include the signer's name, date and time of signing, and the meaning associated with the signature.
2. Implement procedures for initial identity verification and periodic re-verification of individuals using electronic signatures.
3. Maintain records of electronic signatures for audit purposes.

Training and Documentation:

1. Develop and implement training programs to educate personnel on the requirements of 21 CFR Part 11.
2. Maintain comprehensive SOPs that outline the procedures for system validation, audit trail management, record retention, security controls, and the use of electronic signatures.
3. Regularly review and update training materials and SOPs to ensure they remain current and effective.

3.6 General Checklist for 21 CFR Part 11

21 CFR Part 11 compliance is crucial for ensuring that electronic records and electronic signatures are trustworthy, reliable, and equivalent to paper records and handwritten signatures. To aid in achieving and maintaining compliance, a general checklist can serve as a valuable tool for organizations. This checklist outlines the key areas and specific items that need to be addressed to meet the requirements of 21 CFR Part 11. Below is a comprehensive checklist categorized by critical compliance areas.

System Validation:

1. **Validation Plan:**

   - Develop and maintain a comprehensive validation plan.
   - Define the scope, objectives, methodology, and responsibilities.

2. **Installation Qualification (IQ):**

   - Verify that systems are installed according to specifications.
   - Document all installation procedures and configurations.

3. **Operational Qualification (OQ):**

   - Test system functionalities to ensure they operate as intended.
   - Document all operational tests and results.

4. **Performance Qualification (PQ):**

   - Verify that systems perform consistently under real-world conditions.
   - Document performance tests and review results regularly.

5. **Validation Documentation:**

   - Maintain detailed records of all validation activities.
   - Ensure documentation is readily available for review.

Audit Trails:

1. **Implementation:**

   - Implement secure, computer-generated, time-stamped audit trails.
   - Ensure audit trails capture all record creation, modification, and deletion events.

2. **Security:**

   - Protect audit trails from unauthorized access or alterations.
   - Ensure audit trails are tamper-evident.

3. **Review:**

   - Regularly review audit trails for compliance and anomalies.
   - Document audit trail reviews and findings.

Electronic Records:

1. **Integrity:**

   - Ensure electronic records are accurate, complete, and consistent.
   - Implement data validation checks to maintain integrity.

2. **Security:**

   - Implement robust security measures to protect electronic records.
   - Control access to records through user authentication and role-based permissions.

3. **Retention:**

   - Establish and maintain records retention policies in compliance with regulatory requirements.
   - Ensure electronic records are archived securely and remain retrievable for the required retention period.

Electronic Signatures:

1. **Uniqueness:**

   - Ensure each electronic signature is unique to one individual.
   - Prevent the reuse of electronic signatures by others.

2. **Authentication:**

   - Implement procedures for initial identity verification and periodic re-verification.
   - Use strong authentication methods such as passwords, biometrics, or two-factor authentication.

3. **Documentation:**

   - Maintain records of all electronic signatures, including the signer's name, date and time of signing, and the meaning associated with the signature.
   - Ensure electronic signatures are linked to their respective electronic records.

Security Controls:

1. **Access Controls:**

   - Implement physical and logical access controls to protect electronic systems.
   - Define and enforce user access levels based on roles and responsibilities.

2. **User Authentication:**

   - Use strong authentication mechanisms to verify user identity.
   - Implement measures to protect authentication credentials from unauthorized access.

3. **System Security:**

- Conduct regular security assessments to identify and mitigate vulnerabilities.
- Implement measures such as firewalls, encryption, and intrusion detection systems.

Training and Documentation:

1. **Training Programs:**

   - Develop and implement comprehensive training programs on 21 CFR Part 11 requirements.
   - Ensure all personnel are trained on the use of electronic systems, audit trails, and electronic signatures.

2. **Standard Operating Procedures (SOPs):**

   - Develop and maintain SOPs for all aspects of system operation, maintenance, data management, and compliance.
   - Regularly review and update SOPs to ensure they remain current.

3. **Documentation:**

   - Maintain detailed records of training activities, including attendance, assessments, and training materials.
   - Ensure all documentation related to 21 CFR Part 11 compliance is complete and readily accessible.

Compliance and Monitoring:

1. **Internal Audits:**

   - Conduct regular internal audits to assess compliance with 21 CFR Part 11.
   - Document audit findings and corrective actions.

2. **External Inspections:**

- Prepare for FDA inspections and ensure all compliance documentation is up-to-date.
- Address any findings from inspections promptly and thoroughly.

3. **Continuous Improvement:**

- Implement a system for collecting feedback and identifying areas for improvement.
- Regularly review and enhance compliance practices based on feedback and regulatory updates.

General Checklist:

- Develop a comprehensive validation plan.
- Conduct and document IQ, OQ, and PQ for all systems.
- Implement secure, time-stamped audit trails.
- Regularly review audit trails and document findings.
- Ensure the accuracy, completeness, and consistency of electronic records.
- Implement robust security measures for electronic records.
- Establish and follow records retention policies.
- Ensure the uniqueness and security of electronic signatures.
- Implement strong user authentication and access controls.
- Conduct regular security assessments and implement necessary measures.
- Develop and maintain comprehensive SOPs.
- Implement and document training programs for all personnel.
- Conduct regular internal audits and prepare for external inspections.
- Maintain detailed documentation of all compliance activities.
- Implement a continuous improvement process for compliance practices.

3.7 Software Evaluation Checklist

Evaluating software for compliance with **21 CFR Part 11** is essential to ensure that electronic records and electronic signatures are reliable, secure, and compliant with regulatory standards. A comprehensive software evaluation checklist helps organizations systematically assess software functionalities, security measures, and compliance capabilities. Below is a detailed checklist for evaluating software in the context of 21 CFR Part 11.

General Requirements:

- **System Description:**

    ○ Clearly describe the software's purpose, functionalities, and scope of use.

- **Vendor Assessment:**

    ○ Evaluate the vendor's reputation, experience, and support capabilities.
    ○ Review vendor documentation and user testimonials.

System Validation:

- **Validation Plan:**

    ○ Develop a detailed validation plan specific to the software.
    ○ Include objectives, scope, methodology, and responsibilities.

- **Documentation:**

    ○ Ensure comprehensive validation documentation is available, including IQ, OQ, and PQ protocols and results.

- **Performance Testing:**

    ○ Verify the software performs reliably under various conditions.

- Test all critical functionalities and document the results.

Data Integrity:

- **Data Accuracy:**

  - Ensure the software accurately captures and stores data.
  - Validate data entry, modification, and retrieval processes.

- **Data Completeness:**

  - Confirm that the software ensures complete data capture without loss or corruption.
  - Review data handling processes and storage mechanisms.

- **Data Consistency:**

  - Verify that the software maintains consistent data formats and structures.
  - Ensure data consistency across different modules and integrated systems.

Security Controls:

- **User Authentication:**

  - Implement strong user authentication mechanisms (e.g., passwords, biometrics).
  - Ensure user authentication procedures comply with regulatory requirements.

- **Access Controls:**

  - Define and enforce role-based access controls.
  - Ensure access controls restrict users to only necessary functionalities and data.

- **Data Encryption:**

- ◦ Confirm the software uses encryption to protect data at rest and in transit.
- ◦ Review encryption methods and key management practices.

Audit Trails:

- **Implementation:**

  - ◦ Ensure the software generates secure, time-stamped audit trails.
  - ◦ Audit trails should record all relevant actions, including data creation, modification, and deletion.

- **Tamper-Evident:**

  - ◦ Verify that audit trails are tamper-evident and protected from unauthorized access.
  - ◦ Ensure audit trails cannot be modified or deleted.

- **Review and Reporting:**

  - ◦ Implement procedures for regular audit trail reviews.
  - ◦ Ensure the software provides easy access to audit trail reports for inspection.

Electronic Signatures:

- **Uniqueness:**

  - ◦ Confirm that electronic signatures are unique to each individual.
  - ◦ Prevent the reuse or unauthorized use of electronic signatures.

- **Linkage:**

  - ◦ Ensure electronic signatures are linked to their respective electronic records.
  - ◦ Verify that each signature includes the signer's name, date and time of signing, and the meaning of the signature.

- **Authentication:**

  - Implement procedures for verifying the identity of individuals using electronic signatures.
  - Use multi-factor authentication to enhance security.

System Usability:

- **User Interface:**

  - Evaluate the software's user interface for ease of use and clarity.
  - Ensure the interface supports efficient and error-free operation.

- **Training and Support:**

  - Confirm the availability of comprehensive training materials and support resources.
  - Evaluate the vendor's training programs and user support services.

Documentation and Reporting:

- **Compliance Documentation:**

  - Ensure the software includes all necessary compliance documentation.
  - Maintain detailed records of software validation, user training, and operational procedures.

- **Reporting Capabilities:**

  - Evaluate the software's reporting capabilities for generating compliance and operational reports.
  - Ensure reports are customizable and meet regulatory requirements.

Maintenance and Updates:

- **Regular Updates:**

- Confirm the software is regularly updated to address security vulnerabilities and compliance changes.
- Review the vendor's update and patch management processes.

- **Change Control:**

  - Implement a robust change control process for software updates and modifications.
  - Document all changes and ensure they do not compromise compliance.

Vendor Support and Service Level Agreements (SLAs):

- **Support Availability:**

  - Verify the availability and responsiveness of vendor support services.
  - Ensure support is available during critical operational hours.

- **Service Level Agreements:**

  - Review and agree on SLAs with the vendor, specifying response times, resolution times, and performance metrics.

Backup and Recovery:

- **Data Backup:**

  - Ensure the software supports regular and secure data backup processes.
  - Verify backup frequency and storage methods.

- **Disaster Recovery:**

  - Implement a comprehensive disaster recovery plan.
  - Test recovery procedures to ensure data can be restored quickly and accurately in case of an incident.

Regulatory Compliance:

- **21 CFR Part 11 Compliance:**

  - Confirm the software meets all specific requirements of 21 CFR Part 11.
  - Conduct a detailed compliance assessment and document findings.

- **Other Regulatory Standards:**

  - Ensure the software complies with other relevant regulatory standards (e.g., GDPR, HIPAA).
  - Review and document compliance with these standards.

3.8 Relevant ISO and QCI Standards

When implementing **Good Automated Laboratory Practice (GALP)** and ensuring compliance with regulatory frameworks like **21 CFR Part 11**, it is crucial to adhere to relevant standards established by the International Organization for Standardization (ISO) and the Quality Council of India (QCI). These standards provide guidelines and best practices for maintaining quality, reliability, and consistency in laboratory operations. Below is an overview of the key ISO and QCI standards relevant to GALP.

ISO Standards

1. ISO 9001:2015 - Quality Management Systems:

- **Overview:** ISO 9001:2015 specifies requirements for a quality management system (QMS) where an organization needs to demonstrate its ability to consistently provide products and services that meet customer and regulatory requirements.
- **Key Elements:**

  - Quality policy and objectives
  - Risk management and process approach
  - Performance evaluation and continuous improvement
  - Documentation and record-keeping

2. ISO/IEC 17025:2017 - General Requirements for the Competence of Testing and Calibration Laboratories:

- **Overview:** ISO/IEC 17025:2017 outlines the general requirements for the competence, impartiality, and consistent operation of laboratories.
- **Key Elements:**

  - Management system requirements
  - Structural and resource requirements
  - Process requirements, including method validation and measurement traceability
  - Reporting of results and continuous improvement

3. ISO 15189:2012 - Medical Laboratories - Requirements for Quality and Competence:

- **Overview:** ISO 15189:2012 specifies requirements for quality and competence in medical laboratories.
- **Key Elements:**

  - Quality management system specific to medical laboratories
  - Laboratory technical requirements
  - Equipment calibration and maintenance
  - Personnel qualifications and training

4. ISO/IEC 27001:2013 - Information Security Management Systems:

- **Overview:** ISO/IEC 27001:2013 specifies requirements for establishing, implementing, maintaining, and continually improving an information security management system (ISMS).
- **Key Elements:**

  - Information security policies and risk assessment
  - Access control and cryptography
  - Physical and environmental security
  - Security incident management and compliance

5. ISO 13485:2016 - Medical Devices - Quality Management Systems:

- **Overview:** ISO 13485:2016 specifies requirements for a QMS where an organization needs to demonstrate its ability to provide medical devices and related services that consistently meet customer and regulatory requirements.
- **Key Elements:**

  - Risk management and design controls
  - Document and record control
  - Production and process controls
  - Corrective and preventive actions (CAPA)

QCI Standards

1. NABL 112 - Guidelines for Internal Audit and Management Review for Laboratories:

- **Overview:** NABL 112 provides guidelines for laboratories to conduct internal audits and management reviews to ensure continuous improvement and compliance with accreditation criteria.
- **Key Elements:**

  - Planning and conducting internal audits
  - Management review process
  - Identifying non-conformities and corrective actions
  - Continuous improvement initiatives

2. NABL 122 - Specific Criteria for Accreditation of Medical Laboratories:

- **Overview:** NABL 122 outlines specific criteria for the accreditation of medical laboratories, ensuring they meet the necessary standards for quality and competence.
- **Key Elements:**

  - Quality management system requirements
  - Personnel qualifications and training
  - Equipment and calibration standards
  - Laboratory safety and hygiene

3. NABH - Accreditation Standards for Hospitals:

- **Overview:** NABH (National Accreditation Board for Hospitals & Healthcare Providers) provides a set of standards for hospitals to ensure high-quality healthcare services.
- **Key Elements:**

  - Patient safety and care
  - Hospital infrastructure and facilities
  - Quality management and improvement
  - Documentation and record-keeping

4. QCI Scheme for Laboratory Accreditation:

- **Overview:** QCI's scheme for laboratory accreditation aims to improve the quality and reliability of laboratories through accreditation based on internationally accepted standards.
- **Key Elements:**

  - Assessment of technical competence
  - Quality management system requirements
  - Regular surveillance and reassessment
  - Training and capacity building

Implementation of ISO and QCI Standards in GALP

1. **Quality Management System (QMS):**

   - Implement a QMS based on ISO 9001:2015 and ISO/IEC 17025:2017 to ensure consistent quality in laboratory processes.
   - Document quality policies, objectives, and procedures.
   - Conduct regular internal audits and management reviews as per NABL 112 guidelines.

2. **Competence and Training:**

   - Ensure personnel are trained and qualified according to ISO 15189:2012 and ISO/IEC 17025:2017 standards.
   - Maintain records of training and competency assessments.
   - Implement continuous training programs and competency evaluations.

3. **Information Security:**

   - Establish an ISMS following ISO/IEC 27001:2013 to protect electronic records and data.
   - Implement access controls, encryption, and security policies.
   - Conduct regular security risk assessments and incident management.

4. **Equipment Calibration and Maintenance:**

- Calibrate and maintain laboratory equipment in compliance with ISO/IEC 17025:2017 and NABL standards.
- Keep detailed records of calibration activities and maintenance schedules.
- Perform regular validation and verification of equipment performance.

5. **Regulatory Compliance:**

- Ensure electronic records and electronic signatures comply with 21 CFR Part 11 and ISO 9001:2015 requirements.
- Implement audit trails, data integrity checks, and secure data storage.
- Regularly review and update compliance documentation.

6. **Continuous Improvement:**

- Implement CAPA procedures based on ISO 13485:2016 to address non-conformities and improve processes.
- Collect and analyze feedback from audits, inspections, and user experiences.
- Foster a culture of continuous improvement and innovation.

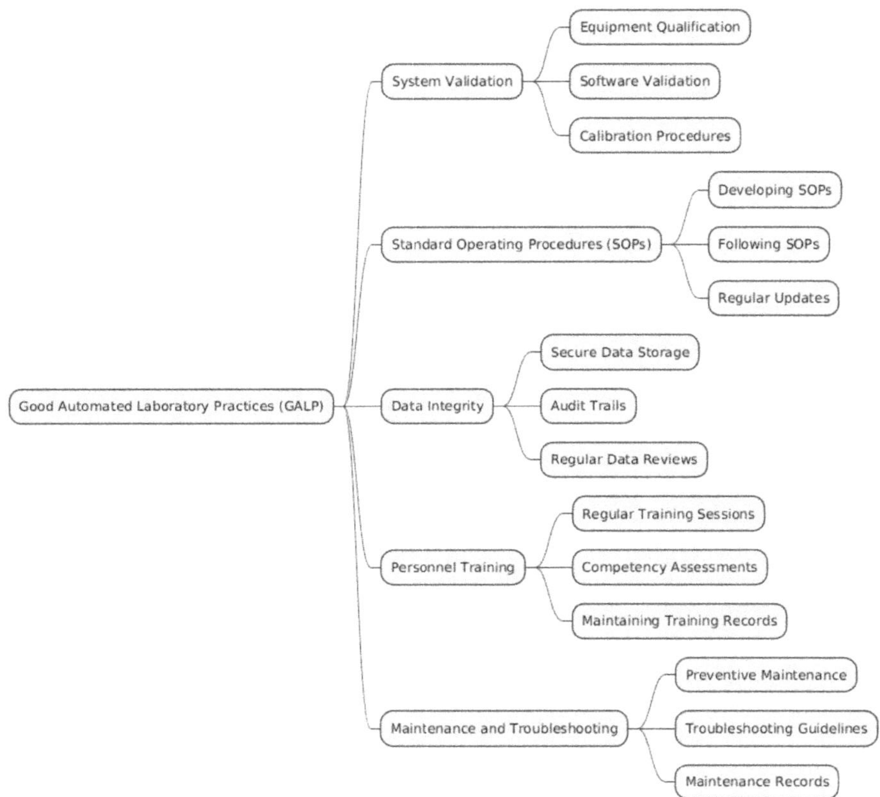

Overview of Good Automated Laboratory Practices (GALP) Key Activities and Interactions

Good Distribution Practices

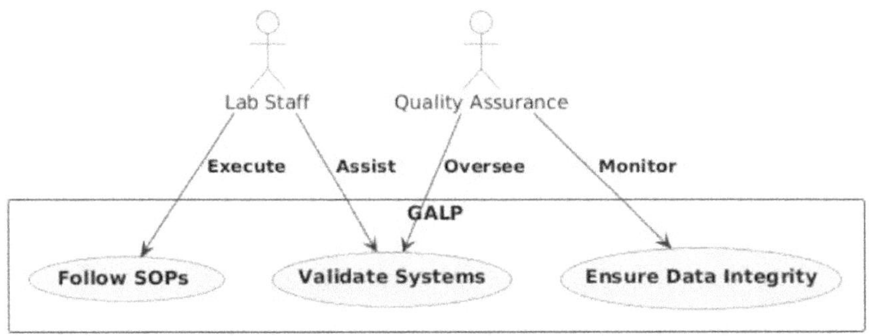

GALP: Roles and Responsibilities of Lab Staff and Quality Assurance

4.1 Introduction to GDP

Gross Domestic Product (GDP) is one of the most crucial indicators used to gauge the health and size of a country's economy. **GDP** represents the total monetary value of all goods and services produced within a nation's borders over a specific period, usually calculated annually or quarterly. This measure includes everything produced by all the people and companies within a country, providing a comprehensive snapshot of its economic activity.

Importance and Components of GDP

The importance of **GDP** lies in its ability to provide a clear picture of the economic performance of a country. Policymakers, economists, and analysts use **GDP** to assess economic growth, make comparisons between different economies, and formulate economic policies. **GDP** can be broken down into four main components: consumption, investment, government spending, and net exports.

Consumption is the largest component and includes all private expenditures by households on goods and services, such as food, clothing, and healthcare. **Investment** encompasses business expenditures on capital goods like machinery and buildings, as well as residential construction and changes in inventories. **Government spending** covers expenditures on goods and services that government agencies provide, excluding transfer payments like pensions and unemployment benefits. **Net exports** are calculated as the difference between a country's exports and imports.

Methods of Calculating GDP

There are three primary methods to calculate **GDP**: the production approach, the income approach, and the expenditure approach.

1. **Production Approach**: Also known as the output approach, this method sums the value added at each stage of production. Value added is the market value of a firm's output minus the value of inputs bought from other firms. For example, if a baker produces bread worth ₹1,000 using flour and other ingredients worth ₹600, the value added by the baker is ₹400.

2. **Income Approach**: This method calculates **GDP** by summing up all the incomes earned by individuals and businesses in an economy, including wages, profits, rents, and taxes, minus subsidies. It essentially measures **GDP** by the total income generated by production. For instance, if workers earn ₹500 in wages, companies earn ₹300 in profits, and landlords earn ₹200 in rent, the **GDP** using the income approach would be ₹1,000.

3. **Expenditure Approach**: The most commonly used method, this approach sums the total spending on the nation's final goods and services. It follows the formula: **GDP** = Consumption (C) + Investment (I) + Government Spending (G) + Net Exports (NX). If households spend ₹500, businesses invest ₹200, the government spends ₹150, and

the net exports are ₹50, the **GDP** would be ₹900.

Real vs. Nominal GDP

Nominal GDP measures a country's total economic output without adjusting for inflation. It is calculated using current market prices, which means it can be influenced by changes in price levels. **Real GDP**, on the other hand, adjusts for inflation and reflects the true value of goods and services at constant prices. This adjustment allows for more accurate comparisons over time by removing the effects of price changes.

GDP Growth Rate

The **GDP growth rate** is an important indicator of economic health. It measures how fast a country's economy is growing by comparing **GDP** from one period to another. A positive growth rate indicates a growing economy, while a negative rate may signify economic troubles. For instance, if India's **GDP** was ₹100 trillion last year and grew to ₹105 trillion this year, the growth rate would be 5%.

GDP Per Capita

GDP per capita divides the total **GDP** by the population, providing an average economic output per person. This measure helps compare the standard of living across different countries. For example, if India's **GDP** is ₹150 trillion and the population is 1.5 billion, the **GDP per capita** would be ₹100,000.

Limitations of GDP

Despite its widespread use, **GDP** has several limitations. It does not account for the distribution of income among residents of a country, nor does it consider whether the nation's rate of growth is sustainable in the long term. Additionally, **GDP** does not measure the informal economy or non-market transactions, such as volunteer work and household labor, which can be significant in some countries.

GDP also does not take into account the negative effects of economic growth on the environment. For example, if a factory increases production, it may boost **GDP**, but if this results in significant pollution, the environmental damage is not reflected in the **GDP** figures.

4.2 Legal GDP Requirements Worldwide

Introduction

Gross Domestic Product (GDP), as a critical measure of economic performance, is subject to various legal requirements and standards worldwide. These regulations ensure the accuracy, consistency, and transparency of GDP calculations, enabling reliable comparisons between different countries and over time. Understanding these legal requirements is essential for policymakers, economists, and international organizations.

International Standards for GDP Calculation

The calculation and reporting of **GDP** are governed by international standards to maintain consistency across countries. The most widely adopted framework is the **System of National Accounts (SNA)**, developed jointly by several international organizations, including the United Nations (UN), the International Monetary Fund (IMF), the World Bank, the Organisation for Economic Co-operation and Development (OECD), and the European Union (EU). The latest version, the **2008 SNA**, provides comprehensive guidelines on concepts, definitions, classifications, and accounting rules for national accounting.

Legal Framework in Different Countries

Each country implements the SNA guidelines through its own legal and institutional frameworks. The national statistical offices (NSOs) are typically responsible for compiling and reporting **GDP** data. These offices must adhere to their country's statistical laws and regulations, which often mandate the collection, processing, and dissemination of economic data.

United States

In the United States, the **Bureau of Economic Analysis (BEA)** is responsible for producing **GDP** estimates. The **BEA** follows the guidelines provided by the **Office of Management and Budget (OMB)** and complies with the principles of the **SNA**. The **GDP** data must be reported quarterly and annually, with detailed breakdowns by sector and industry. The legal basis for these activities is provided by the **Economics and Statistics Administration (ESA) of the Department of Commerce**.

European Union

The European Union requires its member states to follow the **European System of Accounts (ESA)**, which is aligned with the **SNA**. The **Eurostat**, the statistical office of the EU, oversees the implementation of the **ESA** and ensures the quality and comparability of **GDP** data across member countries. Legal requirements for national accounts in the EU are outlined in the **Council Regulation (EC) No 2223/96**, which mandates regular reporting and adherence to specific methodological standards.

India

In India, the **Central Statistics Office (CSO)** under the Ministry of Statistics and Programme Implementation (MoSPI) is responsible for calculating **GDP**. The CSO follows the guidelines of the **SNA** and the recommendations of the National Statistical Commission (NSC). The **Collection of Statistics Act, 2008**, provides the legal framework for the collection of economic data, ensuring accuracy and reliability. The **CSO** publishes **GDP** estimates on a quarterly and annual basis, with detailed sectoral breakdowns.

China

China's **National Bureau of Statistics (NBS)** is tasked with compiling **GDP** figures. The **NBS** follows the principles of the **SNA** and adheres to the regulations set forth by the **Statistics Law of the People's Republic of China**. The law mandates the collection, verification, and publication of economic data to ensure transparency and accuracy. The **NBS** publishes **GDP** data quarterly and annually, providing insights into the country's economic performance.

Transparency and Accountability

Transparency and accountability are crucial components of the legal requirements for **GDP** calculations. Countries are required to provide detailed documentation of their methodologies, data sources, and any adjustments made to ensure the accuracy and reliability of **GDP** figures. This transparency helps build trust among stakeholders, including investors, policymakers, and international organizations.

International organizations such as the **IMF** and the **World Bank** conduct regular reviews and audits of countries' **GDP** compilation processes. These reviews assess the adherence to international standards and provide recommendations for improvement. For instance, the **IMF's Data Quality Assessment Framework (DQAF)** evaluates the quality of national accounts data based on criteria such as integrity, methodological soundness, and accuracy.

Challenges and Compliance

Despite the comprehensive legal frameworks, countries may face challenges in complying with **GDP** calculation standards. These challenges can include data availability, resource constraints, and differences in economic structures. For example, measuring the informal economy, which can be significant in developing countries, poses a challenge for accurate **GDP** estimation. To address these challenges, countries often collaborate with international organizations for technical assistance and capacity building.

4.3 Principles and Personnel in GDP

Introduction

The calculation and analysis of **Gross Domestic Product (GDP)** involve adherence to certain fundamental principles and the engagement of skilled personnel. These principles ensure the accuracy and reliability of **GDP** as an economic measure, while the personnel involved play a critical role in collecting, processing, and interpreting the data.

Fundamental Principles of GDP Calculation

Several key principles underpin the calculation of **GDP**. These principles are designed to ensure that **GDP** figures are consistent, comparable, and reflective of true economic activity.

1. **Comprehensive Coverage**: GDP should cover all economic activities within a country's borders, including the production of goods and services, both market and non-market. This includes agriculture, manufacturing, services, government activities, and the informal sector.
2. **Market Valuation**: Economic activities should be valued at market prices, which reflect the amount people are willing to pay for goods and services. This principle ensures that **GDP** accurately represents the economic value of production.
3. **Double Counting Avoidance**: To avoid double counting, only the value added at each stage of production is included in **GDP**. This principle ensures that intermediate goods, which are used to produce other goods, are not counted multiple times.
4. **Consistency and Comparability**: GDP calculations should be consistent over time and comparable across countries. This requires the use of standardized methods and classifications as outlined in international frameworks like the **System of National Accounts (SNA)**.
5. **Accuracy and Timeliness**: Accurate and timely data collection is crucial for reliable **GDP** estimates. Regular updates and revisions are necessary to reflect the most current economic conditions.

Personnel Involved in GDP Calculation

The accurate calculation of **GDP** requires the involvement of various skilled personnel, including statisticians, economists, data analysts, and field surveyors. Each of these roles plays a vital part in the **GDP** estimation process.

1. **Statisticians**: Statisticians are responsible for designing surveys, sampling methods, and data collection instruments. They ensure that the data collected is representative of the entire economy and meets statistical standards.
2. **Economists**: Economists interpret the data and apply economic theories to ensure that the **GDP** figures accurately reflect economic activity. They also analyze trends, make forecasts, and provide insights that inform policy decisions.
3. **Data Analysts**: Data analysts process and analyze the raw data collected from various sources. They use statistical software and techniques to clean, validate, and aggregate the data, ensuring its accuracy and consistency.
4. **Field Surveyors**: Field surveyors collect primary data from households, businesses, and government agencies. Their role is crucial in gathering firsthand information on production, consumption, investment, and other economic activities.
5. **National Statistical Offices (NSOs)**: NSOs coordinate the entire **GDP** estimation process. They oversee data collection, processing, and dissemination, ensuring adherence to international standards and national regulations.

Training and Capacity Building

Continuous training and capacity building are essential for the personnel involved in **GDP** calculation. International organizations such as the **International Monetary Fund (IMF)** and the **World Bank** provide technical assistance and training programs to enhance the skills of statisticians and economists. These programs focus on best practices in national accounting, data collection methodologies, and the use of statistical software.

4.4 Documentation in GDP

Introduction

Documentation plays a vital role in the calculation and reporting of **Gross Domestic Product (GDP)**. Proper documentation ensures transparency, accuracy, and consistency in **GDP** estimation, facilitating reliable comparisons over time and across countries. This section explores the importance of documentation, the types of documents involved, and the procedures for maintaining and accessing these records.

Importance of Documentation

1. **Transparency**: Detailed documentation provides transparency in the **GDP** calculation process. It allows stakeholders, including policymakers, researchers, and the public, to understand how **GDP** figures are derived and the methodologies used.
2. **Accuracy**: Proper documentation ensures that all steps in the **GDP** calculation process are recorded and can be reviewed for accuracy. It helps identify and correct any errors or discrepancies in the data.
3. **Consistency**: Documentation ensures that consistent methods and procedures are used over time. This consistency is crucial for making reliable comparisons of **GDP** data across different periods.
4. **Compliance**: Detailed records help ensure compliance with national and international standards for **GDP** calculation. They provide evidence that the data collection and processing methods adhere to prescribed guidelines.

Types of Documentation

Several types of documents are involved in the **GDP** calculation process. These documents provide a comprehensive record of the methodologies, data sources, and procedures used.

1. **Methodological Documents**: These documents outline the methods and procedures used for **GDP** calculation. They include details on the data collection instruments, sampling methods, and statistical techniques employed.
2. **Data Collection Forms**: Forms used to collect primary data from households, businesses, and government agencies. These forms capture information on production, consumption, investment, and other economic activities.
3. **Data Processing Records**: Documentation of the data processing steps, including data cleaning, validation, and aggregation procedures. These records ensure that the raw data is accurately transformed into usable statistics.
4. **Quality Assurance Reports**: Reports that detail the quality assurance measures taken to ensure the accuracy and reliability of **GDP** data. These reports include information on data validation checks, error correction procedures, and review processes.
5. **Revision Logs**: Logs that document any revisions made to **GDP** figures. They provide details on the reasons for the revisions and the impact on previously reported data.
6. **Dissemination Reports**: Reports that outline the procedures for disseminating **GDP** data to the public. They include information on the formats and channels used for data release, as well as the timing and frequency of updates.

Documentation Procedures

Proper procedures must be followed to ensure that documentation is maintained accurately and is easily accessible. These procedures include:

1. **Standardized Formats**: Using standardized formats for all documentation ensures consistency and makes it easier to review and understand the records.
2. **Regular Updates**: Documentation should be updated regularly to reflect any changes in methodologies, data sources, or procedures. This ensures that the records are always current and accurate.
3. **Secure Storage**: Documentation should be stored securely to prevent loss or unauthorized access. Digital records should be backed up

regularly, and physical documents should be kept in a secure location.

4. **Access and Review**: Procedures should be in place to allow authorized personnel to access and review the documentation. Regular reviews help ensure that the records are complete and accurate.

5. **Training**: Personnel involved in **GDP** calculation should be trained on the importance of documentation and the procedures for maintaining it. This training helps ensure that all steps in the process are properly recorded.

4.5 Premises and Equipment for GDP

Introduction

The accurate calculation of **Gross Domestic Product (GDP)** relies heavily on the infrastructure and equipment used in data collection, processing, and analysis. Proper premises and state-of-the-art equipment ensure that the data is collected efficiently, processed accurately, and analyzed correctly. This section delves into the types of premises and equipment necessary for **GDP** estimation, their importance, and how they contribute to the overall accuracy and reliability of **GDP** figures.

Premises for GDP Calculation

1. **National Statistical Offices (NSOs)**: The central hub for GDP calculation is the National Statistical Office. This office is responsible for coordinating all activities related to GDP estimation, including data collection, processing, analysis, and dissemination. The NSO must be equipped with adequate space and facilities to house various departments and personnel involved in these activities.
2. **Data Collection Centers**: These centers are dedicated to collecting raw data from various sources, such as households, businesses, and government agencies. They should be strategically located to facilitate easy access to different data sources and equipped with facilities for field surveyors and data collectors.
3. **Data Processing Units**: Once the data is collected, it needs to be processed accurately. Data processing units within the NSO should be equipped with modern computer systems and software to handle large volumes of data efficiently. These units also require secure environments to ensure the confidentiality and integrity of the data.
4. **Research and Analysis Departments**: These departments are responsible for analyzing the processed data and generating GDP estimates. They need access to advanced analytical tools and resources, as well as a collaborative workspace where economists and statisticians

can work together.

5. **Training and Development Centers**: Continuous training is crucial for the personnel involved in GDP calculation. Training centers within the NSO provide ongoing education and skill development for staff, ensuring they are up-to-date with the latest methodologies and technologies in national accounting.

Equipment for GDP Calculation

1. **Computing Infrastructure**: Modern computing infrastructure is essential for processing and analyzing large datasets. This includes high-performance servers, workstations, and data storage systems. Reliable and powerful computers enable statisticians and economists to run complex models and simulations necessary for accurate GDP estimation.

2. **Statistical Software**: Specialized statistical software is used to analyze the data and generate GDP estimates. Software such as STATA, SAS, R, and SPSS provide the tools needed for data manipulation, statistical analysis, and visualization. These programs help ensure the accuracy and reliability of the GDP figures.

3. **Data Collection Tools**: Field surveyors and data collectors use various tools to gather primary data. This includes electronic devices such as tablets and laptops equipped with data collection applications, as well as traditional methods like paper questionnaires. Electronic data collection tools increase efficiency and reduce errors in data entry.

4. **Networking and Communication Equipment**: Efficient communication and data transfer are crucial in GDP calculation. Networking equipment such as routers, switches, and secure internet connections facilitate the seamless transfer of data between collection centers, processing units, and analysis departments. Communication tools like video conferencing systems and secure email services enable collaboration among team members.

5. **Data Security Systems**: Ensuring the confidentiality and integrity of the data is paramount. Data security systems, including firewalls, encryption software, and secure access controls, protect sensitive information from unauthorized access and cyber threats. These systems are essential for maintaining the trust and reliability of the GDP data.

6. **Office Equipment**: Basic office equipment, such as printers, scanners, copiers, and telecommunication devices, support the daily operations of the NSO. These tools are necessary for the documentation, dissemination, and administrative tasks involved in GDP calculation.

Importance of Proper Premises and Equipment

1. **Efficiency**: Proper premises and equipment streamline the data collection and processing activities, ensuring that the GDP calculation is completed efficiently and on time. This is particularly important for meeting reporting deadlines and providing timely economic indicators.
2. **Accuracy**: High-quality equipment and a well-organized workspace contribute to the accuracy of the GDP figures. Advanced computing infrastructure and statistical software help minimize errors and enhance the precision of the data analysis.
3. **Security**: Secure premises and robust data security systems protect sensitive economic data from breaches and unauthorized access. This is crucial for maintaining the integrity and confidentiality of the GDP figures.
4. **Collaboration**: Adequate space and modern communication tools facilitate collaboration among different departments and personnel involved in GDP calculation. This collaborative environment helps improve the quality and reliability of the GDP estimates.
5. **Adaptability**: Well-equipped premises and advanced technology enable the NSO to adapt to new methodologies and standards in national accounting. This adaptability is essential for keeping up with international best practices and improving the overall quality of the GDP data.

4.6 Delivery to Customers and Returns

Introduction

In the context of economic data, particularly **Gross Domestic Product (GDP)** calculation and reporting, the "delivery to customers and returns" refers to the dissemination of **GDP** data to stakeholders and the feedback or revisions process that follows. Ensuring the effective delivery of GDP data to its users and managing revisions and corrections based on new information are critical for maintaining the credibility and utility of this vital economic indicator.

Delivery to Customers

GDP data must be delivered efficiently and transparently to a wide range of customers, including government agencies, policymakers, researchers, businesses, and the general public. This dissemination involves several key components:

1. **Publication Channels**: GDP data is published through various channels to reach a broad audience. These channels include official websites of national statistical offices (NSOs), printed reports, press releases, and digital platforms. The use of multiple channels ensures that the data is accessible to all stakeholders.
2. **Regular Updates**: GDP data is typically reported on a quarterly and annual basis. Regular updates provide timely insights into the economic performance of a country, enabling stakeholders to make informed decisions. For example, the United States Bureau of Economic Analysis (BEA) publishes quarterly GDP reports, while the Central Statistics Office (CSO) in India releases both quarterly and annual estimates.
3. **User-Friendly Formats**: To ensure that GDP data is easily understood, it is often presented in user-friendly formats such as charts, graphs, and summary tables. Detailed methodological notes and explanations accompany the data to help users interpret the figures correctly.

4. **Open Data Access**: Many NSOs adopt open data policies, allowing free access to GDP data and related statistical information. This transparency fosters trust and encourages the use of data for research and policy analysis. For example, the European Union's Eurostat provides free access to extensive economic data, including GDP figures.

5. **Interactive Tools**: Some statistical agencies offer interactive tools and dashboards on their websites, enabling users to explore GDP data in more detail. These tools allow users to customize data views, conduct time series analysis, and compare economic performance across different regions and sectors.

Returns and Revisions

Economic data, including **GDP**, is subject to revisions as more accurate or complete information becomes available. Managing these returns and revisions is a critical aspect of maintaining data quality and credibility.

1. **Revision Policies**: National statistical offices have established policies and procedures for revising GDP data. These policies outline the circumstances under which revisions are made, the frequency of revisions, and the communication of these changes to stakeholders. Revisions can result from updated data sources, methodological improvements, or corrections of errors.

2. **Preliminary and Final Estimates**: GDP estimates are often released in stages, starting with preliminary estimates based on partial data, followed by more accurate final estimates as more comprehensive information is obtained. For example, the BEA releases an "advance" estimate of GDP, followed by "second" and "third" estimates as additional data becomes available.

3. **Historical Revisions**: Periodic historical revisions are conducted to incorporate methodological improvements or rebase the GDP calculations to a new reference year. These revisions ensure that GDP data remains relevant and accurate over time. For example, the rebasing of GDP in India in 2015 involved updating the base year from 2004-05 to 2011-12, resulting in significant changes to the GDP estimates.

4. **Transparency in Revisions**: It is crucial for statistical agencies to be transparent about the reasons for revisions and the impact on previously

reported GDP figures. Detailed revision notes and reports are provided to explain the changes, helping users understand the nature and significance of the revisions.

5. **Feedback Mechanisms**: Effective feedback mechanisms allow stakeholders to provide input on GDP data and methodologies. NSOs often engage with users through surveys, consultations, and advisory committees to gather feedback and improve data quality. For instance, the Office for National Statistics (ONS) in the UK regularly seeks feedback from data users to refine its statistical products.

4.7 Self-Inspection and Provision of Information

Introduction

Self-inspection and the **provision of information** are critical processes in ensuring the accuracy, reliability, and transparency of **Gross Domestic Product (GDP)** calculations. Self-inspection involves internal audits and reviews to assess the quality of data and methodologies, while the provision of information pertains to the dissemination of comprehensive and accessible data to stakeholders. These processes help maintain the integrity of GDP figures and build trust among users.

Self-Inspection

Self-inspection refers to the internal review processes that national statistical offices (NSOs) undertake to ensure the quality and accuracy of GDP data. This involves several key activities:

1. **Internal Audits**: Regular internal audits are conducted to evaluate the methodologies and procedures used in GDP calculation. These audits help identify any discrepancies, errors, or areas for improvement. For instance, the United States Bureau of Economic Analysis (BEA) conducts periodic reviews of its data sources and estimation methods to ensure accuracy.

2. **Quality Assurance Programs**: NSOs implement quality assurance programs to systematically monitor and enhance the quality of GDP data. These programs may include peer reviews, cross-checks with other data sources, and the application of statistical quality control techniques. For example, the European Union's Eurostat has established a comprehensive quality framework for its statistical processes.

3. **Training and Capacity Building**: Continuous training and capacity building for staff involved in GDP calculation are essential for maintaining high standards. Training programs focus on the latest methodologies, data collection techniques, and statistical software. The International Monetary Fund (IMF) and the World Bank often provide technical assistance and training to NSOs.

4. **Documentation and Methodological Reviews**: Regular reviews of documentation and methodologies ensure that the GDP calculation process remains up-to-date and in line with international standards. This includes updating manuals, guidelines, and technical notes. The System of National Accounts (SNA) provides a detailed framework for national accounting that NSOs adhere to.

5. **Feedback and Improvement Mechanisms**: Establishing feedback loops within the organization allows for continuous improvement. Suggestions and feedback from staff involved in the GDP calculation process are encouraged and implemented where feasible.

Provision of Information

The provision of information involves the dissemination of GDP data and related information to stakeholders in a clear, accessible, and transparent manner. This process includes several important aspects:

1. **Comprehensive Reporting**: NSOs publish detailed GDP reports that include not only the main GDP figures but also breakdowns by sector, industry, and expenditure components. These reports provide a holistic view of the economy and facilitate detailed analysis. For example, the Central Statistics Office (CSO) in India publishes extensive reports that break down GDP by industry and expenditure.

2. **Accessible Formats**: To ensure that GDP data is accessible to a broad audience, it is provided in multiple formats such as print, online databases, and interactive dashboards. Data visualization tools, such as graphs and charts, make complex data more understandable. The UK's Office for National Statistics (ONS) offers interactive data visualizations on its website.

3. **Timely Updates**: Regular and timely updates of GDP data are crucial for keeping stakeholders informed about the latest economic trends. NSOs typically release GDP estimates on a quarterly and annual basis, with preliminary estimates followed by revised figures as more data becomes available.

4. **Transparency in Methodologies**: NSOs provide detailed explanations of the methodologies used in GDP calculation. This transparency helps users understand the data and trust its accuracy. Methodological notes,

technical papers, and user guides are often published alongside GDP reports. The IMF's Data Quality Assessment Framework (DQAF) emphasizes transparency in statistical processes.

5. **Public Engagement**: Engaging with the public and stakeholders through consultations, surveys, and advisory committees helps NSOs understand the needs of data users and improve the relevance and quality of GDP data. For instance, Statistics Canada regularly conducts user consultations to gather feedback on its economic data products.

6. **Online Data Portals**: Many NSOs have developed online data portals that provide easy access to GDP data and related statistics. These portals often include advanced search functions, downloadable datasets, and customizable data visualization options. Eurostat's online database is an example of a comprehensive and user-friendly data portal.

4.8 Stability Testing Principles

Introduction

Stability testing is a critical process in various fields, particularly in pharmaceuticals, where it ensures the safety, efficacy, and quality of products throughout their shelf life. The principles of stability testing involve systematic approaches to evaluate how different environmental factors affect the quality of a product over time. This section explores the fundamental principles of stability testing, its importance, methodologies, and regulatory requirements.

Importance of Stability Testing

Stability testing is essential for several reasons:

1. **Safety and Efficacy**: Ensuring that a product remains safe and effective throughout its shelf life is crucial. Stability testing helps identify any potential changes in the product that could compromise its safety or therapeutic efficacy.
2. **Regulatory Compliance**: Regulatory agencies require stability data to approve new products and ensure that they meet quality standards. This data is necessary for obtaining and maintaining marketing authorization.
3. **Shelf Life Determination**: Stability testing provides the data needed to determine the shelf life and appropriate storage conditions for products. This helps in setting expiration dates and storage recommendations.
4. **Quality Assurance**: Continuous monitoring of product stability ensures that the quality of the product is maintained throughout its lifecycle, preventing costly recalls and ensuring customer satisfaction.

Fundamental Principles of Stability Testing

The principles of stability testing revolve around understanding how environmental factors affect the product. Key principles include:

1. **Systematic Approach**: Stability testing follows a structured and systematic approach to study the effects of various environmental conditions on the product. This includes predefined protocols, sampling methods, and analytical procedures.

2. **Environmental Factors**: Testing involves exposing the product to different environmental factors such as temperature, humidity, light, and air. These factors can accelerate the degradation process and reveal potential stability issues.

3. **Time Intervals**: Products are tested at various time intervals to monitor changes over time. This helps in understanding the rate of degradation and predicting the product's shelf life.

4. **Analytical Methods**: Accurate and validated analytical methods are used to assess the quality attributes of the product. These methods can include physical, chemical, biological, and microbiological tests.

5. **Documentation and Record Keeping**: Detailed documentation of the testing protocols, results, and observations is crucial for transparency and regulatory compliance. This includes recording all environmental conditions, sampling times, and test results.

Methodologies in Stability Testing

Stability testing methodologies vary depending on the product and regulatory requirements. Common methodologies include:

1. **Real-Time Stability Testing**: This involves storing the product under recommended storage conditions and testing it at specific intervals throughout its shelf life. Real-time data provides a realistic assessment of the product's stability.

2. **Accelerated Stability Testing**: Products are stored under exaggerated conditions (e.g., higher temperatures and humidity) to speed up the degradation process. This method helps predict the long-term stability of the product in a shorter period.

3. **Stress Testing**: Also known as forced degradation testing, this method subjects the product to extreme conditions to identify potential degradation products and understand the degradation pathways. Stress testing helps in the development of robust formulations.

4. **On-Going Stability Testing**: Continuous monitoring of product stability post-approval ensures that the product remains stable throughout its market lifecycle. This is particularly important for products with long shelf lives or those stored under varying conditions.

Regulatory Requirements

Regulatory agencies such as the International Council for Harmonisation (ICH), the U.S. Food and Drug Administration (FDA), and the European Medicines Agency (EMA) have established guidelines for stability testing. Key regulatory requirements include:

1. **ICH Guidelines**: The ICH provides comprehensive guidelines (ICH Q1A to Q1E) for stability testing of new drug substances and products. These guidelines outline the testing protocols, conditions, and documentation requirements.
2. **FDA Requirements**: The FDA requires stability data for the approval of new drug applications (NDAs) and abbreviated new drug applications (ANDAs). The stability testing protocols must comply with FDA regulations, including 21 CFR Part 211.
3. **EMA Guidelines**: The EMA's guidelines on stability testing align with ICH standards and provide additional requirements for the European market. These guidelines cover testing protocols for different product types, including biologicals and generics.
4. **WHO Guidelines**: The World Health Organization (WHO) also provides stability testing guidelines, particularly for products intended for global distribution. These guidelines emphasize the need for stability testing in different climatic zones.

4.9 WHO GDP and USP GDP (Supply Chain Integrity)

Introduction

Supply chain integrity is critical for ensuring that pharmaceutical products remain safe, effective, and of high quality from the point of manufacture to the end user. The **World Health Organization (WHO)** and the **United States Pharmacopeia (USP)** have established guidelines known as **Good Distribution Practices (GDP)** to maintain the integrity of the pharmaceutical supply chain. This section explores the principles of WHO GDP and USP GDP, their importance, and how they contribute to supply chain integrity.

WHO GDP Guidelines

The WHO GDP guidelines provide a framework to ensure that pharmaceutical products are consistently stored, transported, and handled under appropriate conditions. These guidelines cover various aspects of the distribution process, including:

1. **Quality Management System**: WHO GDP requires a robust quality management system (QMS) to oversee the entire distribution process. This includes documented procedures, quality risk management, and regular audits to ensure compliance.
2. **Personnel**: Personnel involved in the distribution process must be adequately trained and qualified. WHO GDP emphasizes the importance of continuous training and competency assessments.
3. **Premises and Equipment**: Storage facilities and transportation equipment must be suitable for maintaining the quality of pharmaceutical products. This includes temperature-controlled environments and proper maintenance of storage areas and vehicles.
4. **Documentation**: Comprehensive documentation is crucial for traceability and accountability. WHO GDP mandates detailed records of all distribution activities, including receiving, storing, and shipping products.
5. **Product Handling**: Proper handling procedures must be in place to prevent contamination, mix-ups, and damage to products. This includes

guidelines for receiving, picking, packing, and dispatching pharmaceutical products.

6. **Transportation**: WHO GDP requires that transportation conditions are monitored and controlled to prevent exposure to conditions that could compromise product quality. This includes temperature monitoring and ensuring products are securely packaged.

7. **Complaints and Recalls**: Effective procedures must be established for handling complaints and executing product recalls. This ensures that any issues are promptly addressed and that affected products are swiftly removed from the market.

USP GDP Guidelines

The USP GDP guidelines, like those of WHO, focus on maintaining the quality and integrity of pharmaceutical products throughout the supply chain. Key aspects of USP GDP include:

1. **Quality Assurance**: A comprehensive quality assurance system must be implemented to oversee the distribution process. This includes standard operating procedures (SOPs), quality audits, and corrective actions.

2. **Personnel and Training**: USP GDP emphasizes the importance of having trained and competent personnel. Ongoing training programs ensure that staff remain knowledgeable about current GDP practices and regulatory requirements.

3. **Facility Requirements**: Distribution facilities must be designed and maintained to protect product quality. This includes ensuring appropriate storage conditions and regular maintenance of facilities and equipment.

4. **Temperature Control**: USP GDP mandates strict control of storage and transportation temperatures to ensure product stability. This involves using validated temperature-controlled storage and transport systems.

5. **Record Keeping**: Detailed records must be maintained for all distribution activities. USP GDP requires documentation of product receipt, storage conditions, transportation, and delivery to ensure full traceability.

6. **Security Measures**: To prevent theft and unauthorized access, USP GDP requires robust security measures. This includes physical security for

storage facilities and secure transportation practices.

7. **Incident Management**: Procedures must be in place for managing incidents such as product recalls, counterfeit detection, and deviations from established protocols. Prompt action and thorough investigation are essential for resolving issues.

Importance of GDP Guidelines

Adhering to WHO and USP GDP guidelines is crucial for several reasons:

1. **Ensuring Product Quality**: By following GDP guidelines, manufacturers and distributors can ensure that pharmaceutical products maintain their quality, safety, and efficacy throughout the supply chain.
2. **Regulatory Compliance**: Compliance with WHO and USP GDP guidelines is often required by regulatory authorities. This ensures that companies meet national and international regulatory standards.
3. **Patient Safety**: Maintaining the integrity of the supply chain helps prevent the distribution of substandard or counterfeit products, thereby protecting patient safety.
4. **Market Confidence**: Adherence to GDP guidelines builds trust among healthcare providers, patients, and regulatory authorities, ensuring confidence in the quality of pharmaceutical products.
5. **Risk Management**: Implementing GDP guidelines helps identify and mitigate risks associated with the distribution of pharmaceutical products. This proactive approach prevents issues that could compromise product integrity.

4.10 Relevant CDSCO Guidance and ISO Standards

Introduction

The **Central Drugs Standard Control Organization (CDSCO)** in India and the **International Organization for Standardization (ISO)** have established guidelines and standards to ensure the quality, safety, and efficacy of pharmaceutical products. These guidelines and standards are crucial for maintaining high standards in the pharmaceutical industry and ensuring compliance with regulatory requirements. This section explores the relevant CDSCO guidance and ISO standards that contribute to the integrity of the pharmaceutical supply chain.

CDSCO Guidance

The CDSCO is the national regulatory authority for pharmaceuticals and medical devices in India. It is responsible for ensuring that medicines and medical devices meet the required standards of quality, safety, and efficacy. Key guidance documents issued by the CDSCO include:

1. **Good Manufacturing Practices (GMP)**: The CDSCO has adopted GMP guidelines, which outline the requirements for manufacturing processes and facilities. These guidelines ensure that pharmaceutical products are consistently produced and controlled to meet quality standards.
2. **Good Distribution Practices (GDP)**: Similar to the WHO and USP GDP guidelines, the CDSCO has issued GDP guidelines to ensure the quality of pharmaceutical products during distribution. These guidelines cover aspects such as transportation, storage, and handling of pharmaceutical products.
3. **Clinical Trial Regulations**: The CDSCO provides comprehensive guidance on the conduct of clinical trials in India. This includes requirements for ethical considerations, informed consent, trial design, and reporting of adverse events.
4. **Medical Device Regulations**: The CDSCO has established guidelines for the regulation of medical devices, including requirements for

registration, quality control, and post-market surveillance.

5. **Pharmacovigilance**: The CDSCO's guidance on pharmacovigilance outlines the requirements for monitoring the safety of pharmaceutical products once they are on the market. This includes the collection and analysis of adverse event data and the implementation of risk management plans.

ISO Standards

The International Organization for Standardization (ISO) develops and publishes international standards to ensure the quality, safety, and efficiency of products and services. Relevant ISO standards for the pharmaceutical industry include:

1. **ISO 9001: Quality Management Systems**: ISO 9001 specifies the requirements for a quality management system (QMS) that organizations can use to ensure they consistently provide products and services that meet customer and regulatory requirements. It emphasizes continuous improvement and customer satisfaction.
2. **ISO 13485: Medical Devices**: This standard specifies requirements for a QMS specific to the medical device industry. It ensures that medical devices are designed, developed, produced, and delivered to meet regulatory requirements and customer needs.
3. **ISO 14001: Environmental Management Systems**: ISO 14001 sets out the criteria for an environmental management system. It helps organizations improve their environmental performance through more efficient use of resources and reduction of waste.
4. **ISO 27001: Information Security Management**: This standard provides a framework for managing and protecting sensitive information. It is crucial for maintaining data integrity and security in the pharmaceutical industry.
5. **ISO 45001: Occupational Health and Safety**: ISO 45001 specifies requirements for an occupational health and safety (OH&S) management system, providing a framework to improve employee safety, reduce workplace risks, and create better, safer working conditions.

6. **ISO 17025: Testing and Calibration Laboratories**: This standard specifies the general requirements for the competence of testing and calibration laboratories. It ensures that laboratories can produce valid and reliable results, which is essential for pharmaceutical testing and quality control.

Importance of CDSCO Guidance and ISO Standards

Adhering to CDSCO guidance and ISO standards is crucial for several reasons:

1. **Regulatory Compliance**: Compliance with CDSCO guidelines ensures that pharmaceutical products meet national regulatory requirements, facilitating their approval and market access in India.
2. **Quality Assurance**: ISO standards provide a framework for establishing robust quality management systems, ensuring that products are consistently produced to high standards.
3. **International Recognition**: Adherence to ISO standards enhances the credibility and global recognition of pharmaceutical products, facilitating their acceptance in international markets.
4. **Risk Management**: Implementing ISO standards helps identify and mitigate risks associated with pharmaceutical production and distribution, ensuring product safety and efficacy.
5. **Continuous Improvement**: Both CDSCO guidance and ISO standards emphasize continuous improvement, helping organizations enhance their processes and maintain high-quality standards.

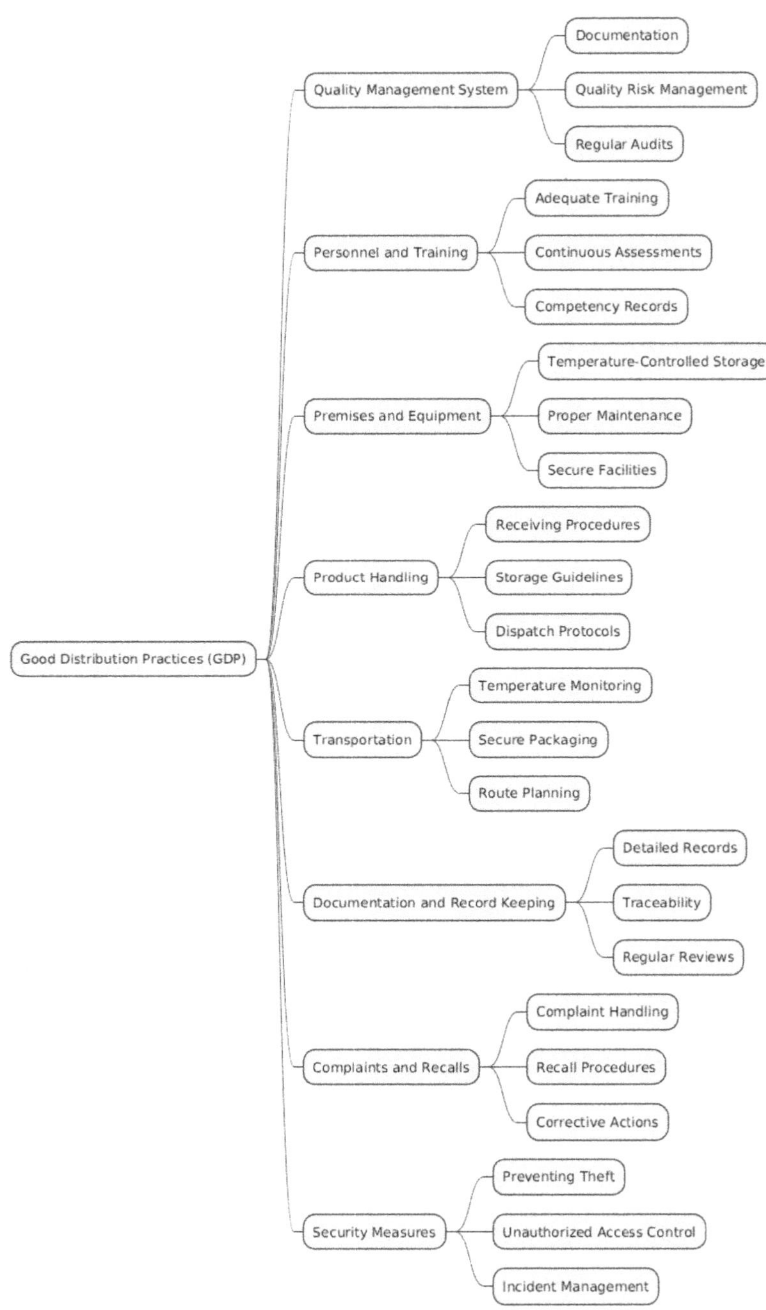

Key Activities and Interactions in Good Distribution Practices (GDP

• 127 •

CHAPTER FIVE

Quality Management Systems

Fig: Quality Management Process

5.1 Concept of Quality and Total Quality Management

The concept of **quality** in the pharmaceutical industry is multifaceted and critical to ensuring that products are safe, effective, and meet the requirements of patients and regulatory authorities. Quality can be defined as the degree to which a product or service meets specified requirements and is free from defects, deficiencies, and significant variations. In the context of pharmaceuticals, quality encompasses the **purity, potency, efficacy, safety, and consistency** of the products. Ensuring high-quality pharmaceuticals is not just about meeting the regulatory standards but also about gaining the trust and confidence of healthcare professionals and patients.

Total Quality Management (TQM) is an integrated approach that aims at improving quality at every level of the organization. TQM focuses on continuous improvement in all aspects of operations and involves every employee, from the top management to the frontline workers. The primary objective of TQM is to enhance customer satisfaction by systematically improving processes, products, and services.

The core principles of TQM include:

1. **Customer Focus**: The primary focus of TQM is on meeting or exceeding customer expectations. This involves understanding the needs and requirements of customers and striving to deliver products and services that fulfill these needs.

2. **Total Employee Involvement**: TQM requires the involvement of all employees in the organization. This means fostering a culture where everyone is responsible for quality, encouraging teamwork, and providing the necessary training and tools to enable employees to contribute to quality improvement.

3. **Process-Centered Approach**: TQM emphasizes the importance of processes in achieving quality outcomes. By understanding and optimizing processes, organizations can reduce variability, eliminate waste, and improve efficiency.

4. **Integrated System**: All aspects of an organization's operations are interconnected, and TQM promotes an integrated approach to quality management. This involves aligning the organization's objectives, processes, and resources towards the common goal of quality improvement.

5. **Strategic and Systematic Approach**: TQM requires a strategic approach to quality management, which involves setting long-term goals, developing a comprehensive plan, and systematically implementing quality initiatives.

6. **Continual Improvement**: A cornerstone of TQM is the concept of continuous improvement, which means that organizations should always strive to improve their processes, products, and services. This can be achieved through regular evaluation, feedback, and innovation.

7. **Fact-Based Decision Making**: Effective quality management relies on data and analysis. TQM promotes the use of data to make informed decisions, identify areas for improvement, and measure the effectiveness of quality initiatives.

8. **Communication**: Open and effective communication is essential for the success of TQM. This involves clear communication of goals,

expectations, and feedback among all levels of the organization.

*The **methodology** of implementing TQM involves several steps:*

1. **Commitment from Top Management**: Successful implementation of TQM starts with the commitment of top management. Leaders must demonstrate their commitment to quality by providing the necessary resources, setting clear quality objectives, and leading by example.
2. **Formation of Quality Management Teams**: Establishing cross-functional teams that include representatives from various departments is crucial. These teams are responsible for identifying areas for improvement, developing action plans, and monitoring progress.
3. **Training and Development**: Providing training to employees at all levels is essential for building a culture of quality. Training programs should focus on quality management principles, tools, and techniques.
4. **Process Mapping and Analysis**: Understanding the existing processes is a critical step in TQM. This involves mapping out processes, identifying bottlenecks, and analyzing them to find areas for improvement.
5. **Setting Quality Objectives and Goals**: Clear, measurable quality objectives and goals should be established. These should align with the organization's overall strategy and customer requirements.
6. **Implementation of Quality Improvement Initiatives**: Based on the analysis, specific initiatives should be implemented to improve processes and product quality. This can include adopting new technologies, revising standard operating procedures, and enhancing quality control measures.
7. **Monitoring and Measurement**: Continuous monitoring and measurement of processes and quality outcomes are vital. This involves collecting data, analyzing performance, and using metrics to track progress towards quality objectives.
8. **Continuous Feedback and Improvement**: Establishing mechanisms for continuous feedback and improvement ensures that TQM is an ongoing process. This includes regular review meetings, audits, and encouraging suggestions from employees.

5.2 Quality by Design and Six Sigma Concept

Quality by Design (QbD) is a systematic approach to pharmaceutical development that emphasizes designing and understanding processes to ensure the predefined quality of the final product. The fundamental idea behind QbD is that quality cannot be tested into products but must be built into them by design. This approach focuses on a thorough understanding of the processes and controls needed to produce high-quality pharmaceuticals consistently.

Key components of Quality by Design include:

1. **Defining Quality Target Product Profile (QTPP)**: The QTPP outlines the desired quality characteristics that a product should possess to ensure it meets the needs of patients and regulatory requirements. This includes aspects such as dosage form, route of administration, strength, and shelf-life.
2. **Identifying Critical Quality Attributes (CQAs)**: CQAs are the physical, chemical, biological, or microbiological properties that need to be controlled to ensure the product meets its quality standards. Identifying CQAs is crucial for understanding which attributes impact the product's safety and efficacy.
3. **Determining Critical Process Parameters (CPPs)**: CPPs are the variables within the manufacturing process that have a significant impact on CQAs. Understanding the relationship between CPPs and CQAs helps in controlling the manufacturing process to ensure consistent product quality.
4. **Risk Assessment and Management**: QbD involves identifying potential risks to product quality and implementing strategies to mitigate these risks. Risk assessment tools such as Failure Modes and Effects Analysis (FMEA) and Hazard Analysis and Critical Control Points (HACCP) are often used.
5. **Design of Experiments (DoE)**: DoE is a statistical approach used to systematically investigate the effects of multiple factors on CQAs. This helps in understanding the interactions between different process variables and optimizing the manufacturing process.

6. **Control Strategy**: A control strategy is a planned set of controls derived from current product and process understanding that ensures process performance and product quality. It includes specifications, process controls, and monitoring plans.
7. **Continuous Improvement**: QbD is an iterative process that involves continuous monitoring and improvement of the manufacturing process to ensure that the product consistently meets quality standards.

Six Sigma is a data-driven methodology aimed at improving the quality of processes by identifying and eliminating defects and variability. The goal of Six Sigma is to achieve near-perfect quality, with a defect rate of fewer than 3.4 defects per million opportunities. This methodology uses a set of quality management tools and statistical methods to improve processes.

The Six Sigma process typically follows the **DMAIC** cycle, which stands for Define, Measure, Analyze, Improve, and Control:

1. **Define**: The first step is to clearly define the problem, goals, and customer requirements. This involves creating a project charter, mapping the process, and identifying key stakeholders.
2. **Measure**: In this phase, the current process performance is measured to establish a baseline. This involves collecting data on process inputs, outputs, and key performance indicators (KPIs).
3. **Analyze**: The analysis phase involves identifying the root causes of defects and process variability. Tools such as root cause analysis, regression analysis, and hypothesis testing are used to understand the underlying issues.
4. **Improve**: Based on the analysis, improvements are designed and implemented to address the root causes of defects. This can involve process redesign, optimizing process parameters, and implementing best practices.
5. **Control**: The final phase is to ensure that the improvements are sustained over time. This involves establishing control plans, monitoring process performance, and making adjustments as needed to maintain the desired quality level.

Integration of QbD and Six Sigma: Combining QbD and Six Sigma can provide a robust framework for achieving high-quality pharmaceutical products. While QbD focuses on designing quality into products from the beginning, Six Sigma provides a structured approach to process improvement and defect reduction. Together, they ensure a comprehensive approach to quality management, from development through manufacturing and continuous improvement.

For example, during the pharmaceutical development process, QbD principles can be applied to design a robust formulation and manufacturing process. Subsequently, Six Sigma tools can be used to monitor and improve these processes, ensuring that they remain within control and continue to produce high-quality products.

5.3 Out of Specifications (OOS) and Change Control

Out of Specifications (OOS) refers to test results that fall outside the predefined acceptance criteria established in the drug product specifications, regulatory filings, or standard operating procedures. In the pharmaceutical industry, OOS results are a significant concern as they may indicate issues with the manufacturing process, raw materials, or final product quality. Addressing OOS results is critical to ensure that only high-quality, safe, and effective products reach patients.

Key Aspects of Out of Specifications (OOS):

1. **Identification and Reporting**: When a test result is identified as OOS, it must be immediately reported and documented. This includes details such as the batch number, specific test, observed result, and acceptance criteria.
2. **Investigation Process**:

   - **Initial Laboratory Investigation**: The first step is to confirm whether the OOS result is due to a laboratory error. This involves reviewing the test method, equipment calibration, analyst training, and any deviations from the standard procedure.
   - **Full-Scale Investigation**: If the initial investigation rules out laboratory error, a full-scale investigation is conducted. This includes reviewing the entire manufacturing process, raw material quality, process controls, and environmental conditions.

3. **Root Cause Analysis**: Identifying the root cause of the OOS result is crucial. This may involve techniques such as cause-and-effect analysis, failure mode and effects analysis (FMEA), and statistical analysis. Common causes include raw material variability, equipment malfunction, human error, and inadequate process controls.
4. **Corrective and Preventive Actions (CAPA)**: Once the root cause is identified, appropriate corrective and preventive actions must be implemented to prevent recurrence. This may involve process modifications, additional training, equipment maintenance, or changes to raw material specifications.

5. **Documentation and Reporting**: All findings from the OOS investigation and CAPA implementation must be thoroughly documented. This documentation is essential for regulatory compliance and provides a record for future reference.

6. **Regulatory Compliance**: Regulatory agencies, such as the FDA, require detailed reporting of OOS results and the corresponding investigations. Failure to adequately address OOS results can lead to regulatory actions, including product recalls, warning letters, and penalties.

Change Control

Change Control is a systematic approach to managing all changes made to a product or process to ensure that no unintended consequences affect the quality, safety, or efficacy of the product. Change control is an essential element of Good Manufacturing Practice (GMP) and is critical for maintaining consistency and compliance in pharmaceutical manufacturing.

Key Components of Change Control:

1. **Change Request**: The change control process begins with a formal change request, which includes a detailed description of the proposed change, the reason for the change, and the expected impact on the product or process. This request can originate from various sources, such as process improvement initiatives, regulatory requirements, or problem resolution efforts.

2. **Change Assessment**:

   - **Impact Assessment**: A thorough evaluation of the potential impact of the proposed change on product quality, regulatory compliance, manufacturing processes, and other critical areas. This includes assessing the risks and benefits of the change.
   - **Stakeholder Review**: Input from all relevant stakeholders, including quality assurance, regulatory affairs, production, and research and development, is gathered to ensure a comprehensive assessment.

3. **Approval Process**: Based on the assessment, the change request is reviewed and approved by a designated change control committee or authority. Approval is granted only if the change is deemed necessary and its impact is fully understood and manageable.

4. **Implementation Plan**: An implementation plan is developed, outlining the steps needed to execute the change. This includes updating standard operating procedures (SOPs), training personnel, modifying equipment, and performing any necessary validation or qualification activities.

5. **Communication**: Effective communication of the change to all affected parties is critical. This ensures that everyone involved understands the change, their responsibilities, and the timelines for implementation.

6. **Monitoring and Review**: After the change is implemented, it is closely monitored to ensure it achieves the desired outcome without any negative impact. This includes collecting data, performing additional testing if necessary, and conducting post-implementation reviews.

7. **Documentation**: Comprehensive documentation of the entire change control process is maintained. This includes the initial change request, impact assessments, approval records, implementation plans, training records, and monitoring results. Proper documentation ensures traceability and regulatory compliance.

8. **Regulatory Notification**: In some cases, significant changes may require notification to regulatory authorities. This ensures that all changes remain within the scope of the approved product specifications and regulatory filings.

5.4 Types of Validation and Qualification

Validation and qualification are fundamental components of the pharmaceutical industry, ensuring that processes, systems, and equipment perform as expected and produce high-quality products consistently. Validation involves establishing documented evidence that a specific process or system consistently produces results meeting predetermined specifications. Qualification is a part of validation that focuses on ensuring that equipment and systems are installed and operate correctly. Here, we will discuss the different types of validation and qualification in detail.

Types of Validation

1. **Process Validation:**

   - **Prospective Validation**: Conducted before a new product is introduced or a process is implemented. It involves planning and conducting tests to ensure the process produces the desired outcome.
   - **Concurrent Validation**: Performed during actual production of the product. Data is collected and evaluated to confirm that the process operates within predefined limits.
   - **Retrospective Validation**: Carried out for established products and processes by reviewing historical data. It helps in confirming that the process has been consistently producing quality products.
   - **Revalidation**: Conducted periodically or when there are significant changes to the process, equipment, or product. It ensures continued process control and product quality.

2. **Analytical Method Validation:**

   - Ensures that the analytical methods used in testing are accurate, reliable, and reproducible. Key parameters include accuracy, precision, specificity, linearity, range, and robustness.

3. **Cleaning Validation:**

- ◦ Confirms that cleaning procedures effectively remove residues from equipment to acceptable levels. It ensures no cross-contamination between products and that the equipment is safe for the next production run.

4. **Computer System Validation (CSV):**

- ◦ Ensures that computer systems used in manufacturing and quality control operate as intended and comply with regulatory requirements. This includes software applications, hardware, and data integrity.

5. **Equipment Validation:**

- ◦ Verifies that equipment used in the manufacturing process performs consistently and as intended. This includes various stages such as Installation Qualification (IQ), Operational Qualification (OQ), and Performance Qualification (PQ).

Types of Qualification

1. **Design Qualification (DQ):**

- ◦ Verifies that the design of facilities, equipment, or systems meets all regulatory and operational requirements. It ensures that the design specifications align with the intended use.

2. **Installation Qualification (IQ):**

- ◦ Confirms that equipment or systems are installed correctly according to manufacturer specifications and regulatory requirements. This includes checking all components, connections, and documentation.

3. **Operational Qualification (OQ):**

- Verifies that the equipment or system operates according to the established operational parameters. It includes testing under various conditions to ensure consistent performance.

4. **Performance Qualification (PQ):**

- Ensures that equipment or systems perform effectively and reproducibly in the actual production environment. It involves testing the equipment under normal operating conditions to verify consistent output quality.

Detailed Procedures and Documentation

Process Validation Procedure:

1. **Planning**: Develop a validation plan outlining objectives, responsibilities, and testing methods.
2. **Protocol Development**: Create detailed protocols specifying test methods, acceptance criteria, and documentation requirements.
3. **Execution**: Conduct validation tests according to the protocol, recording all data and observations.
4. **Analysis and Reporting**: Analyze the data, compare results with acceptance criteria, and compile a validation report.
5. **Approval**: Review and approve the validation report, ensuring all criteria are met and any deviations are addressed.

Analytical Method Validation Procedure:

1. **Define Scope**: Identify the purpose of the analytical method and the specific parameters to be validated.
2. **Develop Protocol**: Outline the validation procedures, including test methods, acceptance criteria, and documentation requirements.

3. **Conduct Tests**: Perform validation tests such as accuracy, precision, specificity, and robustness.
4. **Document Results**: Record all test results, observations, and any deviations from the protocol.
5. **Evaluate Data**: Analyze the results, ensuring they meet predefined acceptance criteria.
6. **Report**: Compile a comprehensive validation report, including all data, analysis, and conclusions.

Cleaning Validation Procedure:

1. **Develop Cleaning Protocol**: Outline the cleaning procedures, including cleaning agents, methods, and acceptance criteria for residues.
2. **Execute Cleaning**: Perform the cleaning process as specified in the protocol.
3. **Sampling**: Collect samples from equipment surfaces to test for residues.
4. **Testing**: Analyze samples for the presence of residues using validated analytical methods.
5. **Documentation**: Record all cleaning activities, sample collection, and test results.
6. **Evaluation**: Compare results with acceptance criteria and document findings in a validation report.

Importance and Benefits

Importance:

- **Regulatory Compliance**: Validation and qualification are essential for compliance with regulatory requirements set by authorities such as the FDA, EMA, and other regulatory bodies.
- **Product Quality**: Ensures that processes consistently produce high-quality products, minimizing risks of defects and recalls.

- **Patient Safety**: By ensuring the quality and safety of pharmaceutical products, validation and qualification protect patient health.
- **Operational Efficiency**: Well-validated processes and qualified equipment operate more efficiently, reducing downtime and increasing productivity.

Benefits:

- **Consistency**: Provides assurance that processes and equipment perform consistently, leading to uniform product quality.
- **Risk Mitigation**: Identifies and addresses potential risks, reducing the likelihood of product failures and non-compliance.
- **Cost Savings**: Prevents costly errors, rework, and recalls by ensuring processes and equipment are reliable from the start.
- **Enhanced Reputation**: Demonstrates commitment to quality and regulatory compliance, enhancing the company's reputation in the industry.

5.5 Validation Master Plan (VMP)

The **Validation Master Plan (VMP)** is a comprehensive document that outlines the principles, approaches, and procedures for validating processes, equipment, and systems within a pharmaceutical manufacturing facility. It serves as a roadmap for ensuring that all aspects of the manufacturing environment operate in compliance with regulatory standards and produce high-quality products consistently. The VMP provides a structured framework for planning, executing, and documenting validation activities.

Components of the Validation Master Plan

1. Introduction and Purpose

- **Introduction**: The VMP begins with an introduction that provides an overview of the document, its scope, and its relevance to the organization's quality assurance program. It explains the importance of validation in maintaining product quality and regulatory compliance.
- **Purpose**: This section outlines the main objectives of the VMP, including ensuring consistency in validation activities, defining roles and responsibilities, and providing a structured approach to validation.

2. Scope

- **Scope Definition**: The scope of the VMP describes the areas, processes, equipment, and systems covered by the validation plan. This includes manufacturing processes, analytical methods, cleaning procedures, computer systems, and more.
- **Exclusions**: Any processes, equipment, or systems not covered by the VMP should be explicitly stated.

3. Organizational Structure and Responsibilities

- **Roles and Responsibilities**: This section defines the roles and responsibilities of key personnel involved in the validation process. It includes responsibilities of the validation team, quality assurance, production, engineering, and other relevant departments.
- **Validation Team**: Details about the composition of the validation team, including qualifications and experience of team members, are provided.

4. Validation Strategy

- **Validation Approach**: Describes the overall approach to validation, including the use of risk-based methodologies, prospective, concurrent, and retrospective validation strategies.
- **Risk Assessment**: Explains how risk assessment tools and techniques will be used to prioritize validation activities and ensure critical aspects are addressed.

5. Validation Activities and Deliverables

- **Types of Validation**: Outlines the different types of validation to be performed, such as process validation, analytical method validation, cleaning validation, computer system validation, and equipment validation.
- **Validation Protocols**: Describes the development and approval process for validation protocols, which detail the specific tests and acceptance criteria for each validation activity.
- **Execution of Validation**: Provides guidelines for executing validation activities, including test execution, data collection, and deviation management.

6. Documentation and Reporting

- **Validation Documentation**: Lists the types of documents to be generated during the validation process, such as validation plans, protocols, test results, deviation reports, and validation reports.
- **Record Keeping**: Specifies the procedures for maintaining and storing validation documents to ensure traceability and compliance with regulatory requirements.

7. Change Control

- **Change Management**: Details the change control procedures for managing changes to processes, equipment, or systems that may impact the validated state. This includes the process for evaluating, approving, and documenting changes.
- **Revalidation**: Describes the circumstances under which revalidation is required, such as significant changes to processes, equipment, or regulatory requirements.

8. Training and Competency

- **Training Programs**: Outlines the training programs for personnel involved in validation activities. This includes initial training, ongoing training, and competency assessments to ensure personnel have the necessary skills and knowledge.

9. Quality Assurance and Compliance

- **Quality Assurance Role**: Describes the role of the quality assurance department in overseeing validation activities, ensuring compliance with regulatory standards, and reviewing validation documentation.

- **Audits and Inspections**: Provides information on internal audits and external inspections related to validation activities, including preparation, conduct, and follow-up actions.

10. Review and Approval

- **VMP Approval**: Details the process for reviewing and approving the VMP, including the responsibilities of key stakeholders and the frequency of review.
- **Revisions and Updates**: Explains how and when the VMP will be reviewed and updated to reflect changes in processes, equipment, regulations, or organizational structure.

Implementation and Benefits of the Validation Master Plan

Implementation:

- **Planning**: Developing a VMP begins with careful planning, involving all relevant departments to ensure a comprehensive approach.
- **Execution**: Implementation involves executing validation activities according to the VMP, adhering to protocols, and documenting results.
- **Monitoring**: Continuous monitoring and periodic review of validation activities ensure ongoing compliance and identification of areas for improvement.
- **Continuous Improvement**: The VMP is a living document, updated regularly to incorporate new regulations, technologies, and best practices.

Benefits:

- **Regulatory Compliance**: A well-documented VMP ensures compliance with regulatory requirements from authorities such as the FDA, EMA, and other global regulatory bodies.
- **Product Quality**: By ensuring processes, equipment, and systems are validated, the VMP helps maintain high product quality and consistency.
- **Risk Management**: The risk-based approach of the VMP helps prioritize critical areas, reducing the likelihood of failures and non-compliance.
- **Operational Efficiency**: Standardized validation procedures streamline operations, reduce variability, and improve efficiency.
- **Documentation and Traceability**: Comprehensive documentation provides a clear audit trail, facilitating inspections and audits.
- **Organizational Alignment**: The VMP aligns validation activities with organizational goals and regulatory requirements, promoting a culture of quality and continuous improvement.

5.6 Analytical Method Validation

Analytical Method Validation is a critical process in the pharmaceutical industry that ensures the reliability, accuracy, and consistency of analytical methods used to test drugs and their components. This validation process is essential for confirming that the methods produce results that meet the predetermined quality standards and regulatory requirements. Analytical method validation provides confidence in the data generated, ensuring that it accurately reflects the quality of the product being tested.

Components of Analytical Method Validation

1. Accuracy

- **Definition**: Accuracy refers to the closeness of the test results to the true value or the standard reference value.
- **Procedure**: Accuracy is assessed by analyzing known quantities of the analyte (standard solutions) and comparing the measured values with the true values. Typically, multiple concentrations are tested, and the percentage recovery is calculated.
- **Importance**: Ensures that the method can produce correct results, reflecting the true concentration of the analyte in the sample.

2. Precision

- **Definition**: Precision refers to the consistency of the test results when the method is applied repeatedly under the same conditions.
- **Types**:

  - **Repeatability**: Intra-assay precision, where the method is tested multiple times within a short period using the same equipment and analyst.
  - **Intermediate Precision**: Inter-assay precision, which includes variations over different days, analysts, and equipment within the same laboratory.
  - **Reproducibility**: Precision between different laboratories.

- **Procedure**: Precision is evaluated by analyzing multiple replicates of a sample and calculating the standard deviation and relative standard deviation (RSD).
- **Importance**: Ensures the method produces consistent and reliable results.

3. Specificity

- **Definition**: Specificity is the ability of the method to accurately measure the analyte in the presence of other components, such as impurities, degradants, and matrix components.
- **Procedure**: Specificity is assessed by analyzing the sample containing the analyte along with potential interfering substances and demonstrating that these substances do not affect the result.
- **Importance**: Ensures the method can distinguish the analyte from other substances.

4. Linearity

- **Definition**: Linearity is the method's ability to produce results directly proportional to the concentration of the analyte within a given range.
- **Procedure**: Linearity is evaluated by analyzing a series of standard solutions of different concentrations and plotting the response versus concentration. The correlation coefficient (R^2) is calculated.
- **Importance**: Ensures the method can accurately quantify the analyte across a specified range.

5. Range

- **Definition**: The range is the interval between the upper and lower concentration levels of the analyte that have been demonstrated to be accurately and precisely measured by the method.
- **Procedure**: The range is established during the evaluation of linearity, accuracy, and precision.
- **Importance**: Defines the limits within which the method is effective.

6. Detection Limit (LOD)

- **Definition**: LOD is the lowest amount of the analyte that can be detected but not necessarily quantified under the stated experimental conditions.
- **Procedure**: LOD is typically determined based on the signal-to-noise ratio, often using a ratio of 3:1.
- **Importance**: Determines the method's sensitivity to detect low levels of the analyte.

7. Quantitation Limit (LOQ)

- **Definition**: LOQ is the lowest amount of the analyte that can be quantitatively determined with suitable precision and accuracy.
- **Procedure**: LOQ is determined similarly to LOD but using a higher signal-to-noise ratio, often 10:1.
- **Importance**: Establishes the method's capability to quantify low levels of the analyte.

8. Robustness

- **Definition**: Robustness is the method's capacity to remain unaffected by small but deliberate variations in method parameters.
- **Procedure**: Robustness is assessed by making slight changes to method parameters such as pH, temperature, or flow rate and evaluating the effect on the results.
- **Importance**: Ensures the method remains reliable under varying conditions.

Validation Procedure

1. **Develop Validation Plan**

   - A validation plan is created outlining the objectives, scope, responsibilities, and detailed procedures for the validation study.

2. **Prepare Validation Protocol**

- The protocol includes specific details on the validation parameters to be tested, acceptance criteria, sample preparations, and test procedures.

3. **Perform Validation Tests**

- Execute the validation tests according to the protocol. This involves analyzing samples, collecting data, and performing calculations to assess each validation parameter.

4. **Analyze Data**

- The data collected from the validation tests are analyzed to determine if the method meets the predefined acceptance criteria for accuracy, precision, specificity, linearity, range, LOD, LOQ, and robustness.

5. **Compile Validation Report**

- A comprehensive validation report is prepared, documenting the validation plan, protocol, test results, data analysis, and conclusions. Any deviations from the protocol and their impact on the validation are also documented.

6. **Review and Approval**

- The validation report is reviewed and approved by the quality assurance and regulatory departments to ensure compliance with regulatory standards and internal quality requirements.

Importance of Analytical Method Validation

Regulatory Compliance

- Regulatory agencies such as the FDA, EMA, and other global authorities require validated analytical methods to ensure the reliability and accuracy of test results. Compliance with these requirements is essential for product approval and market authorization.

Product Quality

- Validated methods ensure that the quality of pharmaceutical products is consistently monitored and maintained, minimizing the risk of releasing substandard products.

Patient Safety

- Accurate and reliable analytical methods are crucial for detecting impurities, contaminants, and ensuring the correct dosage of active ingredients, thereby protecting patient health and safety.

Cost Efficiency

- Reliable analytical methods reduce the need for re-testing, minimize waste, and enhance the overall efficiency of the quality control process.

Operational Consistency

- Validation provides a standardized approach to analytical testing, ensuring consistent results across different batches, laboratories, and over time.

5.7 Validation of Utilities (Compressed Air, Steam, Water Systems, HVAC)

Validation of Utilities is a critical aspect of pharmaceutical manufacturing that ensures utilities such as compressed air, steam, water systems, and HVAC (Heating, Ventilation, and Air Conditioning) consistently meet predefined quality standards and do not compromise the quality of the pharmaceutical products. Each of these utilities plays a vital role in maintaining the controlled environment necessary for manufacturing, and their validation ensures they perform effectively and reliably.

Compressed Air Validation

Compressed air is used in various processes in pharmaceutical manufacturing, including as a direct contact utility in product processing, packaging, and cleaning. Validation of compressed air systems ensures that the air is free from contaminants such as particulates, oil, and microorganisms.

Key Aspects of Compressed Air Validation:

1. **Specification Development**: Define the quality requirements for compressed air, including acceptable limits for particulates, oil, moisture, and microbial contamination.
2. **Installation Qualification (IQ)**: Verify that the compressed air system is installed correctly according to design specifications and manufacturer guidelines.
3. **Operational Qualification (OQ)**: Test the system to ensure it operates within specified parameters. This includes testing pressure, flow rate, and air quality.
4. **Performance Qualification (PQ)**: Conduct routine sampling and testing of compressed air at various points of use to confirm it consistently meets quality specifications.
5. **Monitoring and Maintenance**: Implement a regular monitoring program to ensure ongoing compliance, including periodic testing and maintenance of filters and dryers.

Steam System Validation

Steam is used for sterilization, cleaning, and in some cases, as a heating medium in pharmaceutical processes. Steam quality is crucial for ensuring effective sterilization and preventing contamination.

Key Aspects of Steam System Validation:

1. **Specification Development**: Define the quality requirements for steam, such as temperature, pressure, dryness fraction, and absence of non-condensable gases.
2. **Installation Qualification (IQ)**: Verify that the steam generation and distribution system is installed according to design specifications.
3. **Operational Qualification (OQ)**: Test the system to ensure it operates within specified parameters, including steam pressure, temperature, and quality.
4. **Performance Qualification (PQ)**: Conduct routine testing of steam at various points of use to confirm it consistently meets quality specifications. This includes testing for non-condensable gases, superheat, and dryness.
5. **Monitoring and Maintenance**: Implement a monitoring program to ensure ongoing compliance, including regular testing and maintenance of steam traps, filters, and condensate systems.

Water Systems Validation

Water is one of the most critical utilities in pharmaceutical manufacturing, used in various forms such as purified water (PW), water for injection (WFI), and clean steam. Validation ensures that water systems produce water of consistent quality suitable for its intended use.

Key Aspects of Water Systems Validation:

1. **Specification Development**: Define the quality requirements for different types of water, including chemical and microbial purity, endotoxin levels, and conductivity.
2. **Installation Qualification (IQ)**: Verify that the water generation and distribution system is installed according to design specifications.
3. **Operational Qualification (OQ)**: Test the system to ensure it operates within specified parameters, including flow rates, pressure, temperature, and water quality.
4. **Performance Qualification (PQ)**: Conduct routine sampling and testing of water at various points of use to confirm it consistently meets quality specifications. This includes chemical and microbial testing.
5. **Monitoring and Maintenance**: Implement a comprehensive monitoring program to ensure ongoing compliance, including regular testing, cleaning, and maintenance of water purification systems and distribution loops.

HVAC System Validation

HVAC systems are critical for maintaining controlled environments in pharmaceutical manufacturing, including cleanrooms and other controlled areas. Validation ensures that HVAC systems effectively control temperature, humidity, and airborne particulates.

Key Aspects of HVAC System Validation:

1. **Specification Development**: Define the quality requirements for the controlled environment, including temperature, humidity, air change rates, and particle counts.
2. **Installation Qualification (IQ)**: Verify that the HVAC system is installed according to design specifications and that all components are properly installed.
3. **Operational Qualification (OQ)**: Test the system to ensure it operates within specified parameters. This includes testing air flow, filtration efficiency, temperature and humidity control, and pressure differentials.
4. **Performance Qualification (PQ)**: Conduct routine environmental monitoring to confirm that the HVAC system consistently maintains

the required conditions. This includes testing for airborne particulates, microbial contamination, and environmental parameters.

5. **Monitoring and Maintenance**: Implement a monitoring program to ensure ongoing compliance, including regular testing, calibration, and maintenance of HVAC components such as filters, sensors, and air handling units.

Detailed Validation Procedure

1. **Develop Validation Plan:**

   - Create a detailed validation plan outlining the objectives, scope, responsibilities, and procedures for each utility system validation.

2. **Prepare Validation Protocol:**

   - Develop specific validation protocols for each utility, specifying the tests to be performed, acceptance criteria, sample points, and testing frequency.

3. **Conduct Validation Tests:**

   - Execute the validation tests according to the protocols. This involves collecting samples, performing tests, and recording data.

4. **Analyze Data:**

   - Analyze the test results to determine if the utility systems meet the predefined acceptance criteria.

5. **Compile Validation Report:**

   - Prepare comprehensive validation reports for each utility system, documenting the validation plan, protocols, test results, data analysis, and conclusions.

6. **Review and Approval**:

   ◦ The validation reports are reviewed and approved by the quality assurance and regulatory departments to ensure compliance with regulatory standards and internal quality requirements.

Importance and Benefits of Utility Validation

Regulatory Compliance:

- Utility validation is essential for compliance with regulatory requirements from authorities such as the FDA, EMA, and other global regulatory bodies. It demonstrates that utility systems are capable of consistently providing the necessary conditions for manufacturing high-quality pharmaceutical products.

Product Quality:

- Validated utilities ensure that the quality of the pharmaceutical products is not compromised by contamination or environmental factors, maintaining the safety and efficacy of the products.

Patient Safety:

- Ensuring that utilities like water, steam, and compressed air meet stringent quality standards protects patient health by preventing contamination and ensuring the sterility and purity of the final products.

Operational Efficiency:

- Properly validated utilities operate more efficiently, reducing downtime, maintenance costs, and variability in the manufacturing process.

Risk Management:

- Validation identifies and mitigates potential risks associated with utility systems, ensuring that any deviations are promptly addressed and corrected.

5.8 Cleaning Validation

Cleaning Validation is a critical process in pharmaceutical manufacturing that ensures cleaning procedures effectively remove residues of active pharmaceutical ingredients (APIs), excipients, cleaning agents, and microbial contaminants from equipment and facilities. This process is vital for preventing cross-contamination between different products and ensuring that subsequent batches of pharmaceuticals meet stringent quality and safety standards.

Components of Cleaning Validation

1. Establishing Acceptance Criteria

- **Residue Limits**: Define acceptable residue limits based on toxicological data, therapeutic dose, and potential for cross-contamination. The most commonly used approaches include the **10 ppm criterion**, **0.1% dose criterion**, and **health-based exposure limits (HBELs)**.
- **Microbial Limits**: Set limits for microbial contamination, ensuring that cleaning procedures effectively control bioburden.

2. Cleaning Procedures

- **Standard Operating Procedures (SOPs)**: Develop detailed SOPs outlining the cleaning methods, cleaning agents, contact times, temperatures, and equipment used. SOPs should also specify how often cleaning should be performed and any special instructions.
- **Manual vs. Automated Cleaning**: Define whether cleaning will be done manually or using automated systems such as Clean-In-Place (CIP) or Steam-In-Place (SIP).

3. Sampling Methods

- **Swab Sampling**: Involves using a swab to collect residue samples from specific locations on the equipment surfaces. Swabs are chosen based on their compatibility with the analyte and solvent.
- **Rinse Sampling**: Involves collecting a portion of the final rinse solution used in the cleaning process. This method helps evaluate the overall

cleanliness of the equipment.

- **Placebo Batch Sampling**: Involves running a placebo batch through the equipment after cleaning and testing the batch for residues.

4. Analytical Methods

- **Selection of Methods**: Choose appropriate analytical methods to detect and quantify residues. Common methods include High-Performance Liquid Chromatography (HPLC), Gas Chromatography (GC), Total Organic Carbon (TOC) analysis, and microbial testing.
- **Method Validation**: Ensure the analytical methods are validated for specificity, sensitivity, accuracy, precision, and reproducibility.

5. Validation Protocols

- **Development of Protocols**: Create detailed validation protocols that describe the objectives, scope, acceptance criteria, sampling methods, analytical methods, and cleaning procedures.
- **Execution of Protocols**: Perform the cleaning validation according to the protocols, documenting all steps and results.

6. Data Analysis and Documentation

- **Data Analysis**: Analyze the results of the residue and microbial tests to determine if they meet the predefined acceptance criteria.
- **Validation Report**: Compile a comprehensive validation report that includes the validation plan, protocols, test results, data analysis, deviations, and conclusions. The report should be reviewed and approved by quality assurance.

Steps in Cleaning Validation

1. **Risk Assessment**

    ◦ Conduct a risk assessment to identify potential risks associated with cleaning procedures. Consider factors such as the toxicity of residues, the complexity of the equipment, and the difficulty of cleaning.

2. Development of Cleaning Procedures

- Based on the risk assessment, develop or refine cleaning procedures. This includes selecting appropriate cleaning agents and methods that are effective for the residues of concern.

3. Initial Cleaning Studies

- Perform initial studies to optimize cleaning procedures. This involves testing different cleaning agents, methods, and parameters to determine the most effective approach.

4. Preparation of Validation Protocols

- Develop detailed cleaning validation protocols that outline the objectives, scope, acceptance criteria, sampling methods, analytical methods, and cleaning procedures.

5. Execution of Cleaning Validation

- Perform the cleaning validation according to the protocols. This involves cleaning the equipment, sampling for residues, and analyzing the samples.

6. Evaluation of Results

- Analyze the data from the cleaning validation to determine if the cleaning procedures meet the predefined acceptance criteria. Address any deviations or failures and implement corrective actions as necessary.

7. Documentation and Approval

- Compile a comprehensive cleaning validation report, documenting all steps, results, and conclusions. The report should be reviewed and approved by quality assurance and other relevant stakeholders.

8. Routine Monitoring and Revalidation

- ○ Implement routine monitoring to ensure ongoing compliance with cleaning procedures. Periodic revalidation should be performed to confirm the effectiveness of cleaning procedures over time.

Importance and Benefits of Cleaning Validation

Regulatory Compliance

- Regulatory agencies such as the FDA, EMA, and other global authorities require cleaning validation to ensure that manufacturing processes meet stringent quality and safety standards. Compliance with these requirements is essential for product approval and market authorization.

Product Quality

- Effective cleaning validation ensures that equipment is free from residues and contaminants, maintaining the quality and integrity of pharmaceutical products. This helps prevent cross-contamination and ensures that products meet their specifications.

Patient Safety

- By ensuring that equipment is properly cleaned, cleaning validation protects patient health by preventing contamination and ensuring that pharmaceutical products are safe for use.

Operational Efficiency

- Properly validated cleaning procedures reduce the risk of contamination and product recalls, minimizing downtime and enhancing the efficiency of the manufacturing process.

Risk Management

- Cleaning validation identifies and mitigates potential risks associated with cleaning procedures, ensuring that any deviations are promptly addressed and corrected.

Challenges in Cleaning Validation

1. **Complex Equipment**

   - Cleaning complex equipment with intricate designs and hard-to-reach areas can be challenging. Ensuring that all surfaces are adequately cleaned and sampled requires careful planning and execution.

2. **Residue Detection**

   - Detecting and quantifying low levels of residues can be difficult, especially for highly potent drugs. Selecting and validating sensitive analytical methods is crucial for accurate residue analysis.

3. **Variability in Cleaning Processes**

   - Variability in manual cleaning processes can impact the consistency and effectiveness of cleaning. Implementing automated cleaning systems and standardizing procedures can help reduce variability.

4. **Regulatory Requirements**

   - Keeping up with evolving regulatory requirements and guidelines for cleaning validation can be challenging. Continuous monitoring and updating of cleaning validation procedures are necessary to maintain compliance.

5.9 International Conference on Harmonization (ICH) Process and Guidelines

The **International Conference on Harmonization (ICH)** is a collaborative initiative between regulatory authorities and the pharmaceutical industry to develop common standards and guidelines for the global pharmaceutical market. The main objective of ICH is to ensure that safe, effective, and high-quality medicines are developed and registered efficiently across different countries, reducing duplication of testing and facilitating a faster regulatory process.

Overview of the ICH Process

The ICH process involves the development, consultation, and implementation of guidelines that harmonize the technical requirements for pharmaceutical product registration. The process can be summarized in several key steps:

1. Concept Paper and Business Plan

- **Concept Paper**: The process begins with the drafting of a concept paper, which outlines the scope, objectives, and rationale for developing a new guideline or revising an existing one.
- **Business Plan**: A business plan is then prepared to justify the need for the guideline, including the anticipated benefits and resource requirements.

2. Consensus Building

- **Expert Working Groups (EWGs)**: The ICH assembles Expert Working Groups comprising representatives from regulatory authorities, industry, and other stakeholders. These groups work collaboratively to draft the guideline based on scientific evidence and best practices.
- **Step 1: Draft Guideline**: The EWG develops a draft guideline, incorporating input from all members to reach a consensus on the technical requirements.

3. Regulatory Consultation

- **Step 2a and 2b: Regulatory Consultation and Discussion**: The draft guideline undergoes public consultation in the ICH regions (Europe, Japan, and the United States). Feedback from stakeholders, including industry, academia, and the public, is collected and reviewed.
- **Revision of Draft**: Based on the feedback, the draft guideline is revised and refined to address any concerns or suggestions.

4. Adoption of Guidelines

- **Step 3: Regulatory Adoption**: The final draft guideline is submitted to the ICH Steering Committee for endorsement. Once endorsed, the guideline is adopted by the regulatory authorities in the ICH regions.
- **Implementation**: Regulatory authorities implement the guideline within their respective jurisdictions, ensuring that it becomes part of the regulatory framework for pharmaceutical product registration.

5. Maintenance and Review

- **Step 4: Maintenance and Review**: The ICH guidelines are periodically reviewed and updated to reflect advancements in science and technology, changes in regulatory requirements, and new industry practices.

Key ICH Guidelines

The ICH guidelines are categorized into four main categories: Quality, Safety, Efficacy, and Multidisciplinary. Each category addresses specific aspects of pharmaceutical development and regulatory requirements.

1. Quality Guidelines (Q)

- **Q1: Stability Testing**: Provides guidelines for stability testing of new drug substances and products, including testing conditions, protocols, and data evaluation.
- **Q2: Analytical Validation**: Outlines the validation of analytical methods used in drug development and quality control, including parameters

such as accuracy, precision, specificity, and robustness.

- **Q3: Impurities**: Addresses the identification, qualification, and control of impurities in drug substances and products.
- **Q8: Pharmaceutical Development**: Focuses on the principles of Quality by Design (QbD) in pharmaceutical development, emphasizing the need for a systematic approach to product and process design.
- **Q9: Quality Risk Management**: Provides a framework for identifying, assessing, and controlling risks to product quality using risk management tools and methodologies.
- **Q10: Pharmaceutical Quality System**: Establishes a comprehensive quality management system to ensure consistent production of high-quality pharmaceuticals.

2. Safety Guidelines (S)

- **S1: Carcinogenicity Studies**: Provides guidelines for conducting carcinogenicity studies to assess the potential cancer-causing effects of new drugs.
- **S2: Genotoxicity Testing**: Outlines the testing strategies for evaluating the genotoxic potential of pharmaceutical compounds.
- **S6: Biotechnology Products**: Addresses the preclinical safety evaluation of biotechnology-derived pharmaceuticals, including biologicals and biopharmaceuticals.

3. Efficacy Guidelines (E)

- **E1: Clinical Safety for Drug Trials**: Provides guidelines for determining the size of clinical trials needed to evaluate the safety of new drugs.
- **E6: Good Clinical Practice (GCP)**: Sets international standards for designing, conducting, monitoring, and reporting clinical trials to ensure the protection of trial subjects and the integrity of data.
- **E9: Statistical Principles for Clinical Trials**: Outlines the statistical methodologies and principles for designing and analyzing clinical trials.

4. Multidisciplinary Guidelines (M)

- **M4: Common Technical Document (CTD)**: Provides a standardized format for the submission of regulatory information to health authorities in the ICH regions.
- **M7: Assessment and Control of DNA Reactive (Mutagenic) Impurities**: Offers guidance on assessing and controlling mutagenic impurities in pharmaceuticals.

Importance and Benefits of ICH Guidelines

Regulatory Harmonization

- ICH guidelines harmonize regulatory requirements across different regions, facilitating the global development and registration of pharmaceutical products. This reduces duplication of testing and documentation, speeding up the approval process.

Quality Assurance

- By adhering to ICH guidelines, pharmaceutical companies can ensure that their products meet high standards of quality, safety, and efficacy. This helps maintain public trust and confidence in pharmaceutical products.

Cost Efficiency

- Harmonized guidelines streamline the regulatory process, reducing the need for repeated studies and minimizing resource expenditure. This leads to cost savings for both industry and regulatory authorities.

Global Market Access

- Compliance with ICH guidelines enables pharmaceutical companies to gain access to global markets, as their products meet the regulatory standards of multiple regions. This enhances the availability of medicines worldwide.

Scientific Advancements

- The development and updating of ICH guidelines are based on the latest scientific research and technological advancements. This ensures that regulatory requirements keep pace with innovations in the pharmaceutical industry.

5.10 ISO 13485 and Other Relevant CDSCO Regulatory Guidance Documents

ISO 13485 is an internationally recognized quality management system (QMS) standard specifically for the medical device industry. This standard outlines requirements for a comprehensive QMS that demonstrates the ability to consistently meet customer and regulatory requirements applicable to medical devices and related services. Alongside ISO 13485, the Central Drugs Standard Control Organization (CDSCO) in India provides regulatory guidance documents to ensure the safety, efficacy, and quality of medical devices and pharmaceuticals. This section will explore the key aspects of ISO 13485 and relevant CDSCO guidance documents.

ISO 13485: Quality Management System for Medical Devices

Overview of ISO 13485

- **Purpose**: ISO 13485 specifies requirements for a QMS where an organization needs to demonstrate its ability to provide medical devices and related services that consistently meet customer and applicable regulatory requirements.
- **Scope**: The standard applies to organizations involved in the design, production, installation, and servicing of medical devices, as well as related services.

Key Components of ISO 13485

1. **Quality Management System**: Establishing a QMS that includes documented procedures and processes necessary for the quality and regulatory compliance of medical devices.

2. **Management Responsibility**: Top management's commitment to developing and maintaining an effective QMS, including defining quality policy and objectives, conducting management reviews, and ensuring adequate resource allocation.
3. **Resource Management**: Ensuring the availability of resources, including human resources, infrastructure, and work environment necessary to implement and maintain the QMS.
4. **Product Realization**: Processes for product development, including planning, design and development, purchasing, production, and service provision, to ensure products meet specified requirements.
5. **Measurement, Analysis, and Improvement**: Implementing processes for monitoring and measuring QMS performance, including conducting internal audits, managing nonconformities, and continually improving the effectiveness of the QMS.

Benefits of ISO 13485

- **Regulatory Compliance**: Helps organizations meet regulatory requirements in multiple countries, facilitating market access.
- **Risk Management**: Enhances the ability to identify and mitigate risks associated with medical devices.
- **Quality Assurance**: Ensures consistent product quality, leading to improved patient safety and customer satisfaction.
- **Operational Efficiency**: Streamlines processes and reduces waste, leading to increased efficiency and cost savings.

CDSCO Regulatory Guidance Documents

Central Drugs Standard Control Organization (CDSCO)

- **Role and Responsibilities**: CDSCO is the national regulatory authority (NRA) of India under the Ministry of Health and Family Welfare. It is responsible for the approval, regulation, and control of pharmaceuticals and medical devices in India.

- **Objectives**: Ensuring the safety, efficacy, and quality of medical devices and pharmaceuticals, and promoting public health.

Key CDSCO Guidance Documents for Medical Devices

1. **Medical Device Rules, 2017**

   - **Overview**: The Medical Device Rules, 2017, provide a regulatory framework for the manufacture, import, sale, and distribution of medical devices in India. They classify medical devices based on risk and outline the requirements for registration, licensing, and compliance.
   - **Classification of Devices**: Devices are classified into four categories (Class A, B, C, and D) based on their risk level, with Class A being the lowest risk and Class D the highest.

2. **Guidance on Good Distribution Practices (GDP) for Medical Devices**

   - **Objective**: Ensures that medical devices are consistently stored, transported, and handled under suitable conditions, maintaining their quality and integrity throughout the supply chain.
   - **Key Elements**: Includes requirements for storage conditions, transportation, traceability, handling of complaints and recalls, and training of personnel.

3. **Guidance Document on Essential Principles of Safety and Performance of Medical Devices**

   - **Objective**: Provides guidelines on the essential principles that medical devices must meet to ensure their safety and performance.
   - **Key Principles**: Covers aspects such as design and manufacturing, risk management, labeling and instructions for use, clinical evaluation, and post-market surveillance.

4. **Guidance for Industry on Post-market Surveillance of Medical Devices**

- ◦ **Objective**: Outlines the requirements for post-market surveillance to monitor the safety and performance of medical devices after they have been placed on the market.
- ◦ **Key Elements**: Includes requirements for adverse event reporting, periodic safety update reports (PSURs), and corrective and preventive actions (CAPAs).

5. **Guidance on Technical Documentation for Medical Devices**

- ◦ **Objective**: Provides guidance on the preparation of technical documentation required for the registration and approval of medical devices.
- ◦ **Key Elements**: Includes requirements for device description, design and manufacturing information, risk analysis, product verification and validation, clinical evaluation, and labeling.

Importance and Benefits of CDSCO Guidance Documents

Regulatory Compliance

- Ensures that medical devices meet national regulatory requirements, facilitating their approval and market entry in India.
- Helps manufacturers understand and comply with the specific regulatory requirements for different classes of medical devices.

Patient Safety

- Establishes stringent standards for the safety, efficacy, and performance of medical devices, ensuring that they are safe for use by patients.
- Promotes the monitoring of medical devices through post-market surveillance, helping to identify and mitigate potential risks.

Quality Assurance

- Ensures consistent quality in the manufacturing, distribution, and post-market handling of medical devices, leading to higher levels of patient safety and satisfaction.
- Provides clear guidelines for manufacturers to follow, ensuring that medical devices are produced to the highest standards of quality.

Global Competitiveness

- Aligns Indian regulatory standards with international best practices, enhancing the global competitiveness of Indian medical device manufacturers.
- Facilitates the export of medical devices by ensuring compliance with international regulatory requirements, such as those established by the International Medical Device Regulators Forum (IMDRF).

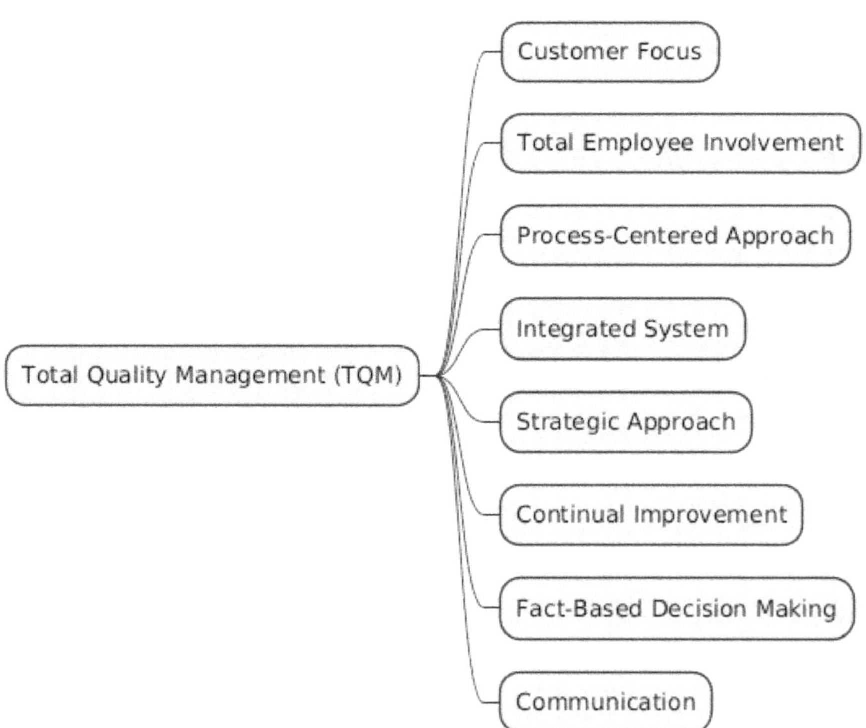

Key principles of Total Quality Management (TQM)

Quality by Design (QbD) and Six Sigma Concept

CHAPTER SIX

Documentation and Regulatory Writing

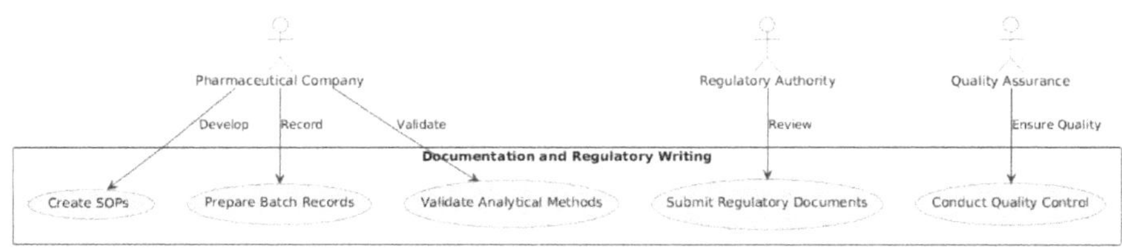

Documentation and Regulatory Writing Process

6.1 Introduction to Documentation in Pharmaceutical Industry

Introduction

Documentation is a critical component of the **pharmaceutical industry**, ensuring the **quality, safety,** and **efficacy** of pharmaceutical products. It involves the systematic creation, organization, maintenance, and storage of all records and data related to drug development, manufacturing, testing, and distribution. Proper documentation serves as a backbone for **regulatory compliance**, traceability, and accountability in the pharmaceutical sector.

Types of Documentation

The pharmaceutical industry relies on various types of documentation, each serving a specific purpose. These include:

- **Standard Operating Procedures (SOPs):** Detailed, written instructions designed to achieve uniformity in the performance of specific functions.
- **Batch Records:** Comprehensive records of the manufacturing history of each batch, including the steps followed, materials used, and results obtained.
- **Analytical Method Validation:** Documents proving that analytical procedures are suitable for their intended use.
- **Quality Control (QC) Records:** Data and reports from testing and analysis of raw materials, in-process materials, and finished products.
- **Regulatory Submissions:** Documentation required by regulatory agencies for the approval of new drugs, including clinical trial data, manufacturing processes, and safety information.

Importance of Documentation

In the pharmaceutical industry, documentation plays a vital role in ensuring product quality and regulatory compliance. It provides a transparent and verifiable record of all activities, enabling effective tracking and auditing. Proper documentation helps in:

- **Compliance:** Ensuring that all processes meet regulatory standards set by authorities like the FDA (Food and Drug Administration) or EMA (European Medicines Agency).
- **Traceability:** Tracking the history, application, or location of a product by means of recorded identification.
- **Accountability:** Providing evidence of compliance with established standards and procedures.
- **Quality Assurance (QA):** Facilitating continuous monitoring and improvement of processes to maintain high-quality standards.

Documentation Process

The process of documentation in the pharmaceutical industry involves several key steps:

1. **Creation:** Drafting detailed documents that accurately describe processes, methods, and results.
2. **Review:** Thoroughly reviewing documents to ensure accuracy, completeness, and compliance with regulatory requirements.
3. **Approval:** Obtaining necessary approvals from authorized personnel before implementation.
4. **Implementation:** Ensuring that the documented procedures are followed during actual operations.
5. **Maintenance:** Regularly updating documents to reflect any changes in processes or regulations.
6. **Storage:** Safely storing documents for future reference and audits.

Methodology and Procedures

Effective documentation requires adherence to specific methodologies and procedures:

- **Clear and Concise Writing:** Documents should be written in a clear and concise manner, avoiding ambiguity.
- **Consistency:** Ensuring consistency in terminology, format, and style across all documents.
- **Traceability:** Including identifiers such as version numbers, dates, and signatures to maintain traceability.
- **Controlled Distribution:** Implementing controlled distribution of documents to ensure that only authorized personnel have access to them.
- **Regular Audits:** Conducting regular audits to verify the accuracy and completeness of documentation.

Challenges and Solutions

Despite its importance, documentation in the pharmaceutical industry faces several challenges:

- **Volume of Documentation:** The sheer volume of required documents can be overwhelming. Implementing electronic documentation systems can streamline this process.
- **Regulatory Changes:** Keeping up with constantly evolving regulatory requirements can be challenging. Regular training and updates can help mitigate this issue.
- **Human Error:** Manual documentation is prone to human error. Automation and electronic documentation systems can reduce the risk of errors.

6.2 Exploratory Product Development Brief (EPDB)

Introduction

The **Exploratory Product Development Brief (EPDB)** is a foundational document in the pharmaceutical industry that outlines the initial stages of product development. It serves as a roadmap, detailing the objectives, strategies, and methodologies that will guide the development of a new pharmaceutical product. The EPDB is crucial for aligning the efforts of various departments, ensuring that the development process is well-coordinated and meets regulatory requirements.

Purpose of EPDB

The primary purpose of the EPDB is to provide a comprehensive overview of the proposed product and its development pathway. It includes:

- **Product Concept:** A clear description of the new product, including its intended use, therapeutic area, and target population.
- **Rationale:** The scientific and clinical basis for developing the product, supported by preliminary research and data.
- **Objectives:** Specific goals to be achieved during the exploratory phase, such as proof of concept, safety assessments, and preliminary efficacy.
- **Development Strategy:** An outline of the development plan, including timelines, key milestones, and critical decision points.

Components of EPDB

An effective EPDB includes several key components, each addressing different aspects of product development:

1. **Executive Summary:** A high-level overview of the project, highlighting the key points of the EPDB.
2. **Background Information:** Detailed information on the disease or condition being targeted, existing treatments, and the unmet medical needs the new product aims to address.

3. **Product Description:** A comprehensive description of the new product, including its formulation, dosage form, and mechanism of action.
4. **Regulatory Considerations:** An outline of the regulatory pathway, including required approvals and compliance with relevant guidelines and standards.
5. **Development Plan:** A detailed plan covering preclinical and clinical development stages, including study designs, endpoints, and anticipated challenges.
6. **Risk Assessment:** Identification of potential risks and challenges, along with mitigation strategies to address them.

Methodology and Procedures

The development of an EPDB involves a systematic approach to ensure that all relevant aspects are thoroughly considered and documented:

- **Interdisciplinary Collaboration:** Engaging various departments such as research and development (R&D), regulatory affairs, clinical operations, and marketing to provide their input and expertise.
- **Data Collection:** Gathering all necessary data from preclinical studies, literature reviews, and expert consultations to support the product concept and development strategy.
- **Drafting and Review:** Creating a draft of the EPDB and circulating it for review among key stakeholders to ensure accuracy and completeness.
- **Approval and Finalization:** Obtaining approvals from senior management and relevant committees before finalizing the document.

Importance of EPDB

The EPDB is critical for several reasons:

- **Strategic Planning:** It provides a clear and structured plan for product development, helping to align resources and efforts towards common goals.
- **Regulatory Compliance:** Ensures that the development process adheres to regulatory requirements and standards, facilitating smoother approval

processes.

- **Risk Management:** Identifies potential risks early in the development process and outlines strategies to mitigate them, reducing the likelihood of costly delays or failures.
- **Stakeholder Communication:** Serves as a communication tool to keep all stakeholders informed and engaged, promoting transparency and collaboration.

Challenges and Solutions

Developing an EPDB can present several challenges, which need to be addressed effectively:

- **Data Gaps:** Incomplete or insufficient data can hinder the development of a robust EPDB. Conducting additional research or feasibility studies can help fill these gaps.
- **Alignment of Stakeholders:** Ensuring that all stakeholders are aligned with the development plan can be challenging. Regular meetings and updates can facilitate better communication and alignment.
- **Regulatory Uncertainty:** Navigating the complex regulatory landscape can be difficult. Engaging regulatory experts and staying updated on guidelines can help mitigate this challenge.

6.3 Product Development Plan (PDP)

Introduction

The **Product Development Plan (PDP)** is an essential document in the pharmaceutical industry that outlines the comprehensive strategy for bringing a new pharmaceutical product from concept to market. It serves as a detailed roadmap, specifying the tasks, timelines, resources, and milestones necessary to achieve successful product development. The PDP ensures that all phases of development are meticulously planned and executed, promoting efficiency, regulatory compliance, and ultimately the delivery of safe and effective pharmaceutical products to patients.

Purpose of PDP

The primary purpose of the PDP is to provide a structured framework for the entire product development lifecycle. It includes:

- **Detailed Project Description:** Clear articulation of the product's purpose, target indications, and intended patient population.
- **Development Goals:** Specific objectives to be achieved at each stage of development, including preclinical studies, clinical trials, and regulatory submissions.
- **Resource Allocation:** Detailed plan for the allocation of financial, human, and material resources throughout the development process.
- **Timelines and Milestones:** Defined timelines for each phase of development, with key milestones to track progress and ensure timely completion.

Components of PDP

An effective PDP encompasses several key components, each addressing critical aspects of product development:

1. **Executive Summary:** A concise overview of the product development project, highlighting key points and objectives.
2. **Background and Rationale:** Explanation of the medical need, current treatment options, and the scientific rationale for the new product.
3. **Product Description:** Detailed information on the product's formulation, dosage form, mechanism of action, and anticipated therapeutic benefits.
4. **Preclinical Development Plan:** Outline of preclinical studies, including in vitro and in vivo tests, to assess the product's safety and efficacy.
5. **Clinical Development Plan:** Detailed plan for clinical trials, including study design, patient population, endpoints, and statistical analysis.
6. **Regulatory Strategy:** Comprehensive plan for navigating regulatory requirements, including interactions with regulatory agencies and preparation of submission dossiers.
7. **Quality Assurance Plan:** Strategies to ensure that all development activities comply with quality standards and regulatory guidelines.
8. **Risk Management Plan:** Identification of potential risks and challenges, along with mitigation strategies to address them.

Methodology and Procedures

The development of a PDP involves a systematic approach to ensure thorough planning and execution:

- **Interdisciplinary Collaboration:** Engaging experts from various fields, including R&D, regulatory affairs, clinical operations, quality assurance, and marketing, to contribute their expertise.
- **Data Integration:** Collecting and integrating data from preclinical and clinical studies, market research, and regulatory guidelines to support the development plan.
- **Drafting and Review:** Creating a draft PDP and subjecting it to rigorous review by key stakeholders to ensure accuracy, feasibility, and alignment with organizational goals.
- **Approval and Implementation:** Securing approvals from senior management and relevant committees before initiating the implementation phase.

Importance of PDP

The PDP is crucial for several reasons:

- **Strategic Alignment:** Ensures that all development activities are aligned with the overall strategic goals of the organization.
- **Regulatory Compliance:** Helps ensure that the development process adheres to regulatory requirements, facilitating smoother approval processes.
- **Resource Optimization:** Enables efficient allocation and utilization of resources, reducing waste and maximizing productivity.
- **Risk Mitigation:** Proactively identifies and addresses potential risks, minimizing the likelihood of costly delays or failures.
- **Project Management:** Provides a clear framework for project management, enabling effective tracking of progress and timely adjustments.

Challenges and Solutions

Developing a PDP can present several challenges, which need to be effectively managed:

- **Complexity of Development:** The complexity of pharmaceutical development requires meticulous planning and coordination. Using project management tools and methodologies can help manage this complexity.
- **Regulatory Changes:** Regulatory requirements can change, impacting the development plan. Staying updated with regulatory guidelines and maintaining flexibility in the PDP can help address this challenge.
- **Unforeseen Risks:** Unexpected issues can arise during development. Regular risk assessments and having contingency plans in place can help mitigate unforeseen risks.

6.4 Product Development Report (PDR)

Introduction

The **Product Development Report (PDR)** is a comprehensive document that provides a detailed account of the product development process in the pharmaceutical industry. It serves as a formal record of all activities, findings, and outcomes related to the development of a new pharmaceutical product. The PDR is crucial for ensuring transparency, traceability, and regulatory compliance, and it plays a vital role in the final stages of product development and approval.

Purpose of PDR

The primary purpose of the PDR is to consolidate and document the entire product development process. This includes:

- **Detailed Record:** Providing a thorough and accurate record of all development activities, including research, testing, and production.
- **Evidence of Compliance:** Demonstrating adherence to regulatory requirements and industry standards.
- **Basis for Approval:** Serving as a key document for regulatory submissions and approvals.
- **Knowledge Repository:** Acting as a repository of knowledge for future reference and continuous improvement.

Components of PDR

An effective PDR includes several key components, each addressing different aspects of product development:

1. **Executive Summary:** A high-level overview of the product development process, highlighting key achievements, milestones, and outcomes.

2. **Introduction and Background:** Detailed information on the product's background, including the medical need, target population, and scientific rationale for its development.

3. **Development Objectives:** Clear articulation of the objectives set for the development process and the extent to which they were achieved.

4. **Preclinical Studies:** Comprehensive documentation of all preclinical studies, including methodologies, results, and conclusions regarding the product's safety and efficacy.

5. **Clinical Trials:** Detailed accounts of clinical trial phases, including study designs, patient demographics, methodologies, results, and interpretations.

6. **Manufacturing and Quality Control:** Information on the manufacturing process, quality control measures, and validation of production methods.

7. **Regulatory Submissions:** Documentation of all interactions with regulatory agencies, including submission dossiers, responses, and approvals.

8. **Risk Management:** Overview of identified risks, mitigation strategies implemented, and outcomes.

9. **Conclusions and Recommendations:** Summarization of the development process, key findings, and recommendations for future steps or improvements.

Methodology and Procedures

The preparation of a PDR involves a systematic approach to ensure accuracy and comprehensiveness:

- **Data Collection:** Gathering all relevant data from preclinical and clinical studies, manufacturing records, and regulatory submissions.
- **Collaboration:** Involving experts from various departments, including R&D, clinical operations, quality assurance, and regulatory affairs, to contribute their insights and data.
- **Drafting and Review:** Creating a detailed draft of the PDR and conducting thorough reviews by key stakeholders to ensure accuracy and completeness.
- **Finalization:** Securing necessary approvals from senior management and relevant committees before finalizing the document.

Importance of PDR

The PDR is essential for several reasons:

- **Regulatory Approval:** It provides the necessary documentation to regulatory agencies, facilitating the approval process.
- **Quality Assurance:** Ensures that all aspects of product development meet the highest standards of quality and safety.
- **Traceability:** Provides a transparent and verifiable record of all development activities, enabling traceability and accountability.
- **Continuous Improvement:** Acts as a valuable resource for identifying areas of improvement in future product development projects.

Challenges and Solutions

Developing a PDR can present several challenges, which need to be effectively managed:

- **Volume of Data:** The extensive amount of data generated during product development can be overwhelming. Implementing data management systems and tools can help organize and streamline this process.
- **Interdepartmental Coordination:** Ensuring effective communication and collaboration across departments can be challenging. Regular meetings and updates can facilitate better coordination.
- **Regulatory Complexity:** Navigating the complex regulatory landscape requires expertise and vigilance. Engaging regulatory experts and maintaining up-to-date knowledge of guidelines can help address this challenge.

6.5 Master Formula Record and Batch Manufacturing Record

Introduction

In the pharmaceutical industry, documentation is paramount to ensure the quality, safety, and consistency of products. Two critical documents in this context are the **Master Formula Record (MFR)** and the **Batch Manufacturing Record (BMR)**. The MFR provides a detailed blueprint for manufacturing a product, while the BMR records the actual production process for each batch. Together, these documents ensure that every batch of a pharmaceutical product is produced according to predefined specifications and complies with regulatory standards.

Master Formula Record (MFR)

Definition and Purpose

The **Master Formula Record (MFR)** is a comprehensive document that outlines the detailed instructions for the production of a pharmaceutical product. It serves as a standardized reference to ensure that each batch of the product is manufactured consistently and according to the same specifications. The MFR is critical for maintaining product quality, meeting regulatory requirements, and ensuring reproducibility in manufacturing.

Components of MFR

An effective MFR includes several key components:

1. **Product Name and Description:** The official name and a detailed description of the product, including its formulation and intended use.
2. **Formula:** A detailed list of all ingredients, including active pharmaceutical ingredients (APIs) and excipients, with their exact quantities.

3. **Manufacturing Instructions:** Step-by-step procedures for the manufacturing process, including equipment and tools required, environmental conditions, and specific techniques.
4. **Packaging Instructions:** Detailed instructions for the packaging of the product, including type of packaging materials, labeling requirements, and packaging process.
5. **Quality Control Tests:** A list of quality control tests to be performed at various stages of the manufacturing process to ensure product quality and compliance with specifications.
6. **Storage Conditions:** Specific storage conditions for the product and its raw materials to maintain their stability and efficacy.

Importance of MFR

The MFR is crucial for several reasons:

- **Consistency:** Ensures that every batch of the product is manufactured consistently, meeting the same quality standards.
- **Regulatory Compliance:** Provides a standardized document that meets regulatory requirements, facilitating inspections and approvals.
- **Quality Assurance:** Serves as a basis for quality assurance, ensuring that all manufacturing processes are controlled and monitored.

Batch Manufacturing Record (BMR)

Definition and Purpose

The **Batch Manufacturing Record (BMR)** is a document that records the actual production details of each batch of a pharmaceutical product. It provides a comprehensive record of the manufacturing process, including any deviations or anomalies that occurred during production. The BMR is essential for traceability, quality control, and regulatory compliance.

Components of BMR

An effective BMR includes several key components:

1. **Batch Number and Product Name:** The unique batch number and the name of the product being manufactured.
2. **Date and Time of Production:** The specific dates and times at which various stages of the production process were carried out.
3. **Equipment and Materials:** Details of the equipment used and the materials consumed during the manufacturing process, including lot numbers and quantities.
4. **Manufacturing Steps:** A step-by-step record of the manufacturing process, including the specific operations performed, conditions maintained, and any deviations from the MFR.
5. **Operator Details:** Names and signatures of the operators and supervisors involved in the production process.
6. **Quality Control Results:** Results of the quality control tests conducted during and after the manufacturing process, ensuring that the batch meets all specifications.

Importance of BMR

The BMR is critical for several reasons:

- **Traceability:** Provides a complete record of the manufacturing process, allowing for traceability in case of any issues or recalls.
- **Quality Control:** Ensures that each batch meets the predefined quality standards and specifications.
- **Regulatory Compliance:** Acts as evidence of compliance with regulatory requirements, facilitating inspections and audits.

Methodology and Procedures

The preparation and maintenance of MFR and BMR involve a systematic approach to ensure accuracy and compliance:

- **Drafting MFR:** Creating a detailed and precise MFR with input from various departments, including R&D, manufacturing, and quality assurance.

- **Review and Approval:** Subjecting the MFR to rigorous review and obtaining necessary approvals from senior management and regulatory authorities.
- **Implementation:** Using the MFR as a reference during the manufacturing process to ensure consistency and adherence to specifications.
- **Recording BMR:** Documenting each step of the manufacturing process in the BMR, ensuring that all details are accurately recorded and any deviations are noted.
- **Auditing:** Regularly auditing the MFR and BMR to ensure compliance with regulatory standards and to identify areas for improvement.

Challenges and Solutions

Maintaining accurate MFR and BMR can present several challenges:

- **Complexity of Processes:** The complexity of pharmaceutical manufacturing processes requires meticulous documentation. Implementing electronic documentation systems can streamline this process.
- **Human Error:** Manual recording is prone to errors. Training personnel and using automated systems can reduce the risk of errors.
- **Regulatory Changes:** Keeping up with changing regulatory requirements can be challenging. Regular updates and training can help mitigate this issue.

6.6 Batch Reconciliation and Batch Packaging Records

Introduction

In the pharmaceutical industry, ensuring the accuracy and integrity of batch records is crucial for maintaining product quality and regulatory compliance. Two important documents in this regard are the **Batch Reconciliation Record** and the **Batch Packaging Record**. These records provide a detailed account of the materials used, quantities produced, and packaging processes, ensuring that all aspects of production and packaging are thoroughly documented and verified.

Batch Reconciliation Record

Definition and Purpose

The **Batch Reconciliation Record** is a document that provides a detailed account of the quantities of materials used and products produced in a specific batch. It serves to ensure that there are no discrepancies between the quantities of materials issued for production and the quantities actually used and produced. This record is essential for maintaining the accuracy and integrity of the manufacturing process, ensuring that all materials are accounted for and that any deviations are identified and addressed.

Components of Batch Reconciliation Record

An effective Batch Reconciliation Record includes several key components:

1. **Batch Number and Product Name:** The unique identifier for the batch and the name of the product being produced.
2. **Material Reconciliation:** A detailed account of the quantities of raw materials and components issued for production, used, and remaining.
3. **Yield Calculation:** The calculation of the actual yield of the product, comparing the expected yield with the actual yield obtained.

4. **Losses and Discrepancies:** Documentation of any losses or discrepancies observed during the production process, with explanations for these variances.
5. **Approval Signatures:** Signatures of authorized personnel confirming the accuracy of the reconciliation process.

Importance of Batch Reconciliation Record

The Batch Reconciliation Record is crucial for several reasons:

- **Accuracy:** Ensures that all materials used in production are accurately accounted for, reducing the risk of errors and discrepancies.
- **Regulatory Compliance:** Provides a documented trail that meets regulatory requirements, facilitating inspections and audits.
- **Quality Control:** Helps identify and address any issues in the production process, ensuring that the final product meets quality standards.
- **Efficiency:** Enables efficient use of materials by tracking and minimizing losses.

Methodology and Procedures

The preparation and maintenance of a Batch Reconciliation Record involve a systematic approach:

- **Material Tracking:** Keeping accurate records of all materials issued for production, used, and remaining.
- **Yield Calculation:** Calculating the expected yield based on the materials used and comparing it with the actual yield obtained.
- **Loss Identification:** Identifying and documenting any losses or discrepancies observed during the production process.

Review and Approval: Conducting a thorough review of the reconciliation record and obtaining necessary approvals from authorized personnel.

Batch Packaging Record

Definition and Purpose

The **Batch Packaging Record** is a document that provides a comprehensive account of the packaging process for a specific batch of a pharmaceutical product. It includes details of the packaging materials used, the packaging operations performed, and the quantities of finished products packaged. This record is essential for ensuring that the packaging process is conducted according to predefined specifications and that all packaged products meet quality standards.

Components of Batch Packaging Record

An effective Batch Packaging Record includes several key components:

1. **Batch Number and Product Name:** The unique identifier for the batch and the name of the product being packaged.
2. **Packaging Materials:** A detailed list of the packaging materials used, including lot numbers and quantities.
3. **Packaging Instructions:** Step-by-step instructions for the packaging process, including equipment used, conditions maintained, and specific techniques applied.
4. **Quantities Packaged:** Documentation of the quantities of products packaged, including the number of units, batches, and any rejects or reworks.
5. **Quality Control Checks:** Results of quality control checks performed during and after the packaging process to ensure compliance with specifications.
6. **Approval Signatures:** Signatures of authorized personnel confirming the accuracy and completeness of the packaging record.

Importance of Batch Packaging Record

The Batch Packaging Record is critical for several reasons:

- **Traceability:** Provides a detailed account of the packaging process, enabling traceability and accountability for each batch.
- **Regulatory Compliance:** Ensures that the packaging process complies with regulatory requirements and standards.
- **Quality Assurance:** Helps maintain the quality of the packaged product by documenting and verifying each step of the packaging process.
- **Documentation:** Acts as a formal record that can be reviewed during audits and inspections.

Methodology and Procedures

The preparation and maintenance of a Batch Packaging Record involve a systematic approach:

- **Material Documentation:** Keeping accurate records of all packaging materials used, including lot numbers and quantities.
- **Process Documentation:** Documenting each step of the packaging process, including equipment used, conditions maintained, and specific techniques applied.
- **Quality Checks:** Conducting and documenting quality control checks to ensure that all packaged products meet predefined specifications.
- **Review and Approval:** Conducting a thorough review of the packaging record and obtaining necessary approvals from authorized personnel.

Challenges and Solutions

Maintaining accurate Batch Reconciliation and Batch Packaging Records can present several challenges:

- **Volume of Data:** The large volume of data generated during production and packaging can be overwhelming. Implementing electronic record-keeping systems can help manage and organize this data.
- **Human Error:** Manual recording is prone to errors. Training personnel and using automated systems can reduce the risk of errors.
- **Regulatory Changes:** Keeping up with changing regulatory requirements can be challenging. Regular updates and training can help

ensure compliance.

6.7 Print Pack Specifications and Distribution Records

Introduction

In the pharmaceutical industry, the accurate and meticulous documentation of packaging and distribution processes is critical for maintaining product quality, ensuring regulatory compliance, and guaranteeing patient safety. Two essential documents in this context are the **Print Pack Specifications** and the **Distribution Records**. These records provide detailed information on the packaging materials, design, and distribution of pharmaceutical products, ensuring that all aspects of packaging and distribution are thoroughly documented and verified.

Print Pack Specifications

Definition and Purpose

The **Print Pack Specifications** document outlines the detailed requirements for the packaging materials used in the production of pharmaceutical products. This includes the design, materials, dimensions, and regulatory information that must be present on the packaging. The primary purpose of this document is to ensure that the packaging is consistent, meets regulatory standards, and effectively protects the product while providing essential information to the user.

Components of Print Pack Specifications

An effective Print Pack Specifications document includes several key components:

1. **Product Name and Description:** The official name and a detailed description of the product.
2. **Packaging Design:** Detailed drawings and descriptions of the packaging design, including dimensions, layout, and graphics.
3. **Material Specifications:** Information on the materials used for the packaging, including type, grade, and any specific requirements for

material properties.

4. **Labeling Requirements:** Detailed instructions on the labeling of the product, including text, font size, color, and placement of regulatory information such as batch numbers, expiration dates, and barcodes.

5. **Regulatory Compliance:** Ensuring that the packaging meets all regulatory requirements, including safety warnings, usage instructions, and compliance marks.

6. **Approval Signatures:** Signatures of authorized personnel confirming the accuracy and approval of the packaging specifications.

Importance of Print Pack Specifications

Print Pack Specifications are crucial for several reasons:

- **Consistency:** Ensures that all packaging is consistent and meets predefined standards.
- **Regulatory Compliance:** Helps ensure that the packaging complies with all relevant regulatory requirements, facilitating approval and inspection processes.
- **Product Protection:** Ensures that the packaging effectively protects the product from damage and contamination.
- **Information Accuracy:** Ensures that all necessary information is accurately presented on the packaging, providing essential information to users and healthcare professionals.

Methodology and Procedures

The preparation and maintenance of Print Pack Specifications involve a systematic approach:

- **Design Collaboration:** Collaborating with design and regulatory teams to create accurate and compliant packaging designs.
- **Material Selection:** Choosing appropriate materials that meet the required specifications and regulatory standards.
- **Drafting and Review:** Creating a detailed draft of the Print Pack Specifications and reviewing it for accuracy and compliance.

- **Approval and Implementation:** Securing necessary approvals from authorized personnel and implementing the specifications in the production process.

Distribution Records

Definition and Purpose

The **Distribution Records** document provides a comprehensive account of the distribution of pharmaceutical products from the manufacturing site to the end user. This includes details of the shipment, storage conditions, and handling of the products during transit. The primary purpose of this document is to ensure that the distribution process is controlled and documented, maintaining the quality and integrity of the products throughout the supply chain.

Components of Distribution Records

An effective Distribution Records document includes several key components:

1. **Product Name and Batch Number:** The official name of the product and the unique batch number of the distributed products.
2. **Distribution Details:** Information on the distribution process, including the dates of shipment, transportation methods, and destinations.
3. **Storage Conditions:** Documentation of the storage conditions maintained during transportation to ensure product stability and integrity.
4. **Handling Instructions:** Specific instructions for handling the products during distribution to prevent damage and contamination.
5. **Receipt Confirmation:** Records of the receipt of the products by the end user, including the date of receipt and the condition of the products upon arrival.
6. **Approval Signatures:** Signatures of authorized personnel confirming the accuracy and completion of the distribution records.

Importance of Distribution Records

Distribution Records are critical for several reasons:

- **Traceability:** Provides a detailed account of the distribution process, enabling traceability and accountability for each batch.
- **Quality Assurance:** Ensures that the products are handled and stored correctly during distribution, maintaining their quality and efficacy.
- **Regulatory Compliance:** Helps ensure that the distribution process complies with regulatory requirements, facilitating inspections and audits.
- **Risk Management:** Identifies and addresses any issues in the distribution process, reducing the risk of product recalls or quality defects.

Methodology and Procedures

The preparation and maintenance of Distribution Records involve a systematic approach:

- **Documentation of Shipments:** Keeping accurate records of all shipments, including dates, transportation methods, and destinations.
- **Storage and Handling Monitoring:** Monitoring and documenting the storage conditions and handling of products during distribution.
- **Receipt Verification:** Confirming and documenting the receipt of products by the end user, including the condition of the products upon arrival.
- **Review and Approval:** Conducting a thorough review of the distribution records and obtaining necessary approvals from authorized personnel.

Challenges and Solutions

Maintaining accurate Print Pack Specifications and Distribution Records can present several challenges:

- **Complex Supply Chains:** The complexity of pharmaceutical supply chains requires meticulous documentation and coordination. Implementing robust supply chain management systems can help streamline this process.
- **Regulatory Changes:** Keeping up with changing regulatory requirements can be challenging. Regular updates and training can ensure compliance.
- **Human Error:** Manual recording is prone to errors. Using automated systems and electronic records can reduce the risk of errors.

6.8 Certificate of Analysis (CoA)

Introduction

In the pharmaceutical industry, the **Certificate of Analysis (CoA)** is a crucial document that certifies the quality and compliance of a pharmaceutical product. It provides detailed information on the tests performed, the specifications set, and the results obtained for a specific batch of a product. The CoA is essential for ensuring that the product meets all regulatory standards and quality requirements, and it plays a significant role in the release and distribution of pharmaceutical products.

Definition and Purpose

The **Certificate of Analysis (CoA)** is a document issued by the manufacturer that accompanies a batch of pharmaceutical product, summarizing the quality control testing conducted on the batch and the results obtained. The primary purpose of the CoA is to provide assurance to regulatory authorities, healthcare providers, and consumers that the product complies with all necessary specifications and quality standards.

Components of Certificate of Analysis

An effective CoA includes several key components:

1. **Product Information:** The official name of the product, its dosage form, and strength.
2. **Batch Number:** The unique identifier for the batch being certified.
3. **Manufacturing Date:** The date on which the batch was manufactured.
4. **Expiration Date:** The date until which the product is expected to remain within its specified quality limits.
5. **Testing Specifications:** Detailed specifications against which the product was tested, including parameters such as identity, purity, potency, and physical characteristics.

6. **Test Methods:** The analytical methods and procedures used to conduct the tests.
7. **Test Results:** The actual results obtained from the tests, compared against the specifications.
8. **Compliance Statement:** A statement confirming that the batch complies with all specified standards and regulatory requirements.
9. **Signatures:** Signatures of authorized personnel who conducted the tests and approved the results.

Importance of Certificate of Analysis

The CoA is crucial for several reasons:

- **Quality Assurance:** Provides documented proof that the batch meets all quality specifications and regulatory standards.
- **Regulatory Compliance:** Ensures that the product complies with regulatory requirements, facilitating approvals and inspections.
- **Traceability:** Enables traceability of the batch, providing a documented trail from production to distribution.
- **Customer Confidence:** Provides assurance to healthcare providers and consumers that the product is safe and effective.

Methodology and Procedures

The preparation of a CoA involves a systematic approach to ensure accuracy and compliance:

- **Sample Collection:** Collecting representative samples from the batch for testing.
- **Testing:** Conducting a series of quality control tests using validated analytical methods.
- **Data Documentation:** Recording the test results and comparing them with the specified limits.
- **Review and Approval:** Reviewing the test results and obtaining necessary approvals from authorized personnel.

- **Issuance:** Preparing the CoA document and issuing it along with the batch.

Challenges and Solutions

Maintaining the accuracy and integrity of the CoA can present several challenges:

- **Analytical Variability:** Variability in test results can occur due to differences in analytical methods or laboratory conditions. Using validated methods and standard operating procedures can minimize this variability.
- **Human Error:** Manual data entry and documentation are prone to errors. Implementing automated systems and electronic records can reduce the risk of errors.
- **Regulatory Changes:** Keeping up with changing regulatory requirements can be challenging. Regular updates and training can help ensure compliance.

6.9 Site Master File and Drug Master Files (DMF)

Introduction

In the pharmaceutical industry, comprehensive documentation is essential for ensuring the quality, safety, and regulatory compliance of drug products. Two critical documents in this context are the **Site Master File (SMF)** and the **Drug Master File (DMF)**. These documents provide detailed information about manufacturing facilities, processes, and product components, facilitating regulatory inspections and approvals.

Site Master File (SMF)

Definition and Purpose

The **Site Master File (SMF)** is a document that provides a comprehensive overview of a pharmaceutical manufacturing facility. It includes detailed information about the site's organizational structure, operations, quality management system, and manufacturing processes. The primary purpose of the SMF is to facilitate regulatory inspections and demonstrate compliance with Good Manufacturing Practices (GMP).

Components of Site Master File

An effective SMF includes several key components:

1. **General Information:** Details about the site, including its name, address, and contact information.
2. **Organizational Structure:** An overview of the organizational structure, including key personnel and their responsibilities.
3. **Quality Management System:** A description of the quality management system in place, including procedures for quality control, quality assurance, and risk management.
4. **Manufacturing Operations:** Detailed information about the manufacturing processes, including equipment used, production flow, and standard operating procedures.

5. **Facilities and Equipment:** Descriptions of the facilities and equipment used in the manufacturing process, including maintenance and calibration procedures.
6. **Utilities:** Information on utilities such as water, air, and power supply systems that support the manufacturing operations.
7. **Documentation:** Details about the documentation practices, including record-keeping, data integrity, and document control.
8. **Sanitation and Hygiene:** Procedures for maintaining sanitation and hygiene in the manufacturing facility.
9. **Personnel:** Information about personnel training and qualifications.
10. **Self-Inspection:** Procedures for internal audits and self-inspection to ensure compliance with GMP.

Importance of Site Master File

The SMF is crucial for several reasons:

- **Regulatory Compliance:** Demonstrates compliance with GMP and facilitates regulatory inspections and approvals.
- **Quality Assurance:** Provides a detailed overview of the quality management system, ensuring that quality standards are consistently met.
- **Operational Transparency:** Offers a comprehensive view of the manufacturing operations, enhancing transparency and accountability.
- **Risk Management:** Helps identify and mitigate potential risks associated with manufacturing processes and facilities.

Methodology and Procedures

The preparation and maintenance of an SMF involve a systematic approach:

- **Data Collection:** Gathering detailed information about the site's organizational structure, operations, and quality management system.
- **Documentation:** Documenting the collected information in a clear and organized manner, following regulatory guidelines.

- **Review and Approval:** Conducting thorough reviews of the SMF and obtaining necessary approvals from authorized personnel.
- **Updating:** Regularly updating the SMF to reflect any changes in the facility, processes, or quality management system.

Drug Master Files (DMF)

Definition and Purpose

The **Drug Master File (DMF)** is a confidential document submitted to regulatory authorities that provides detailed information about the manufacturing, processing, packaging, and storage of drug products or components. The DMF is used to support regulatory submissions for drug applications, ensuring that the components and processes meet regulatory standards.

Components of Drug Master File

An effective DMF includes several key components:

1. **Administrative Information:** Details about the DMF holder, including name, address, and contact information.
2. **Introduction:** A brief introduction to the DMF, including its purpose and scope.
3. **Chemistry, Manufacturing, and Controls (CMC):** Detailed information about the chemistry, manufacturing, and controls of the drug substance or product.
4. **Facilities and Equipment:** Descriptions of the facilities and equipment used in the manufacturing process.
5. **Production Process:** Detailed information about the production process, including raw materials, intermediates, and finished products.
6. **Quality Control:** Information about quality control procedures, including analytical methods, specifications, and testing protocols.
7. **Stability Data:** Stability data demonstrating that the drug product or component remains within specifications throughout its shelf life.
8. **Packaging and Labeling:** Details about packaging materials and labeling procedures.

Types of DMFs

DMFs can be categorized into several types, including:

- **Type I:** Manufacturing site, facilities, operating procedures, and personnel.
- **Type II:** Drug substance, drug substance intermediate, and material used in the preparation of the drug substance.
- **Type III:** Packaging materials.
- **Type IV:** Excipient, colorant, flavor, essence, or material used in the preparation of the drug product.
- **Type V:** FDA-accepted reference information.

Importance of Drug Master File

The DMF is essential for several reasons:

- **Regulatory Compliance:** Ensures that the drug product or component meets regulatory standards, facilitating approvals and inspections.
- **Confidentiality:** Protects proprietary information while allowing regulatory authorities to assess the safety and quality of the product.
- **Support for Applications:** Provides critical information to support regulatory submissions for drug applications.

Methodology and Procedures

The preparation and submission of a DMF involve a systematic approach:

- **Data Collection:** Gathering detailed information about the manufacturing, processing, packaging, and storage of the drug product or component.
- **Documentation:** Documenting the collected information in a clear and organized manner, following regulatory guidelines.
- **Review and Approval:** Conducting thorough reviews of the DMF and obtaining necessary approvals from authorized personnel.

- **Submission:** Submitting the DMF to regulatory authorities and maintaining it to reflect any changes.

Challenges and Solutions

Maintaining accurate SMFs and DMFs can present several challenges:

- **Data Management:** Managing large volumes of data can be challenging. Implementing robust data management systems can help streamline this process.
- **Regulatory Changes:** Keeping up with changing regulatory requirements can be difficult. Regular updates and training can ensure compliance.
- **Confidentiality:** Protecting proprietary information while providing necessary details to regulatory authorities requires careful documentation and submission.

CHAPTER SEVEN

Dossier Preparation and Submission

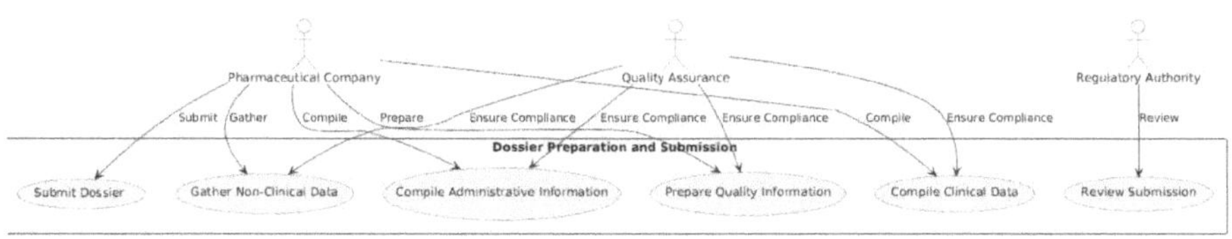

Fig: Dossier Preparation and Submission

7.1 INTRODUCTION AND OVERVIEW OF DOSSIERS

Dossiers are comprehensive collections of documents compiled to provide detailed information about a product or project. In the pharmaceutical industry, dossiers play a crucial role in the regulatory approval process for new drugs, generic drugs, and other pharmaceutical products. These documents are meticulously prepared to ensure they meet the stringent requirements set by regulatory authorities such as the Food and Drug Administration (FDA), European Medicines Agency (EMA), and other national regulatory bodies.

A dossier typically includes a wide range of documents that cover various aspects of the product. These aspects can be broadly categorized into administrative information, quality information, non-clinical studies, and clinical studies. The **administrative section** includes application forms, product labeling, and information about the manufacturer. This section also contains **legal documents** such as patent information and letters of authorization.

The **quality section** of the dossier is one of the most critical components. It provides detailed information about the manufacturing process, controls in place to ensure product quality, and the **chemical composition** of the drug. This section is divided into several parts, including information on raw materials, intermediates, and the finished product. It also includes specifications, test methods, and validation reports to ensure the drug meets all required quality standards. Stability data demonstrating the product's shelf life under various conditions is also included in this section.

In the **non-clinical section**, the dossier contains data from **preclinical studies** conducted on animals or in vitro to evaluate the safety and efficacy of the drug. These studies provide information on the pharmacokinetics, pharmacodynamics, and toxicological profile of the product. The aim is to identify any potential adverse effects before the drug is tested in humans.

The **clinical section** includes detailed reports of **clinical trials** conducted in humans. This part of the dossier is critical for demonstrating the safety and efficacy of the drug in the target population. Clinical trials are conducted in multiple phases, and the dossier includes data from all these phases. Phase I trials primarily focus on safety, Phase II on efficacy and safety, and Phase III on confirming efficacy and monitoring adverse reactions in larger populations. The dossier also includes information on Phase IV post-marketing surveillance studies, which continue to monitor the drug's safety after it has been approved for use.

Methodology and procedures for compiling a dossier are stringent and require meticulous attention to detail. Each document must be prepared following specific guidelines issued by regulatory authorities. The process starts with the **collection of data** from various departments such as research and development, manufacturing, quality assurance, and clinical research. This data is then organized into a coherent and comprehensive document following the format required by the relevant regulatory authority. For instance, the **Common Technical Document (CTD)** format is widely used for regulatory submissions in Europe, Japan, and the United States. The CTD is divided into five modules: administrative information and prescribing information, overview and summaries, quality, non-clinical study reports, and clinical study reports.

The preparation of a dossier requires collaboration among multiple departments within a pharmaceutical company. It involves a thorough review process to ensure all information is accurate, up-to-date, and meets the regulatory standards. Once compiled, the dossier is submitted to the regulatory authority, which reviews the documents to decide whether to grant approval for the product.

7.2 CONTENTS AND ORGANIZATION OF DOSSIER

The **contents and organization** of a dossier are critical to its role in the regulatory approval process. A well-structured dossier not only facilitates the review process by regulatory authorities but also ensures that all necessary information is presented in a clear and logical manner. The structure of a dossier is typically aligned with the Common Technical Document (CTD) format, which is an internationally recognized standard. This format is divided into five main modules, each serving a specific purpose and containing a distinct set of documents.

Module 1: Administrative Information and Prescribing Information This module includes region-specific administrative documents and product labeling. Key contents are:

- **Application forms**: Completed forms required by the regulatory authority.
- **Product labeling**: Information intended for healthcare professionals and patients, including the package insert, summary of product characteristics (SmPC), and patient information leaflet (PIL).
- **Patent information**: Details about patents protecting the product.
- **Letters of authorization**: Documents authorizing the regulatory authority to access or review information related to the product.

Module 2: Overview and Summaries This module provides an overview of the dossier and concise summaries of the data contained in Modules 3, 4, and 5. It includes:

- **Table of contents**: An organized list of all documents included in the dossier.
- **Introduction**: A brief summary of the pharmaceutical product.
- **Quality overall summary (QOS)**: A summary of the quality information presented in Module 3.
- **Non-clinical overview and summaries**: Summaries of non-clinical data, including pharmacology, pharmacokinetics, and toxicology.
- **Clinical overview and summaries**: Summaries of clinical data, including biopharmaceutics, clinical pharmacology, efficacy, and safety.

Module 3: Quality (Chemical, Pharmaceutical, and Biological Information) This module contains detailed information about the quality of the drug substance and drug product. It is divided into:

- **Drug substance:** Information about the active pharmaceutical ingredient (API), including its nomenclature, structure, manufacture, characterization, control of the drug substance, reference standards, and stability.
- **Drug product:** Details about the formulation, manufacture, and quality control of the finished pharmaceutical product. This includes descriptions of excipients, the manufacturing process, specifications, analytical procedures, validation of analytical methods, batch analyses, and stability data.

Module 4: Non-clinical Study Reports This module provides detailed reports of non-clinical studies conducted to assess the safety and efficacy of the drug. Key sections are:

- **Pharmacology:** Studies on the drug's pharmacodynamics and pharmacokinetics.
- **Pharmacokinetics:** Absorption, distribution, metabolism, and excretion (ADME) studies.
- **Toxicology:** Toxicity studies, including single-dose toxicity, repeated-dose toxicity, genotoxicity, carcinogenicity, reproductive and developmental toxicity, and other toxicity studies.

Module 5: Clinical Study Reports This module includes comprehensive data from clinical trials conducted on the drug. It is subdivided into:

- **Biopharmaceutic studies and associated analytical methods:** Studies on the bioavailability and bioequivalence of the drug.
- **Clinical pharmacology studies:** Data on pharmacokinetics and pharmacodynamics in humans.
- **Clinical efficacy and safety studies:** Detailed reports of clinical trials, including Phase I, II, III, and IV studies. These reports provide data on the efficacy and safety of the drug in the target population, along with statistical analyses.

- **Post-marketing data**: Information from post-marketing surveillance studies and any additional clinical information gathered after the drug has been marketed.

Methodology for Compiling Dossiers Compiling a dossier involves a meticulous process of data collection, organization, and documentation. It begins with gathering data from various departments within the pharmaceutical company, including research and development, manufacturing, quality assurance, and clinical research. This data is then organized according to the CTD format.

Each section of the dossier must be prepared following specific guidelines issued by regulatory authorities. For example, the International Council for Harmonisation of Technical Requirements for Pharmaceuticals for Human Use (ICH) provides detailed guidelines on the preparation of CTD modules. Ensuring compliance with these guidelines is essential for the dossier to be accepted by regulatory authorities.

A thorough review process is also crucial. The dossier undergoes multiple rounds of review within the company to ensure all information is accurate, complete, and presented in a clear and logical manner. Any discrepancies or missing information must be addressed before the dossier is submitted to the regulatory authority.

7.3 PAPER SUBMISSIONS AND OVERVIEW OF MODULES OF CTD

Paper Submissions in Dossiers

In the realm of pharmaceutical regulatory affairs, **paper submissions** refer to the traditional method of submitting regulatory dossiers in a printed format. Although the trend is moving towards electronic submissions due to their efficiency and ease of use, some regulatory authorities and situations still require or accept paper submissions. Preparing paper submissions involves meticulously printing, organizing, and binding the extensive documentation that constitutes a dossier. Each page must be carefully reviewed to ensure that it is clear, legible, and free from errors. The submission must also be formatted according to the specific guidelines provided by the regulatory authority to ensure consistency and ease of review.

The primary challenge with paper submissions is managing the vast volume of documents. A typical dossier can consist of thousands of pages, covering a wide array of data and reports. Therefore, it is crucial to implement a robust **document management system** to track and organize all the documents accurately. Additionally, each document must be indexed and cross-referenced to facilitate easy navigation for reviewers. Physical storage and transport of these documents must also be considered, as they require secure and environmentally controlled conditions to prevent damage or loss.

Overview of Modules of Common Technical Document (CTD)

The Common Technical Document (CTD) is an internationally standardized format for regulatory submissions, aimed at streamlining the approval process and facilitating simultaneous submissions to multiple regulatory authorities. The CTD is divided into five main modules, each serving a specific purpose:

Module 1: Administrative Information and Prescribing Information
Module 1 contains region-specific administrative and prescribing

information. This includes documents required by the regulatory authorities, such as:

- **Application forms**: These are the forms that must be filled out according to the specific requirements of the regulatory body.
- **Product labeling**: This includes the Summary of Product Characteristics (SmPC), patient information leaflets (PILs), and labels for packaging.
- **Patent information**: Details about any patents related to the product.
- **Certificates and authorizations**: Letters of authorization, GMP certificates, and other necessary legal documents.

Module 2: Overview and Summaries Module 2 provides a concise overview and summaries of the data contained in Modules 3, 4, and 5. This module includes:

- **Table of contents**: A comprehensive list of all documents included in the dossier.
- **Introduction**: A brief summary of the pharmaceutical product, its development, and intended use.
- **Quality overall summary (QOS)**: A summary of the key quality information presented in Module 3.
- **Non-clinical overview and summaries**: Summaries of the non-clinical data, including pharmacology, pharmacokinetics, and toxicology studies.
- **Clinical overview and summaries**: Summaries of the clinical data, including biopharmaceutics, clinical pharmacology, efficacy, and safety studies.

Module 3: Quality (Chemical, Pharmaceutical, and Biological Information) Module 3 is dedicated to the quality aspects of the drug substance and drug product. It is structured into two main parts:

- **Drug substance**: Information about the active pharmaceutical ingredient (API), including its nomenclature, structure, method of manufacture, characterization, control of the drug substance, reference standards, and stability.
- **Drug product**: Details about the finished pharmaceutical product, including its formulation, manufacturing process, specifications, analytical procedures, validation of analytical methods, batch analyses,

and stability data.

Module 4: Non-clinical Study Reports Module 4 contains the detailed reports of non-clinical studies conducted to assess the safety and efficacy of the drug in animal models and in vitro. This module is divided into several sections:

- **Pharmacology**: Studies on the drug's pharmacodynamics (effects and mechanisms of action) and pharmacokinetics (absorption, distribution, metabolism, and excretion).
- **Toxicology**: Comprehensive toxicological studies, including single-dose and repeated-dose toxicity, genotoxicity, carcinogenicity, reproductive and developmental toxicity, and other relevant toxicity studies.

Module 5: Clinical Study Reports Module 5 includes detailed clinical study reports that provide evidence of the drug's safety and efficacy in humans. This module is organized into sections based on the type of clinical studies conducted:

- **Biopharmaceutic studies and associated analytical methods**: Reports on the bioavailability, bioequivalence, and related analytical methods used.
- **Clinical pharmacology studies**: Data on the pharmacokinetics and pharmacodynamics of the drug in humans.
- **Clinical efficacy and safety studies**: Detailed reports from Phase I, II, III, and IV clinical trials, demonstrating the drug's efficacy and safety in the intended patient population.
- **Post-marketing data**: Information gathered from post-marketing surveillance and additional clinical studies conducted after the drug's approval and market launch.

Methodology for Preparing CTD Modules

The preparation of CTD modules follows a stringent methodology to ensure accuracy, completeness, and compliance with regulatory guidelines. The process involves several steps:

1. **Data Collection**: Gathering relevant data from various departments, including research and development, manufacturing, quality assurance, and clinical research.
2. **Document Preparation**: Drafting and compiling the necessary documents in accordance with the CTD format and regulatory requirements.
3. **Review and Quality Control**: Conducting thorough reviews and quality checks to ensure all documents are accurate, complete, and error-free.
4. **Formatting and Organization**: Ensuring that all documents are properly formatted, indexed, and organized according to the CTD structure.
5. **Submission**: Submitting the completed CTD modules to the regulatory authority, either in paper format or electronically, depending on the requirements.

7.4 ELECTRONIC CTD SUBMISSIONS

Introduction to Electronic CTD Submissions

Electronic Common Technical Document (eCTD) submissions represent a significant advancement in the pharmaceutical regulatory process, streamlining the submission, review, and approval of new drugs. The eCTD format is a standardized electronic version of the traditional paper-based CTD, designed to facilitate the efficient management and transfer of regulatory information between pharmaceutical companies and regulatory authorities. This method of submission offers numerous advantages, including improved efficiency, reduced errors, and enhanced communication.

Advantages of eCTD Submissions

The transition from paper-based to electronic submissions provides several key benefits:

- **Efficiency**: eCTD submissions significantly reduce the time and resources required to compile, submit, and review regulatory documents. Electronic submissions eliminate the need for printing, shipping, and storing large volumes of paper.
- **Accuracy and Consistency**: eCTD formats ensure a standardized presentation of data, minimizing the risk of errors and inconsistencies that can occur with paper submissions. This standardization facilitates easier navigation and review by regulatory authorities.
- **Improved Communication**: The electronic format allows for seamless updates and amendments to submissions. Regulatory authorities can provide feedback and request additional information more efficiently, accelerating the review process.
- **Environmental Impact**: eCTD submissions reduce the environmental footprint associated with paper production, printing, and transportation.

Components of eCTD Submissions

The eCTD format mirrors the structure of the traditional CTD, comprising five modules:

Module 1: Administrative Information and Prescribing Information This module contains region-specific administrative and product labeling documents. In the eCTD format, these documents are submitted electronically, allowing for easy updates and modifications. Key components include:

- **Application forms**: Digital versions of the forms required by regulatory authorities.
- **Product labeling**: Electronic versions of the Summary of Product Characteristics (SmPC), patient information leaflets (PILs), and packaging labels.
- **Certificates and authorizations**: Digital copies of GMP certificates, letters of authorization, and other legal documents.

Module 2: Overview and Summaries Module 2 provides an electronic overview and summaries of the detailed data contained in Modules 3, 4, and 5. It includes:

- **Table of contents**: An electronic, hyperlinked table of contents for easy navigation.
- **Introduction**: A digital summary of the pharmaceutical product.
- **Quality overall summary (QOS)**: An electronic summary of the key quality information presented in Module 3.
- **Non-clinical and clinical overviews and summaries**: Digital summaries of non-clinical and clinical data.

Module 3: Quality (Chemical, Pharmaceutical, and Biological Information) Module 3 contains detailed electronic documents related to the quality of the drug substance and drug product. It includes:

- **Drug substance**: Digital files containing information about the API, including its nomenclature, structure, manufacture, characterization, control, reference standards, and stability.

- **Drug product**: Electronic documents detailing the formulation, manufacturing process, specifications, analytical procedures, validation of analytical methods, batch analyses, and stability data.

Module 4: Non-clinical Study Reports Module 4 includes electronic reports of non-clinical studies. Key sections are:

- **Pharmacology**: Digital studies on the drug's pharmacodynamics and pharmacokinetics.
- **Toxicology**: Electronic toxicology studies, including single-dose and repeated-dose toxicity, genotoxicity, carcinogenicity, reproductive and developmental toxicity, and other relevant studies.

Module 5: Clinical Study Reports Module 5 comprises electronic clinical study reports. It is organized into:

- **Biopharmaceutic studies and associated analytical methods**: Digital reports on bioavailability, bioequivalence, and related analytical methods.
- **Clinical pharmacology studies**: Electronic data on the pharmacokinetics and pharmacodynamics of the drug in humans.
- **Clinical efficacy and safety studies**: Digital reports from Phase I, II, III, and IV clinical trials, along with post-marketing surveillance data.

Methodology for Preparing eCTD Submissions

The preparation of eCTD submissions follows a rigorous methodology to ensure compliance with regulatory standards and guidelines. Key steps include:

1. **Data Collection**: Gathering all necessary data from various departments, including research and development, manufacturing, quality assurance, and clinical research.
2. **Document Preparation**: Creating and formatting documents in compliance with eCTD guidelines. This involves using specialized software to ensure documents are properly structured and hyperlinked.

3. **Validation**: Using eCTD validation tools to check for errors and ensure compliance with technical requirements. This step is crucial for identifying and correcting issues before submission.
4. **Compilation**: Assembling the documents into the eCTD structure. This involves organizing files into the appropriate modules and sections, ensuring that all documents are correctly formatted and hyperlinked.
5. **Submission**: Submitting the eCTD to the regulatory authority through secure electronic submission gateways. Regulatory authorities provide specific guidelines and technical requirements for electronic submissions, which must be adhered to rigorously.

7.5 PLANNING AND REQUIREMENTS FOR ELECTRONIC SUBMISSIONS

Introduction to Planning for Electronic Submissions

Effective planning is crucial for the successful implementation of **electronic submissions** in the pharmaceutical industry. This process involves a thorough understanding of the regulatory requirements, careful organization of documents, and the use of specialized tools and software to ensure compliance with the standards set by regulatory authorities. Proper planning ensures that the submission process is smooth, efficient, and meets all necessary guidelines.

Key Steps in Planning for Electronic Submissions

1. Understanding Regulatory Requirements

Before initiating the electronic submission process, it is essential to familiarize yourself with the specific regulatory requirements of the target authorities. Different regulatory bodies may have varying guidelines for electronic submissions, including formatting, structure, and technical specifications. Key regulatory bodies like the **FDA**, **EMA**, and **PMDA** have detailed guidelines available on their respective websites. Understanding these requirements helps in avoiding common pitfalls and ensuring the submission is acceptable.

2. Establishing a Submission Timeline

Creating a detailed timeline for the submission process is critical. This timeline should account for all phases of the submission, including data collection, document preparation, review, validation, and final submission. Setting realistic deadlines and milestones ensures that the project stays on track and allows for adequate time to address any unforeseen issues.

3. Assembling a Cross-Functional Team

Electronic submissions require collaboration across various departments, including **Regulatory Affairs**, **Quality Assurance**, **Clinical Research**, and **Information Technology**. Assembling a cross-functional team with clear roles and responsibilities ensures that all aspects of the submission are covered. Regular team meetings and updates help in coordinating efforts and maintaining progress.

4. Selecting Appropriate Tools and Software

Choosing the right tools and software is crucial for preparing and managing electronic submissions. **eCTD** submission software is designed to help compile, validate, and submit electronic documents in compliance with regulatory standards. These tools often come with features such as document management, template creation, and automated validation checks. It is important to select software that is compatible with the requirements of the target regulatory authorities and can integrate with existing systems.

5. Training and Support

Providing adequate training for all team members involved in the submission process is essential. Training sessions should cover the use of eCTD software, understanding regulatory guidelines, and best practices for document preparation and submission. Additionally, having technical support available can help address any issues that arise during the submission process.

Requirements for Electronic Submissions

1. Document Formatting and Structure

Documents included in electronic submissions must be formatted according to the specific guidelines provided by the regulatory authorities. This typically includes:

- **File formats**: Commonly accepted formats include PDF for documents, SAS datasets for statistical data, and XML for metadata.
- **Document structure**: Documents must be organized into the appropriate modules and sections as per the eCTD structure.
- **Hyperlinking and bookmarking**: Electronic documents should be hyperlinked and bookmarked for easy navigation, allowing reviewers to quickly access relevant sections.

2. Technical Specifications

Technical specifications are crucial for ensuring the submission is compatible with the regulatory authority's systems. These specifications include:

- **File naming conventions**: Adhering to standard file naming conventions helps maintain consistency and ensures files are easily identifiable.
- **Submission metadata**: Metadata such as submission type, sequence number, and module identifiers must be correctly specified.
- **Validation**: Using eCTD validation tools to check for errors and ensure compliance with technical requirements is essential. This step helps identify and correct issues before submission.

3. Data Integrity and Security

Maintaining the integrity and security of data throughout the submission process is paramount. This involves:

- **Data encryption**: Encrypting sensitive data to protect it from unauthorized access.
- **Access controls**: Implementing access controls to ensure that only authorized personnel can access and modify submission documents.
- **Audit trails**: Keeping detailed audit trails to track changes and ensure data integrity.

4. Submission Gateway

Most regulatory authorities provide electronic submission gateways for the secure transfer of documents. These gateways require:

- **User accounts and access permissions**: Setting up user accounts with the appropriate access permissions for submitting documents.
- **Technical compliance**: Ensuring that the submission package meets the technical requirements for the gateway, including file formats and metadata specifications.

7.6 ELECTRONIC SUBMISSION GATEWAY (ESG)

Introduction to Electronic Submission Gateway (ESG)

The **Electronic Submission Gateway (ESG)** is a secure online portal that facilitates the electronic submission of regulatory documents to authorities such as the FDA (Food and Drug Administration) and other regulatory bodies. The ESG streamlines the submission process, ensuring that documents are transmitted securely and efficiently. It replaces the traditional paper-based submission process, offering numerous advantages in terms of speed, security, and reliability.

Advantages of Using ESG

1. Enhanced Security: The ESG ensures that all data transmitted through the gateway is encrypted and secure, protecting sensitive information from unauthorized access. This is crucial for maintaining the confidentiality and integrity of regulatory submissions.

2. Increased Efficiency: ESG allows for faster submission of documents compared to traditional paper-based methods. This efficiency is beneficial for pharmaceutical companies aiming to accelerate the approval process and bring their products to market more quickly.

3. Reduced Costs: By eliminating the need for physical printing, shipping, and storage of documents, ESG significantly reduces the costs associated with regulatory submissions. Additionally, the streamlined process minimizes the likelihood of errors and the need for re-submissions.

4. Improved Tracking and Management: The ESG provides tools for tracking the status of submissions in real-time. This capability allows companies to monitor the progress of their submissions and respond promptly to any queries or requests from regulatory authorities.

Components and Functionality of ESG

The ESG consists of several components designed to facilitate the secure and efficient submission of documents:

1. User Registration and Account Management Before utilizing the ESG, companies must register and set up user accounts. This process involves:

- **Creating User Accounts**: Companies need to create user accounts with appropriate access permissions for individuals involved in the submission process.
- **Authentication**: Users must authenticate their identities to ensure secure access to the ESG. This typically involves the use of digital certificates.

2. Document Preparation and Submission The ESG supports the submission of various types of documents, including those in eCTD format. Key steps in the document preparation and submission process include:

- **Formatting and Validation**: Documents must be formatted according to regulatory guidelines and validated using eCTD software tools to ensure compliance.
- **Submission Packages**: Documents are compiled into submission packages, which are then uploaded to the ESG. Each package includes metadata to facilitate the organization and review of the documents.

3. Secure Data Transmission The ESG employs robust encryption protocols to ensure the secure transmission of data. This involves:

- **Data Encryption**: All documents and data transmitted through the ESG are encrypted to protect against unauthorized access.
- **Transmission Protocols**: The ESG uses secure transmission protocols, such as HTTPS, to ensure data integrity and confidentiality during transfer.

4. Real-Time Tracking and Notifications The ESG provides tools for tracking the status of submissions in real-time. Features include:

- **Submission Status**: Users can monitor the status of their submissions, including receipt, processing, and review stages.
- **Notifications**: The ESG sends notifications to users regarding the status of their submissions, any issues detected, and requests for additional information from regulatory authorities.

5. Data Integrity and Audit Trails Maintaining the integrity of data and providing a clear audit trail are critical components of the ESG. This includes:

- **Audit Trails**: The ESG maintains detailed audit trails that record all actions taken during the submission process. This ensures transparency and accountability.
- **Data Integrity Checks**: The ESG performs regular checks to ensure that all submitted data is complete, accurate, and has not been tampered with.

Steps to Utilize the ESG

To effectively utilize the ESG, companies must follow several key steps:

1. Registration and Account Setup

- Register with the regulatory authority and create user accounts with appropriate access permissions.
- Obtain and install digital certificates for secure authentication.

2. Document Preparation

- Prepare and format documents according to regulatory guidelines.
- Validate documents using eCTD software to ensure compliance with submission standards.

3. Package Compilation and Submission

- Compile documents into submission packages, including necessary metadata.
- Upload submission packages to the ESG through the secure portal.

4. Monitoring and Responding

- Monitor the status of submissions in real-time using ESG tracking tools.
- Respond promptly to any notifications or requests from regulatory authorities.

7.7 NON-eCTD ELECTRONIC SUBMISSIONS (NeeS)

Introduction to Non-eCTD Electronic Submissions (NeeS)

Non-eCTD Electronic Submissions (NeeS) represent an alternative electronic submission format used by pharmaceutical companies when the Common Technical Document (eCTD) format is not applicable or required. NeeS serves as an interim solution, providing a structured approach to electronic submissions while maintaining flexibility in format and presentation. This method is often used in regions or situations where eCTD is not mandated but electronic submission is preferred over paper-based submissions.

Advantages of NeeS

1. Flexibility: NeeS offers greater flexibility in document formatting and structure compared to eCTD. This allows companies to tailor their submissions according to specific regulatory requirements or internal preferences.

2. Simplicity: The NeeS format is generally simpler to implement and manage than the eCTD format. It does not require the same level of technical sophistication, making it more accessible for companies with limited resources or technical expertise.

3. Cost-Effective: NeeS can be more cost-effective than eCTD, as it often requires fewer resources for document preparation and submission. This makes it an attractive option for smaller companies or those submitting to regions with less stringent regulatory requirements.

Components and Structure of NeeS

The structure of NeeS is designed to organize documents in a logical and accessible manner. While it does not adhere to the rigid format of eCTD, it still follows a systematic approach to ensure clarity and ease of review. Key components of a typical NeeS submission include:

1. Cover Letter The cover letter provides an overview of the submission, including the purpose, scope, and any special considerations. It also includes contact information for the submitter and a summary of the contents of the submission.

2. Table of Contents A detailed table of contents is essential for navigating the NeeS submission. It lists all documents included in the submission, organized by section and sub-section. Hyperlinks are often used to facilitate quick access to specific documents.

3. Administrative Information This section includes administrative documents similar to those found in Module 1 of the eCTD. Key components are:

- **Application Forms**: Completed forms required by the regulatory authority.
- **Product Labeling**: Drafts of the Summary of Product Characteristics (SmPC), patient information leaflets (PILs), and packaging labels.
- **Certificates and Authorizations**: GMP certificates, letters of authorization, and other relevant legal documents.

4. Quality Information The quality information section corresponds to Module 3 of the eCTD, providing details about the drug substance and drug product. It includes:

- **Drug Substance**: Information on the active pharmaceutical ingredient (API), including its manufacture, characterization, and control.
- **Drug Product**: Details about the formulation, manufacturing process, specifications, and stability of the finished product.

5. Non-Clinical Reports This section includes non-clinical study reports, similar to Module 4 of the eCTD. Key components are:

- **Pharmacology Studies**: Data on the pharmacodynamics and pharmacokinetics of the drug in animal models.
- **Toxicology Studies**: Results from single-dose and repeated-dose toxicity studies, genotoxicity, carcinogenicity, and other toxicological assessments.

6. Clinical Reports The clinical reports section corresponds to Module 5 of the eCTD. It includes:

- **Clinical Study Reports**: Detailed reports from clinical trials, including Phase I, II, III, and IV studies.
- **Biopharmaceutic Studies**: Data on bioavailability, bioequivalence, and related analytical methods.

Preparation and Submission of NeeS

1. Document Preparation Preparing documents for NeeS involves organizing them in a clear and logical manner. Each document should be formatted according to regulatory guidelines, with consistent use of headings, subheadings, and pagination. Hyperlinks and bookmarks are used to facilitate navigation within the submission.

2. Compilation of Submission Package The submission package is compiled by organizing documents into the appropriate sections and sub-sections. Each section is clearly labeled, and a comprehensive table of contents is included to guide reviewers.

3. Validation and Quality Control Before submission, the NeeS package undergoes validation and quality control checks to ensure all documents are correctly formatted and organized. This step helps identify and rectify any issues that could impede the review process.

4. Submission to Regulatory Authorities NeeS packages are submitted electronically via secure portals provided by regulatory authorities. These portals ensure the secure transfer of documents and provide tracking capabilities to monitor the status of the submission.

7.8 ASIAN CTD FORMATS (ACTD) SUBMISSION

Introduction to Asian CTD Formats (ACTD)

The **Asian Common Technical Document (ACTD)** is a harmonized format designed to streamline the submission process for pharmaceutical products in the ASEAN (Association of Southeast Asian Nations) region. The ACTD aims to simplify the submission and review process by providing a standardized structure that aligns with international guidelines while accommodating regional requirements. The ACTD format facilitates the efficient assessment and approval of pharmaceutical products across multiple ASEAN member countries, promoting regulatory harmonization and cooperation.

Structure of the ACTD

The ACTD is divided into four main parts, each corresponding to a specific type of information required for regulatory submissions. These parts are designed to provide a comprehensive overview of the pharmaceutical product, ensuring that all critical aspects are thoroughly documented and reviewed.

Part I: Administrative Information

This part includes administrative documents specific to the region. Key components are:

- **Application Form**: Completed form required by the regulatory authority in each ASEAN member country.
- **Introduction**: A brief overview of the pharmaceutical product, including its name, dosage form, strength, and intended use.
- **Product Labeling**: Proposed labeling materials, such as the Summary of Product Characteristics (SmPC), patient information leaflet (PIL), and packaging labels.
- **Patent Information**: Details of patents related to the pharmaceutical product.

- **Certificates and Authorizations**: GMP certificates, letters of authorization, and other relevant legal documents.

Part II: Quality Document

This part contains detailed information about the quality of the drug substance and drug product. It corresponds to the quality section in the eCTD and is divided into several sections:

- **Drug Substance**: Information on the active pharmaceutical ingredient (API), including its nomenclature, structure, method of manufacture, characterization, control, reference standards, and stability.
- **Drug Product**: Details about the finished pharmaceutical product, including its formulation, manufacturing process, specifications, analytical procedures, validation of analytical methods, batch analyses, and stability data.

Part III: Non-Clinical Document

This part includes non-clinical study reports that assess the safety and efficacy of the drug in animal models and in vitro. Key sections are:

- **Pharmacology**: Studies on the drug's pharmacodynamics and pharmacokinetics.
- **Toxicology**: Toxicology studies, including single-dose and repeated-dose toxicity, genotoxicity, carcinogenicity, reproductive and developmental toxicity, and other relevant toxicology studies.

Part IV: Clinical Document

This part contains clinical study reports that provide evidence of the drug's safety and efficacy in humans. It is divided into several sections:

- **Clinical Overview and Summaries**: Summaries of clinical data, including biopharmaceutics, clinical pharmacology, efficacy, and safety.

- **Clinical Study Reports**: Detailed reports from Phase I, II, III, and IV clinical trials, along with post-marketing surveillance data.

Preparation and Submission of ACTD

1. Understanding Regulatory Requirements

Before preparing the ACTD submission, it is crucial to understand the specific regulatory requirements of each ASEAN member country. These requirements may vary slightly, and understanding them ensures that the submission meets all necessary guidelines.

2. Document Preparation

Preparing documents for ACTD involves organizing them according to the standardized format. Each document must be clearly labeled and formatted according to the guidelines provided by the ASEAN harmonization initiative. Key steps include:

- **Collecting Data**: Gathering relevant data from various departments, including research and development, manufacturing, quality assurance, and clinical research.
- **Formatting Documents**: Ensuring that all documents are formatted according to the ACTD guidelines, with consistent use of headings, subheadings, and pagination.

3. Compilation of Submission Package

The submission package is compiled by organizing documents into the appropriate parts and sections. Each part is clearly labeled, and a comprehensive table of contents is included to guide reviewers. Hyperlinks and bookmarks may be used to facilitate easy navigation within the submission.

4. Validation and Quality Control

Before submission, the ACTD package undergoes validation and quality control checks to ensure all documents are correctly formatted and organized. This step helps identify and rectify any issues that could impede the review process.

5. Submission to Regulatory Authorities

ACTD packages are submitted to regulatory authorities in each ASEAN member country, either electronically or in paper format, depending on the specific requirements. The submission process involves:

- **Secure Data Transmission**: Ensuring that all documents are transmitted securely to protect sensitive information.
- **Tracking and Monitoring**: Using tools provided by the regulatory authorities to track the status of submissions and respond promptly to any queries or requests.

7.9 ORGANIZING, PROCESS, AND VALIDATION OF SUBMISSION

Introduction to Organizing, Process, and Validation of Submission

The successful submission of regulatory dossiers, whether in eCTD, NeeS, or ACTD formats, hinges on meticulous organization, a streamlined submission process, and thorough validation. These steps ensure that the submission is complete, accurate, and compliant with the requirements of the regulatory authorities. Properly organizing and validating the submission can significantly reduce review times and increase the likelihood of approval.

Organizing the Submission

1. Comprehensive Planning

The first step in organizing a submission is comprehensive planning. This involves:

- **Defining Objectives**: Clearly outlining the goals of the submission, including the specific regulatory approval sought.
- **Developing a Timeline**: Creating a detailed timeline that includes all key milestones and deadlines for data collection, document preparation, internal reviews, and final submission.
- **Assigning Responsibilities**: Designating tasks to specific team members, ensuring all aspects of the submission are covered by individuals with the appropriate expertise.

2. Document Collection and Management

Efficient document collection and management are crucial for organizing a submission:

- **Data Collection**: Gathering all necessary data from various departments, such as research and development, manufacturing, quality assurance, and clinical research.

- **Document Management System**: Implementing a robust document management system (DMS) to store, organize, and track documents. A good DMS allows for easy retrieval, version control, and ensures that all documents are up-to-date.

3. Formatting and Structuring Documents

Proper formatting and structuring of documents are essential for compliance and ease of review:

- **Standardized Formats**: Ensuring all documents follow the standardized format required by the regulatory authority, such as eCTD, NeeS, or ACTD.
- **Clear Headings and Subheadings**: Using clear and consistent headings and subheadings to organize content logically.
- **Hyperlinks and Bookmarks**: Adding hyperlinks and bookmarks to facilitate easy navigation within the submission.

The Submission Process

1. Compilation of Submission Package

Compiling the submission package involves organizing documents into the appropriate sections and subsections as per the chosen format (eCTD, NeeS, ACTD). Each section should be clearly labeled, and a comprehensive table of contents should be included to guide reviewers.

2. Internal Review and Quality Control

Before submission, the compiled package undergoes internal review and quality control:

- **Peer Review**: Conducting peer reviews to ensure the accuracy and completeness of each document.
- **Quality Control Checks**: Performing quality control checks to verify that all documents are correctly formatted, labeled, and free of errors.

3. Secure Submission

Submitting the package securely is crucial for protecting sensitive information:

- **Electronic Submission Gateways**: Using secure electronic submission gateways (ESG) provided by regulatory authorities to transmit documents. These gateways ensure data integrity and confidentiality during transfer.
- **Tracking and Acknowledgment**: Monitoring the submission process and obtaining acknowledgment receipts from regulatory authorities to confirm successful submission.

Validation of Submission

1. Pre-Validation

Pre-validation involves initial checks to ensure the submission meets all technical requirements:

- **Validation Tools**: Using eCTD validation tools to perform pre-submission checks. These tools identify formatting errors, missing documents, and other issues that need to be addressed before submission.
- **Regulatory Compliance**: Ensuring that all documents comply with the regulatory guidelines of the target authority.

2. Technical Validation

Technical validation is a critical step to ensure the submission is technically sound and free of errors:

- **Automated Validation Checks**: Running automated validation checks using specialized software to detect any technical issues in the submission package.
- **Manual Review**: Conducting a manual review to cross-check automated validation results and ensure all issues are resolved.

3. Post-Submission Validation

After submission, regulatory authorities may perform their own validation checks:

- **Response to Queries**: Being prepared to respond promptly to any queries or requests for additional information from regulatory authorities.

- **Ongoing Monitoring**: Continuously monitoring the status of the submission and addressing any issues that arise during the review process.

7.10 SUBMISSION IN SUGAM SYSTEM OF CDSCO

Introduction to the Sugam System

The **Sugam System** is an online portal developed by the Central Drugs Standard Control Organization (CDSCO) of India to streamline the submission, review, and approval processes for pharmaceutical products. This system aims to facilitate electronic submissions, reduce the time required for regulatory approvals, and improve transparency and efficiency in the drug approval process. The Sugam System provides a single window for various regulatory activities, including applications for clinical trials, import and export licenses, and new drug approvals.

Advantages of Using the Sugam System

1. Efficiency: The Sugam System enhances the efficiency of the submission process by allowing for electronic submission and tracking of applications. This reduces the time and effort required compared to traditional paper-based methods.

   2. Transparency: The system provides real-time updates on the status of applications, improving transparency and allowing applicants to monitor the progress of their submissions.

   3. Accessibility: The online platform is accessible from anywhere, enabling applicants to submit and manage their applications remotely.

   4. Streamlined Process: The Sugam System integrates various regulatory processes into a single platform, simplifying the overall submission and approval workflow.

Components of the Sugam System

The Sugam System encompasses several key components designed to facilitate different types of regulatory submissions:
   1. Registration and User Management

- **User Registration**: Applicants must register on the Sugam portal to create an account. The registration process requires basic information about the organization and the individual users.
- **User Roles and Permissions**: The system allows for the creation of multiple user roles within an organization, each with specific permissions. This helps in managing and delegating tasks effectively.

2. Application Submission

- **Form Selection**: Depending on the type of submission, applicants can select the appropriate application form from the portal. The forms are categorized based on the type of product or regulatory activity, such as new drug applications, clinical trial approvals, or import/export licenses.
- **Document Upload**: Applicants can upload the required documents directly to the portal. The system supports various file formats and provides guidelines on the specific documents needed for each type of application.
- **Data Entry**: The portal allows for the electronic entry of application data, ensuring that all necessary information is captured accurately.

3. Tracking and Monitoring

- **Real-Time Status Updates**: The Sugam System provides real-time updates on the status of each application, including receipt, processing, and approval stages.
- **Notifications**: Applicants receive notifications via email and the portal regarding any updates or requests for additional information from CDSCO.

4. Communication and Query Resolution

- **Query Management**: The system includes a module for managing queries and communications between applicants and CDSCO. This allows for timely resolution of any issues or additional information requests.
- **Document Revisions**: Applicants can submit revised documents or additional information in response to queries raised by CDSCO.

5. Compliance and Validation

- **Pre-Submission Validation**: The Sugam System includes validation checks to ensure that all required fields are completed and that documents meet the necessary format and content requirements.
- **Regulatory Compliance**: The system helps ensure that submissions comply with CDSCO guidelines and regulations, reducing the likelihood of errors or omissions.

Process for Submission in the Sugam System

1. Registration and Account Setup

- Register on the Sugam portal and create user accounts for all relevant personnel.
- Obtain and configure the necessary digital certificates for secure login and data submission.

2. Preparation of Submission Package

- Gather all required documents and data for the application.
- Format documents according to CDSCO guidelines, ensuring clarity and completeness.

3. Online Submission

- Log in to the Sugam portal and select the appropriate application form.
- Enter all required data and upload supporting documents.
- Review the submission for accuracy and completeness before finalizing.

4. Monitoring and Responding

- Track the status of the submission through the portal and respond promptly to any queries or requests for additional information from CDSCO.
- Use the query management module to communicate with CDSCO and submit any required revisions or additional documents.

5. Final Approval

- Once the application is approved, receive the approval documents and any related licenses or certificates electronically through the portal.
- Ensure compliance with any post-approval requirements or conditions specified by CDSCO.

CHAPTER EIGHT

Audits

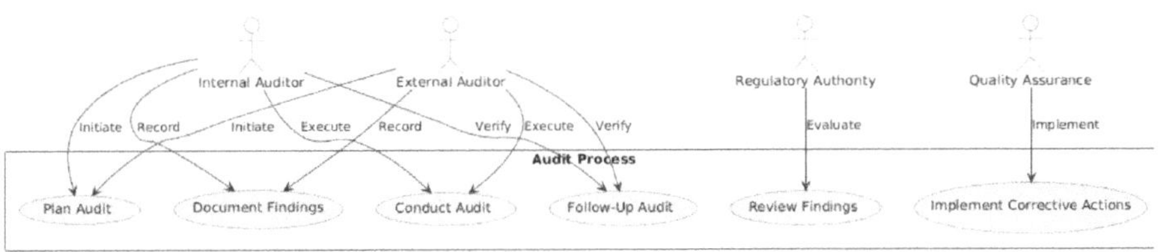

Audits in the Pharmaceutical Industry

8.1 Introduction to Audits

Audits play a crucial role in ensuring the *quality*, *compliance*, and *efficiency* of various processes within an organization. An **audit** is a systematic and independent examination of books, accounts, statutory records, documents, and vouchers of an organization to ascertain how far the financial statements as well as non-financial disclosures present a true and fair view of the concern. It also ensures that the records are maintained as per the required norms and regulations. The *objective* of an audit is to express an opinion on the fairness of the information presented and to ensure compliance with established standards and regulations.

In the pharmaceutical industry, **audits** are particularly significant due to the stringent regulatory requirements that govern the manufacture, storage, and distribution of medicinal products. These audits can be classified into several types, such as *internal audits*, *external audits*, *regulatory audits*, and *customer audits*. Each type of audit has its unique purpose and methodology, although they share common procedures and objectives.

Internal audits are conducted by the organization's own staff or internal auditors. The primary objective is to review and assess the internal controls and processes to ensure that they are adequate and functioning effectively. These audits help in identifying any weaknesses or areas of improvement within the system. For instance, an internal audit might examine the *inventory management* process to ensure that materials are being tracked accurately and that there is no *discrepancy* between physical and recorded inventory.

External audits, on the other hand, are conducted by independent auditing firms. These audits provide an unbiased evaluation of the company's financial and operational status. External auditors examine financial statements, *compliance* with legal requirements, and overall organizational performance. They provide a report that is often used by stakeholders, including shareholders, regulatory bodies, and potential investors, to make informed decisions.

Regulatory audits are mandatory inspections carried out by regulatory authorities such as the *Food and Drug Administration (FDA)* or the *European Medicines Agency (EMA)*. These audits ensure that the company complies with the regulations and guidelines set forth by the authority. Regulatory audits can be very detailed and cover all aspects of the pharmaceutical operations, including *good manufacturing practices (GMP)*, *quality control*, and *safety protocols*. The process usually involves a thorough review of documentation, interviews with personnel, and physical inspections of the facilities.

Customer audits are performed by the customers or clients of a company to ensure that their specific requirements and standards are being met. In the pharmaceutical industry, this could involve audits by hospitals, clinics, or other organizations that purchase and use the company's products. These audits focus on aspects such as *product quality*, *delivery timelines*, and *compliance* with contractual terms.

The **audit process** typically involves several stages. The first stage is **planning**, where the scope and objectives of the audit are defined. This involves understanding the processes and systems to be audited, identifying key areas of risk, and developing an audit plan. Detailed checklists and *audit trails* are often prepared to ensure that all relevant aspects are covered during the audit.

The next stage is **execution**, where the auditors carry out the examination according to the audit plan. This involves collecting evidence through various methods such as *document reviews*, *interviews*, and *physical inspections*. The auditors evaluate the evidence against established criteria to identify any *non-conformances* or areas for improvement.

Reporting is the third stage, where the findings of the audit are documented and communicated to the relevant stakeholders. The audit report typically includes an *executive summary*, detailed findings, and recommendations for corrective actions. The report aims to provide a clear and concise account of the audit results, highlighting both strengths and areas that require attention.

The final stage is **follow-up**, where the implementation of corrective actions is monitored to ensure that the issues identified during the audit are addressed effectively. This stage is critical to the success of the audit process, as it ensures that improvements are made and sustained over time.

8.2 Types of Audits

Audits in the pharmaceutical industry are essential for ensuring that all processes comply with regulatory standards, thereby guaranteeing the safety and efficacy of medicinal products. Different types of audits serve various purposes, each with its specific focus and methodology. The main types of audits include **GMP Compliance Audits**, **Internal Audits**, and **External Audits**.

8.2.1 GMP Compliance Audits

Good Manufacturing Practices (GMP) compliance audits are critical in the pharmaceutical industry. These audits are conducted to ensure that manufacturing processes adhere to the stringent regulations and guidelines established by regulatory authorities like the **Food and Drug Administration (FDA)** and the **European Medicines Agency (EMA)**. The primary objective is to confirm that the products are consistently produced and controlled according to quality standards appropriate for their intended use.

The **methodology** of GMP compliance audits involves a comprehensive review of the entire manufacturing process. Auditors examine the production facilities, equipment, and personnel practices to ensure that they meet GMP requirements. This includes inspecting the cleanliness of the facilities, the suitability of the equipment used, and the training and hygiene practices of the staff. Documentation plays a crucial role, and auditors scrutinize records related to production batches, quality control tests, and standard operating procedures (SOPs). Any **non-conformance** found during the audit needs immediate corrective action to ensure compliance and avoid potential regulatory penalties.

8.2.2 Internal Audits

Internal audits are conducted by the organization's own staff or internal audit team. These audits are proactive measures to ensure that internal processes and controls are functioning effectively. The primary goal of internal audits is to identify areas of improvement within the organization and ensure adherence to internal policies and procedures.

The **procedure** for internal audits starts with planning, where the scope and objectives of the audit are defined. This involves selecting the areas to be audited, developing an audit plan, and preparing checklists. During the execution phase, auditors collect data through document reviews, interviews, and observations. They evaluate the evidence against internal policies and industry standards to identify any discrepancies or areas for enhancement. The findings are then documented in an audit report, which includes recommendations for corrective actions. The final phase involves follow-up to ensure that the recommended actions are implemented effectively.

8.2.3 External Audits

External audits are performed by independent auditing firms or regulatory bodies. The main purpose of these audits is to provide an unbiased evaluation of the organization's compliance with external regulations and standards. External audits are crucial for validating the integrity and reliability of the company's financial statements, operational processes, and regulatory compliance.

The **methodology** for external audits involves a thorough examination of the organization's records and processes. External auditors review financial statements, compliance with regulatory requirements, and overall operational efficiency. They conduct detailed interviews with key personnel, inspect facilities, and review documentation. The findings are compiled into a comprehensive audit report, which is shared with stakeholders such as shareholders, regulatory authorities, and potential investors. This report provides an independent assessment of the organization's performance and compliance, highlighting both strengths and areas that need improvement.

8.2.4 Comparative Analysis of Audit Types

Each type of audit has its unique focus and significance:

- **GMP Compliance Audits** are primarily focused on ensuring that the manufacturing processes meet regulatory standards. They are critical for maintaining product quality and regulatory compliance.

- **Internal Audits** are aimed at improving internal processes and controls. They help in identifying inefficiencies and potential risks within the organization, allowing for timely corrective actions.
- **External Audits** provide an independent assessment of the organization's compliance with external regulations and standards. They are essential for building trust with stakeholders and ensuring transparency.

8.3 Audit Policy and Strategies

An **audit policy** is a framework that outlines the principles, objectives, and procedures for conducting audits within an organization. In the pharmaceutical industry, having a robust audit policy is essential for maintaining regulatory compliance, ensuring product quality, and fostering continuous improvement. This section delves into the components of an effective audit policy and the strategies employed to execute audits efficiently and effectively.

8.3.1 Components of an Audit Policy

A comprehensive audit policy typically includes the following components:

- **Objectives and Scope**: Clearly define the purpose of the audit, whether it is to ensure compliance with regulations, assess internal controls, or evaluate financial statements. The scope outlines the areas and processes to be audited.
- **Roles and Responsibilities**: Specify the roles and responsibilities of the audit team, including internal auditors, external auditors, and other stakeholders involved in the audit process.
- **Standards and Guidelines**: Reference the standards and guidelines that will be followed during the audit, such as GMP guidelines, ISO standards, and regulatory requirements.
- **Audit Plan and Schedule**: Develop a detailed audit plan that includes the timeline, frequency of audits, and specific areas to be audited. The schedule ensures that audits are conducted regularly and systematically.
- **Documentation and Reporting**: Establish procedures for documenting audit findings, preparing audit reports, and communicating results to relevant stakeholders. This includes maintaining records of audit plans, checklists, and corrective actions.
- **Follow-up and Corrective Actions**: Define the process for follow-up audits to verify the implementation of corrective actions and ensure that any identified issues are resolved promptly.

8.3.2 Strategies for Effective Audits

To conduct audits effectively, organizations employ various strategies that enhance the efficiency and thoroughness of the audit process. Key strategies include:

8.3.2.1 Risk-Based Auditing

Risk-based auditing involves focusing audit efforts on areas with the highest risk of non-compliance or operational inefficiency. By prioritizing high-risk areas, auditors can allocate resources more effectively and address critical issues that could impact the organization's performance and compliance.

8.3.2.2 Continuous Monitoring and Improvement

Continuous monitoring involves regularly reviewing and assessing processes to identify potential issues before they escalate. This proactive approach allows organizations to implement corrective actions promptly and continuously improve their operations. Tools such as real-time data analytics and automated monitoring systems can support continuous monitoring efforts.

8.3.2.3 Training and Development

Investing in the training and development of the audit team is crucial for ensuring that auditors have the necessary skills and knowledge to conduct thorough and effective audits. Regular training sessions, workshops, and certifications help auditors stay updated with the latest industry standards and best practices.

8.3.2.4 Use of Technology

Leveraging technology can significantly enhance the efficiency and accuracy of the audit process. Audit management software, data analytics tools, and automated checklists streamline data collection, analysis, and reporting. These technologies also facilitate better communication and collaboration among audit team members.

8.3.2.5 Collaboration and Communication

Effective collaboration and communication among audit team members and stakeholders are essential for a successful audit. Regular meetings, clear communication channels, and collaborative tools help ensure that everyone is on the same page and that audit findings are addressed promptly.

8.3.2.6 Follow-up and Accountability

Ensuring accountability for implementing corrective actions is critical for the success of the audit process. Regular follow-up audits and tracking the progress of corrective actions help ensure that identified issues are resolved and that improvements are sustained over time.

8.3.3 Implementation of Audit Policies and Strategies

Implementing audit policies and strategies involves several steps:

1. **Policy Development**: Develop a comprehensive audit policy that includes all the necessary components outlined above. Ensure that the policy is aligned with regulatory requirements and organizational objectives.
2. **Training and Awareness**: Train employees and audit team members on the audit policy, procedures, and the importance of compliance. This helps create a culture of accountability and continuous improvement within the organization.
3. **Execution of Audits**: Conduct audits according to the established plan and schedule. Use the strategies outlined above to ensure that audits are thorough and effective.
4. **Reporting and Documentation**: Document audit findings and prepare detailed reports. Communicate the results to relevant stakeholders and ensure that all findings are addressed promptly.
5. **Follow-up and Review**: Conduct follow-up audits to verify the implementation of corrective actions. Regularly review and update the audit policy and procedures to reflect changes in regulations and industry best practices.

8.4 Preparation and Conducting Audit

8.4.1 Preparation for an Audit

Preparation is a crucial phase in the audit process, laying the groundwork for a thorough and effective examination. Proper preparation involves several steps to ensure that the audit team is well-equipped and that the audit objectives are clearly defined.

8.4.1.1 Defining the Scope and Objectives

The first step in preparing for an audit is to define its **scope** and **objectives**. The scope outlines the areas, processes, or departments that will be audited, while the objectives clarify the purpose of the audit, such as ensuring regulatory compliance, assessing the effectiveness of internal controls, or evaluating financial performance. Clear objectives help in focusing the audit and ensuring that all relevant aspects are covered.

8.4.1.2 Developing an Audit Plan

An **audit plan** is a detailed roadmap that guides the audit process. It includes the audit schedule, the specific areas to be audited, the methods to be used, and the resources required. The plan should also include a timeline, detailing the start and end dates of the audit and the deadlines for completing different phases of the audit. A well-structured audit plan ensures that the audit process is organized and systematic.

8.4.1.3 Assembling the Audit Team

The **audit team** should be composed of individuals with the appropriate skills and expertise relevant to the audit scope. This may include internal auditors, external auditors, and subject matter experts. The team should be briefed on the audit plan, the scope and objectives, and the specific roles and responsibilities of each member. Effective team assembly ensures that the audit is conducted efficiently and that all relevant areas are examined thoroughly.

8.4.1.4 Preparing Audit Checklists

Audit checklists are valuable tools that help auditors ensure that all critical areas are covered during the audit. The checklists should be tailored to the specific audit scope and include detailed criteria for each area to be examined. These checklists serve as a guide for auditors, helping them to systematically review each aspect of the audit and document their findings.

8.4.1.5 Gathering Preliminary Information

Before the audit begins, auditors should gather **preliminary information** about the areas to be audited. This may include reviewing relevant documents such as policies and procedures, previous audit reports, financial records, and regulatory guidelines. Gathering this information helps auditors understand the context and prepare for a more focused and informed audit.

8.4.2 Conducting an Audit

Once the preparation phase is complete, the audit moves into the **execution** phase, where the actual examination takes place. This phase involves several key activities to ensure a thorough and effective audit.

8.4.2.1 Opening Meeting

The audit typically begins with an **opening meeting**, where the audit team meets with the auditee (the organization or department being audited). The purpose of this meeting is to introduce the audit team, review the audit plan and objectives, and discuss the audit process. The opening meeting helps set the tone for the audit and ensures that everyone is on the same page.

8.4.2.2 Data Collection and Analysis

During the audit, the team collects **data** through various methods, including document reviews, interviews, observations, and inspections. This data is analyzed to identify any **non-conformances**, **weaknesses**, or areas for improvement. The audit team should use the prepared checklists to guide their examination and ensure that all critical areas are covered. Effective data collection and analysis are crucial for identifying issues and providing accurate findings.

8.4.2.3 Interviews and Observations

Interviews with key personnel and **observations** of processes in action are essential components of the audit. Interviews help auditors understand the procedures, gather insights from employees, and clarify any ambiguities. Observations allow auditors to see firsthand how processes are implemented and identify any deviations from established procedures. These techniques provide valuable insights and help validate the information gathered from documents and records.

8.4.2.4 Documentation of Findings

As the audit progresses, auditors should meticulously document their **findings**. This includes recording observations, identifying non-conformances, and noting any areas of excellence. Detailed documentation is essential for preparing the final audit report and for providing a clear record of the audit process. The findings should be supported by evidence, such as copies of documents, photographs, or interview notes.

8.4.2.5 Closing Meeting

After the data collection and analysis phase, the audit team conducts a **closing meeting** with the auditee. The purpose of this meeting is to present the preliminary findings, discuss any identified issues, and provide an opportunity for the auditee to respond or clarify. The closing meeting helps ensure transparency and allows for a collaborative approach to addressing any issues identified during the audit.

8.4.3 Post-Audit Activities

Following the audit, several post-audit activities are conducted to finalize the process and ensure that corrective actions are implemented.

8.4.3.1 Audit Report Preparation

The audit team prepares a comprehensive **audit report** that summarizes the findings, identifies non-conformances, and provides recommendations for corrective actions. The report should be clear, concise, and well-organized, with each finding supported by evidence. The report serves as a formal record of the audit and provides a basis for follow-up actions.

8.4.3.2 Communication of Findings

The audit report is communicated to relevant **stakeholders**, including senior management, the auditee, and any regulatory bodies, if applicable. Clear and timely communication ensures that the findings are understood and that the necessary actions can be taken promptly. Effective communication is key to ensuring that the audit results in meaningful improvements.

8.4.3.3 Implementation of Corrective Actions

The auditee is responsible for implementing the recommended **corrective actions** to address the issues identified during the audit. This may involve revising procedures, conducting additional training, or making operational changes. The implementation of corrective actions should be monitored to ensure that they are effective and sustainable.

8.4.3.4 Follow-up Audit

A **follow-up audit** is conducted to verify that the corrective actions have been implemented and that the issues identified in the original audit have been resolved. This follow-up helps ensure that improvements are made and sustained over time. It also provides an opportunity to assess the effectiveness of the corrective actions and make any additional adjustments as needed.

8.5 Audit Analysis and Report

The final stages of the audit process, **Audit Analysis** and **Report Preparation**, are critical for synthesizing the findings, drawing conclusions, and communicating results to stakeholders. This phase involves thorough data analysis, careful report drafting, and clear communication of the audit outcomes.

8.5.1 Audit Analysis

8.5.1.1 Data Compilation and Review

Once the fieldwork is completed, the first step in audit analysis is to compile and review all the collected **data**. This includes documents, interview notes, observation records, and any other evidence gathered during the audit. The audit team ensures that the data is organized and complete, allowing for a comprehensive review. Proper data management is essential to facilitate accurate analysis and reporting.

8.5.1.2 Identifying Non-Conformances and Observations

During the review process, the audit team identifies any **non-conformances**—instances where the processes or practices do not meet the established standards or regulatory requirements. Additionally, the team notes any **observations**—areas where improvements could be made, even if they do not constitute a formal non-conformance. Both non-conformances and observations are documented with supporting evidence to provide a clear understanding of the issues.

8.5.1.3 Root Cause Analysis

For each identified non-conformance, the audit team conducts a **root cause analysis** to determine the underlying reasons for the issue. Understanding the root cause is crucial for developing effective corrective actions. This analysis involves looking beyond the symptoms of the problem to uncover the fundamental factors contributing to the non-conformance. Techniques such as the **5 Whys** or **Fishbone Diagrams** can be used to facilitate this analysis.

8.5.1.4 Risk Assessment

The audit team assesses the **risk** associated with each non-conformance and observation. This involves evaluating the potential impact of the issue on the organization's operations, compliance, and overall objectives. Risks are typically categorized based on their severity and likelihood, helping prioritize the areas that require immediate attention. A risk assessment ensures that the most critical issues are addressed first.

8.5.1.5 Formulating Recommendations

Based on the root cause analysis and risk assessment, the audit team formulates **recommendations** for corrective actions. These recommendations should be practical, specific, and actionable, providing clear guidance on how to address the identified issues. The aim is to eliminate the root causes and prevent recurrence, thereby improving the organization's processes and compliance.

8.5.2 Audit Report Preparation

The audit report is the formal document that communicates the audit findings, analysis, and recommendations to the stakeholders. Preparing a comprehensive and clear audit report is essential for ensuring that the audit results are understood and acted upon.

8.5.2.1 Structure of the Audit Report

A well-structured audit report typically includes the following sections:

- **Executive Summary**: A concise overview of the audit scope, objectives, key findings, and overall conclusions. This section provides a snapshot of the audit for senior management and other stakeholders who may not read the entire report.
- **Introduction**: A detailed description of the audit's purpose, scope, and methodology. This section sets the context for the findings and explains

how the audit was conducted.

- **Audit Findings**: A comprehensive presentation of the non-conformances and observations identified during the audit. Each finding should be clearly described, with supporting evidence and references to the relevant standards or regulations.
- **Root Cause Analysis**: An explanation of the underlying causes for each non-conformance, demonstrating the thoroughness of the audit analysis.
- **Risk Assessment**: An evaluation of the risks associated with each finding, highlighting the potential impact on the organization.
- **Recommendations**: Practical and actionable recommendations for corrective actions, designed to address the root causes and mitigate risks.
- **Conclusion**: A summary of the audit's overall conclusions, reinforcing the importance of the findings and the need for corrective actions.

8.5.2.2 Writing the Audit Report

When writing the audit report, clarity and precision are paramount. The language should be clear and straightforward, avoiding jargon and overly technical terms unless necessary. Each section should be logically organized, with headings and subheadings used to enhance readability. The use of bullet points, tables, and charts can help present complex information in a more digestible format.

8.5.2.3 Reviewing and Finalizing the Report

Before finalizing the audit report, it is essential to review it for accuracy, completeness, and clarity. The audit team should cross-check the findings and recommendations to ensure they are supported by the evidence collected. Any ambiguities or inconsistencies should be resolved, and the report should be proofread to eliminate grammatical and typographical errors.

8.5.3 Communication of Audit Results

8.5.3.1 Distribution of the Report

Once the audit report is finalized, it is distributed to the relevant **stakeholders**. This typically includes senior management, the auditee, and any regulatory bodies if applicable. The distribution should be timely to ensure that the findings and recommendations can be addressed promptly.

8.5.3.2 Presenting the Findings

In addition to distributing the written report, the audit team may present the findings to stakeholders through meetings or presentations. This provides an opportunity to discuss the findings in detail, answer questions, and clarify any points of confusion. Effective presentation of the findings helps ensure that the stakeholders fully understand the audit results and the importance of the recommended actions.

8.5.3.3 Follow-up on Corrective Actions

Effective communication also involves **follow-up** to ensure that the recommended corrective actions are implemented. The audit team should establish a process for tracking the progress of these actions and verifying their implementation. Regular follow-up audits or reviews help ensure that the issues identified in the original audit are addressed and that improvements are sustained.

In conclusion, audit analysis and report preparation are critical stages in the audit process, providing a thorough examination of findings and clear communication of results. By following a structured approach to analysis and reporting, organizations can ensure that audits lead to meaningful improvements, enhanced compliance, and better overall performance.

8.6 Audit Follow-Up

Audit follow-up is an essential phase in the audit process, ensuring that the findings and recommendations from the audit are addressed effectively and that improvements are implemented and sustained over time. This phase involves verifying that corrective actions have been taken, assessing their effectiveness, and ensuring that the organization remains compliant with relevant standards and regulations.

8.6.1 Importance of Audit Follow-Up

The **importance** of audit follow-up cannot be overstated. Without follow-up, the audit process would be incomplete, as there would be no mechanism to ensure that the issues identified during the audit are resolved. Follow-up helps in closing the loop on the audit process by ensuring that corrective actions are not only implemented but also effective in addressing the root causes of the identified issues. This phase enhances the overall impact of the audit, contributing to continuous improvement, risk mitigation, and regulatory compliance.

8.6.2 Planning for Follow-Up

Planning for follow-up starts immediately after the audit report is finalized and communicated to the relevant stakeholders. The audit team should develop a follow-up plan that outlines the timeline for follow-up activities, the specific areas to be reviewed, and the methods to be used. The plan should be detailed and tailored to the nature and severity of the findings, prioritizing high-risk areas and critical non-conformances.

8.6.2.1 Timeline for Follow-Up

The **timeline** for follow-up should be clearly defined, with specific dates for follow-up reviews or audits. The timing of follow-up activities depends on the nature of the findings and the complexity of the corrective actions. For instance, critical non-conformances that pose significant risks may require immediate follow-up, while less severe issues may be scheduled for review after a few months. A well-defined timeline ensures that follow-up activities are conducted in a timely manner, preventing delays in resolving issues.

8.6.2.2 Methods for Follow-Up

The **methods** for follow-up can vary depending on the nature of the findings and the corrective actions. Common methods include document reviews, interviews, observations, and re-audits. Document reviews involve examining records and documentation related to the corrective actions to verify their implementation. Interviews with key personnel can provide insights into the effectiveness of the actions taken and any challenges faced during implementation. Observations of processes and practices can help assess whether the corrective actions have been integrated into daily operations. In some cases, a **re-audit** may be necessary to conduct a comprehensive review of the affected areas and ensure that the issues have been fully resolved.

8.6.3 Conducting Follow-Up Activities

Once the follow-up plan is in place, the audit team proceeds with conducting the follow-up activities. This phase involves several steps to ensure that the corrective actions are thoroughly reviewed and assessed.

8.6.3.1 Verification of Corrective Actions

The primary objective of follow-up is to **verify** that the corrective actions have been implemented as recommended. The audit team reviews the evidence provided by the auditee, such as updated procedures, training records, and process changes. The team checks for compliance with the recommended actions and ensures that the issues identified in the original audit have been addressed. Verification involves a detailed examination of the corrective actions to confirm their implementation and effectiveness.

8.6.3.2 Assessing Effectiveness

Beyond verifying implementation, it is crucial to **assess the effectiveness** of the corrective actions. This involves evaluating whether the actions have successfully addressed the root causes of the non-conformances and have led to sustainable improvements. The audit team assesses the impact of the corrective actions on the organization's processes, quality, and compliance. For instance, if a finding related to inadequate training was identified, the team would evaluate whether the new training programs have improved employee competence and reduced errors.

8.6.3.3 Continuous Monitoring

Continuous monitoring is an integral part of the follow-up process. It involves regularly reviewing the affected areas to ensure that the corrective actions remain effective over time. Continuous monitoring helps in identifying any new issues or emerging risks, allowing for timely interventions. Tools such as real-time data analytics, key performance indicators (KPIs), and internal audits can support continuous monitoring efforts. This proactive approach helps maintain high standards of quality and compliance.

8.6.4 Reporting Follow-Up Results

The results of the follow-up activities are documented in a **follow-up report**, which provides a detailed account of the verification and assessment processes. The follow-up report should include:

- **Summary of Follow-Up Activities**: A brief overview of the follow-up activities conducted, including the methods used and the areas reviewed.
- **Status of Corrective Actions**: A detailed status update on the implementation of each corrective action, indicating whether the action has been completed, is in progress, or has not been started.
- **Effectiveness Assessment**: An evaluation of the effectiveness of the corrective actions, highlighting any improvements observed and any remaining issues or new risks identified.
- **Recommendations**: Additional recommendations for further actions, if necessary, to address any unresolved issues or to enhance the effectiveness of the corrective actions.
- **Conclusion**: A summary of the overall follow-up process, reinforcing the importance of continuous improvement and compliance.

8.6.5 Communication and Follow-Up Closure

The follow-up report is communicated to the relevant **stakeholders**, including senior management and the auditee. Clear and timely communication ensures that the findings and recommendations are understood and acted upon. The audit team discusses the follow-up results with the auditee, addressing any concerns or questions. The follow-up process is considered **closed** once all corrective actions have been implemented and verified, and the issues identified during the original audit have been resolved.

8.7 Auditing/Inspection of Manufacturing Facilities by Regulatory Agencies

Auditing and inspection of manufacturing facilities by regulatory agencies are critical components of the pharmaceutical industry's compliance framework. These audits and inspections ensure that manufacturing processes meet stringent regulatory standards, safeguarding the quality, safety, and efficacy of pharmaceutical products. Regulatory agencies such as the **Food and Drug Administration (FDA)**, the **European Medicines Agency (EMA)**, and other national health authorities conduct these audits to enforce Good Manufacturing Practices (GMP) and other regulatory requirements.

8.7.1 Purpose and Importance

The primary **purpose** of regulatory audits and inspections is to verify that pharmaceutical manufacturers comply with applicable laws, regulations, and guidelines. These audits assess whether manufacturing facilities adhere to GMP standards, which cover all aspects of production, including raw material sourcing, equipment maintenance, personnel training, hygiene practices, and quality control. Ensuring compliance with these standards is crucial to prevent contamination, mix-ups, deviations, and other issues that could compromise product quality and patient safety.

Importance of regulatory audits lies in their role in maintaining public health and confidence in pharmaceutical products. Regulatory audits help identify deficiencies in manufacturing processes and systems, prompting corrective actions to rectify these issues. They also serve as a deterrent against non-compliance, encouraging manufacturers to maintain high standards continuously. Additionally, regulatory audits support the approval process for new drugs and the ongoing compliance of marketed products, ensuring that they meet the required standards throughout their lifecycle.

8.7.2 Types of Regulatory Audits and Inspections

Regulatory agencies conduct various types of audits and inspections based on their objectives and the specific circumstances. These include:

8.7.2.1 Routine Inspections

Routine inspections are scheduled visits conducted at regular intervals to assess ongoing compliance with GMP and other regulatory requirements. These inspections are comprehensive, covering all aspects of the manufacturing process. They are usually announced, allowing manufacturers to prepare and ensure that all documentation and processes are in order. Routine inspections help maintain consistent compliance and identify any emerging issues before they escalate.

8.7.2.2 Pre-Approval Inspections

Pre-approval inspections (PAIs) are conducted before the regulatory agency grants approval for a new drug or a significant manufacturing change. The purpose of these inspections is to verify that the facility is capable of producing the drug according to the submitted application and that it meets GMP standards. PAIs focus on validating the processes, controls, and documentation associated with the new product or change, ensuring that the manufacturer can consistently produce a high-quality product.

8.7.2.3 For-Cause Inspections

For-cause inspections are initiated in response to specific concerns or complaints about a manufacturing facility. These concerns may arise from adverse event reports, product recalls, or other indications of potential non-compliance. For-cause inspections are typically unannounced and targeted, focusing on the specific issues that prompted the inspection. The objective is to investigate the root cause of the problem and determine whether there are broader compliance issues within the facility.

8.7.2.4 Follow-Up Inspections

Follow-up inspections are conducted to verify that a manufacturer has implemented corrective actions in response to previous inspection findings. These inspections ensure that the identified deficiencies have been addressed effectively and that the facility is now in compliance with regulatory requirements. Follow-up inspections are crucial for ensuring that corrective actions lead to sustained improvements in manufacturing practices.

8.7.3 Preparation for Regulatory Inspections

Proper **preparation** is essential for successfully navigating regulatory inspections. Manufacturers must ensure that all aspects of their operations are compliant with GMP and other regulatory standards.

8.7.3.1 Documentation and Record Keeping

Maintaining comprehensive and accurate **documentation** is critical for regulatory compliance. This includes standard operating procedures (SOPs), batch records, training logs, equipment maintenance records, and quality control data. Documentation should be organized and easily accessible, allowing inspectors to verify compliance quickly. Regular reviews and updates of documents ensure that they reflect current practices and regulatory requirements.

8.7.3.2 Staff Training and Awareness

Personnel should be well-trained and aware of their roles and responsibilities during regulatory inspections. Regular **training** sessions and mock inspections can help staff understand what to expect and how to interact with inspectors. Ensuring that employees are knowledgeable about GMP and their specific duties fosters a culture of compliance and readiness.

8.7.3.3 Facility Cleanliness and Maintenance

Regulatory inspectors pay close attention to the **cleanliness** and **maintenance** of manufacturing facilities. Ensuring that the facility is clean, well-organized, and in good repair is crucial for demonstrating compliance. Routine cleaning, preventive maintenance, and prompt repairs help maintain a state of readiness for inspections.

8.7.4 Conducting Regulatory Inspections

During the inspection, regulatory inspectors follow a structured process to evaluate the facility's compliance with regulatory standards.

8.7.4.1 Opening Meeting

The inspection typically begins with an **opening meeting**, where the inspectors introduce themselves, outline the inspection scope and objectives, and review the inspection agenda. This meeting provides an opportunity for the manufacturer to ask questions and clarify any concerns about the inspection process.

8.7.4.2 Facility Tour and Observations

Inspectors conduct a **tour** of the facility to observe manufacturing processes, equipment, and hygiene practices. They may take notes, photographs, and samples to document their observations. Inspectors look for compliance with GMP standards, identifying any deviations or deficiencies.

8.7.4.3 Document Review

A significant portion of the inspection involves reviewing **documentation**. Inspectors examine SOPs, batch records, quality control data, and other records to verify that processes are documented correctly and that the facility operates in compliance with regulatory requirements. They may also request additional documents or clarifications as needed.

8.7.4.4 Interviews with Personnel

Inspectors may conduct **interviews** with key personnel to assess their understanding of GMP requirements and their roles in maintaining compliance. These interviews help inspectors gauge the effectiveness of the training programs and the overall compliance culture within the organization.

8.7.4.5 Closing Meeting

The inspection concludes with a **closing meeting**, where inspectors present their preliminary findings and discuss any identified deficiencies. This meeting provides an opportunity for the manufacturer to respond to the findings, provide additional information, or clarify any misunderstandings. Inspectors may issue a formal inspection report detailing their findings and any required corrective actions.

8.7.5 Post-Inspection Activities

Following the inspection, manufacturers must address any identified deficiencies and implement corrective actions.

8.7.5.1 Corrective Action Plan

Manufacturers should develop a **corrective action plan** to address the deficiencies identified during the inspection. The plan should outline the specific actions to be taken, the timeline for implementation, and the personnel responsible for each action. Effective corrective action plans address the root causes of the deficiencies and prevent recurrence.

8.7.5.2 Implementation and Monitoring

The corrective actions should be **implemented** promptly and monitored for effectiveness. Regular reviews and internal audits can help ensure that the actions lead to sustained improvements in compliance. Continuous monitoring helps identify any new issues and allows for timely interventions.

8.7.5.3 Communication with Regulatory Agencies

Manufacturers should maintain open communication with regulatory agencies throughout the post-inspection process. Providing regular updates on the implementation of corrective actions and addressing any additional concerns helps build a collaborative relationship with regulators. This communication demonstrates the manufacturer's commitment to compliance and continuous improvement.

8.8 Timelines for Audits/Inspections

Timelines for audits and inspections are essential to ensure that the process is systematic, organized, and efficient. Establishing clear timelines helps in planning, executing, and following up on audits and inspections, ensuring that all necessary activities are completed within the stipulated time. This section discusses the typical timelines for various types of audits and inspections, highlighting the key stages and their respective durations.

8.8.1 Pre-Audit/Inspection Phase

The **pre-audit/inspection phase** involves planning and preparation, which are crucial for the success of the audit or inspection.

8.8.1.1 Planning and Scheduling

The initial step is **planning and scheduling**, which includes defining the audit scope, objectives, and methodology. This phase typically takes about **2 to 4 weeks**. During this period, the audit team coordinates with the auditee to schedule the audit dates, ensuring minimal disruption to regular operations.

8.8.1.2 Notification

For scheduled audits, the auditee is usually notified **2 to 3 weeks** in advance. This notification period allows the auditee to prepare necessary documentation, inform relevant personnel, and make logistical arrangements. However, for unannounced audits, there is no notification period.

8.8.1.3 Team Assembly and Preparation

Assembling the audit team and conducting preparatory meetings usually takes about **1 to 2 weeks**. During this time, the team reviews the audit plan, prepares checklists, and gathers preliminary information about the auditee's operations.

8.8.2 Audit/Inspection Phase

The **audit/inspection phase** is the actual execution of the audit or inspection, where data is collected, reviewed, and analyzed.

8.8.2.1 On-Site Audit/Inspection

The duration of the on-site audit or inspection varies depending on the scope and complexity. Typically, it lasts between **3 to 10 days**. For routine inspections, this phase may take **3 to 5 days**, while more comprehensive audits, such as GMP compliance audits, may extend to **7 to 10 days**.

8.8.2.2 Data Collection and Analysis

During the on-site phase, auditors collect and analyze data through document reviews, interviews, and observations. This period overlaps with the on-site audit and is integral to ensuring that all relevant information is thoroughly examined.

8.8.2.3 Daily Wrap-Up Meetings

Daily wrap-up meetings with the auditee help in discussing preliminary findings and addressing any immediate concerns. These meetings typically last about **30 minutes to 1 hour** each day.

8.8.3 Post-Audit/Inspection Phase

The **post-audit/inspection phase** involves compiling findings, reporting, and follow-up activities to ensure that corrective actions are implemented.

8.8.3.1 Report Preparation

Preparing the audit report is a detailed process that usually takes **1 to 2 weeks**. The report includes a summary of findings, non-conformances, root cause analysis, and recommendations for corrective actions. The draft report is reviewed internally before being finalized.

8.8.3.2 Closing Meeting

A closing meeting is held at the end of the on-site audit to present the preliminary findings to the auditee. This meeting typically lasts about **1 to 2 hours** and is crucial for discussing the immediate observations and next steps.

8.8.3.3 Report Issuance

The final audit report is issued to the auditee within **2 to 3 weeks** after the closing meeting. This period allows for any final adjustments to the report based on feedback from the closing meeting and internal reviews.

8.8.3.4 Corrective Action Plan Submission

The auditee is usually required to submit a corrective action plan (CAP) within **2 to 4 weeks** of receiving the audit report. This plan outlines the steps that will be taken to address the identified non-conformances and improve compliance.

8.8.3.5 Implementation and Follow-Up

The implementation of corrective actions is typically monitored over a period of **3 to 6 months**. During this time, the audit team conducts follow-up reviews to ensure that the corrective actions are effective and sustainable. For critical non-conformances, follow-up audits may be scheduled within **3 months** to verify compliance.

8.8.4 Regulatory Agency Timelines

Regulatory agencies often have specific timelines for conducting and reporting on inspections.

8.8.4.1 Routine Inspections

Routine inspections by regulatory agencies, such as the FDA, are typically scheduled every **2 to 3 years**. The on-site inspection usually lasts about **5 to 7 days**, followed by the issuance of an inspection report within **30 days**.

8.8.4.2 Pre-Approval Inspections

Pre-approval inspections (PAIs) are conducted within **3 to 6 months** before the expected approval date of a new drug application. The inspection duration is similar to routine inspections, lasting about **5 to 7 days**.

8.8.4.3 For-Cause Inspections

For-cause inspections are initiated promptly in response to specific concerns and are usually unannounced. The timeline for these inspections is shorter, often lasting **3 to 5 days**, with expedited reporting and follow-up.

8.8.5 Continuous Improvement

In addition to the formal timelines, continuous improvement activities are ongoing. Organizations are encouraged to conduct internal audits and self-inspections regularly, typically **annually** or **semi-annually**, to identify and address issues proactively. These activities help maintain a state of readiness for external audits and inspections and promote a culture of continuous improvement.

8.8 Timelines for Audits/Inspections

Timelines for audits and inspections are crucial in ensuring that the process is systematic, organized, and efficient. Establishing clear timelines helps in planning, executing, and following up on audits and inspections, ensuring that all necessary activities are completed within the stipulated time. This section discusses the typical timelines for various types of audits and inspections, highlighting the key stages and their respective durations.

8.8.1 Pre-Audit/Inspection Phase

The **pre-audit/inspection phase** involves planning and preparation, which are crucial for the success of the audit or inspection.

8.8.1.1 Planning and Scheduling

The initial step is **planning and scheduling**, which includes defining the audit scope, objectives, and methodology. This phase typically takes about **2 to 4 weeks**. During this period, the audit team coordinates with the auditee to schedule the audit dates, ensuring minimal disruption to regular operations.

8.8.1.2 Notification

For scheduled audits, the auditee is usually notified **2 to 3 weeks** in advance. This notification period allows the auditee to prepare necessary documentation, inform relevant personnel, and make logistical arrangements. However, for unannounced audits, there is no notification period.

8.8.1.3 Team Assembly and Preparation

Assembling the audit team and conducting preparatory meetings usually takes about **1 to 2 weeks**. During this time, the team reviews the audit plan, prepares checklists, and gathers preliminary information about the auditee's operations.

8.8.2 Audit/Inspection Phase

The **audit/inspection phase** is the actual execution of the audit or inspection, where data is collected, reviewed, and analyzed.

8.8.2.1 On-Site Audit/Inspection

The duration of the on-site audit or inspection varies depending on the scope and complexity. Typically, it lasts between **3 to 10 days**. For routine inspections, this phase may take **3 to 5 days**, while more comprehensive audits, such as GMP compliance audits, may extend to **7 to 10 days**.

8.8.2.2 Data Collection and Analysis

During the on-site phase, auditors collect and analyze data through document reviews, interviews, and observations. This period overlaps with the on-site audit and is integral to ensuring that all relevant information is thoroughly examined.

8.8.2.3 Daily Wrap-Up Meetings

Daily wrap-up meetings with the auditee help in discussing preliminary findings and addressing any immediate concerns. These meetings typically last about **30 minutes to 1 hour** each day.

8.8.3 Post-Audit/Inspection Phase

The **post-audit/inspection phase** involves compiling findings, reporting, and follow-up activities to ensure that corrective actions are implemented.

8.8.3.1 Report Preparation

Preparing the audit report is a detailed process that usually takes **1 to 2 weeks**. The report includes a summary of findings, non-conformances, root cause analysis, and recommendations for corrective actions. The draft report is reviewed internally before being finalized.

8.8.3.2 Closing Meeting

A closing meeting is held at the end of the on-site audit to present the preliminary findings to the auditee. This meeting typically lasts about **1 to 2 hours** and is crucial for discussing the immediate observations and next steps.

8.8.3.3 Report Issuance

The final audit report is issued to the auditee within **2 to 3 weeks** after the closing meeting. This period allows for any final adjustments to the report based on feedback from the closing meeting and internal reviews.

8.8.3.4 Corrective Action Plan Submission

The auditee is usually required to submit a corrective action plan (CAP) within **2 to 4 weeks** of receiving the audit report. This plan outlines the steps that will be taken to address the identified non-conformances and improve compliance.

8.8.3.5 Implementation and Follow-Up

The implementation of corrective actions is typically monitored over a period of **3 to 6 months**. During this time, the audit team conducts follow-up reviews to ensure that the corrective actions are effective and sustainable. For critical non-conformances, follow-up audits may be scheduled within **3 months** to verify compliance.

8.8.4 Regulatory Agency Timelines

Regulatory agencies often have specific timelines for conducting and reporting on inspections.

8.8.4.1 Routine Inspections

Routine inspections by regulatory agencies, such as the FDA, are typically scheduled every **2 to 3 years**. The on-site inspection usually lasts about **5 to 7 days**, followed by the issuance of an inspection report within **30 days**.

8.8.4.2 Pre-Approval Inspections

Pre-approval inspections (PAIs) are conducted within **3 to 6 months** before the expected approval date of a new drug application. The inspection duration is similar to routine inspections, lasting about **5 to 7 days**.

8.8.4.3 For-Cause Inspections

For-cause inspections are initiated promptly in response to specific concerns and are usually unannounced. The timeline for these inspections is shorter, often lasting **3 to 5 days**, with expedited reporting and follow-up.

8.8.5 Continuous Improvement

In addition to the formal timelines, continuous improvement activities are ongoing. Organizations are encouraged to conduct internal audits and self-inspections regularly, typically **annually** or **semi-annually**, to identify and address issues proactively. These activities help maintain a state of readiness for external audits and inspections and promote a culture of continuous improvement.

8.9 GHTF Study Group 4 Guidance Document

The **Global Harmonization Task Force (GHTF)** was established to harmonize medical device regulations across different regions. One of its key outputs is the **Study Group 4 (SG4) Guidance Document**, which provides comprehensive guidelines on the auditing of quality management systems for medical device manufacturers. This document aims to standardize audit practices, improve audit quality, and facilitate mutual recognition of audit results among regulatory authorities.

8.9.1 Purpose and Objectives

The **purpose** of the GHTF SG4 Guidance Document is to provide a unified approach to auditing quality management systems in the medical device industry. The document's primary **objectives** include:

- Establishing a common framework for conducting audits.
- Enhancing the consistency and reliability of audit outcomes.
- Facilitating international trade by promoting mutual recognition of audit reports.
- Supporting regulatory authorities in ensuring that medical devices are safe and effective.

8.9.2 Structure of the Guidance Document

The GHTF SG4 Guidance Document is structured into several sections, each addressing different aspects of the audit process. The key sections include:

8.9.2.1 Audit Planning

This section outlines the steps involved in **audit planning**, including defining the audit scope, objectives, and criteria. It emphasizes the importance of understanding the auditee's quality management system and relevant regulatory requirements. Effective planning helps ensure that the audit is focused and covers all critical areas.

8.9.2.2 Audit Team Selection

Audit team selection is crucial for the success of the audit. The guidance document provides criteria for selecting auditors, including qualifications, experience, and independence. It also highlights the importance of team composition, ensuring that the team has the necessary skills and knowledge to conduct a thorough audit.

8.9.2.3 Conducting the Audit

This section provides detailed guidance on **conducting the audit**, covering activities such as document review, interviews, and observations. It outlines the principles of auditing, including objectivity, evidence-based evaluation, and confidentiality. The document also provides templates for audit checklists and reports to standardize the audit process.

8.9.2.4 Reporting Audit Findings

Reporting audit findings is a critical aspect of the audit process. The guidance document emphasizes the need for clear, concise, and accurate reporting of audit results. It includes guidelines for categorizing findings, documenting non-conformances, and providing recommendations for corrective actions. The document also highlights the importance of timely communication of audit findings to the auditee.

8.9.2.5 Follow-Up and Verification

This section focuses on the **follow-up and verification** of corrective actions. It provides guidelines for assessing the implementation and effectiveness of corrective actions taken by the auditee. The guidance document emphasizes the need for continuous monitoring and periodic re-audits to ensure sustained compliance.

8.9.3 Key Principles and Best Practices

The GHTF SG4 Guidance Document incorporates several key principles and best practices to enhance the quality and consistency of audits.

8.9.3.1 Risk-Based Approach

A **risk-based approach** is central to the guidance document. It recommends prioritizing audit activities based on the risk associated with different processes and products. This approach helps auditors focus on areas that have the highest potential impact on product quality and patient safety.

8.9.3.2 Auditor Competence

The document emphasizes the importance of **auditor competence**. It provides detailed criteria for auditor qualifications, including education, training, and experience. Continuous professional development and periodic evaluations are recommended to maintain auditor competence and ensure high-quality audits.

8.9.3.3 Evidence-Based Auditing

Evidence-based auditing is a fundamental principle outlined in the guidance document. Auditors are encouraged to base their conclusions on objective evidence obtained through observations, measurements, and records. This approach ensures that audit findings are accurate, reliable, and defendable.

8.9.3.4 Transparency and Confidentiality

The guidance document stresses the importance of **transparency and confidentiality** in the audit process. Auditors should maintain open communication with the auditee while respecting confidentiality requirements. Transparency helps build trust and facilitates the effective implementation of corrective actions.

8.9.4 Implementation and Impact

The implementation of the GHTF SG4 Guidance Document has a significant impact on the global medical device industry.

8.9.4.1 Harmonization of Audit Practices

The guidance document promotes the **harmonization** of audit practices across different regions. By providing a standardized approach to auditing, it helps reduce variability in audit outcomes and enhances the reliability of audit reports. This harmonization facilitates mutual recognition of audit results, reducing the need for multiple audits by different regulatory authorities.

8.9.4.2 Improved Compliance and Quality

The document's emphasis on best practices and continuous improvement helps medical device manufacturers achieve higher levels of **compliance and quality**. By following the guidelines, manufacturers can enhance their quality management systems, identify and mitigate risks, and ensure the safety and effectiveness of their products.

8.9.4.3 Support for Regulatory Authorities

Regulatory authorities benefit from the standardized audit framework provided by the guidance document. It supports their efforts to oversee the medical device industry effectively and ensures that audit findings are consistent and reliable. This consistency helps regulatory authorities make informed decisions about product approvals and market surveillance.

8.10 ISO 13485

ISO 13485 is an internationally recognized standard for quality management systems (QMS) specifically designed for the medical device industry. It provides a comprehensive framework for manufacturers to ensure that their products consistently meet regulatory requirements and customer expectations. This standard is crucial for maintaining the quality and safety of medical devices throughout their lifecycle.

8.10.1 Purpose and Scope of ISO 13485

The **purpose** of ISO 13485 is to establish a quality management system that ensures the consistent design, development, production, installation, and delivery of medical devices that are safe and effective. The **scope** of ISO 13485 extends to organizations involved in one or more stages of the lifecycle of a medical device, including design, development, production, storage, distribution, installation, servicing, and final decommissioning and disposal.

8.10.2 Key Requirements of ISO 13485

ISO 13485 is structured around several key requirements that form the foundation of a robust quality management system:

8.10.2.1 Quality Management System

Organizations must establish and maintain a documented **quality management system** that is tailored to their specific processes and products. This includes creating a quality manual, defining quality policies and objectives, and ensuring that all processes are effectively controlled and documented.

8.10.2.2 Management Responsibility

Management responsibility is a critical component of ISO 13485. Top management must demonstrate their commitment to the QMS by establishing a quality policy, setting quality objectives, and ensuring that sufficient resources are available to achieve these objectives. Management is also responsible for conducting regular reviews of the QMS to ensure its continuing suitability, adequacy, and effectiveness.

8.10.2.3 Resource Management

Effective **resource management** is essential for maintaining a quality management system. This includes providing adequate human resources, ensuring personnel are trained and competent, and maintaining the infrastructure and work environment needed to achieve product quality.

8.10.2.4 Product Realization

The **product realization** process encompasses all stages from initial design and development to production and delivery. Organizations must establish processes for planning, designing, developing, producing, and delivering products. This includes risk management, design controls, validation and verification, and control of production and service provision.

8.10.2.5 Measurement, Analysis, and Improvement

ISO 13485 requires organizations to implement processes for **measurement, analysis, and improvement** to ensure the quality of their products and processes. This includes monitoring and measuring product quality, conducting internal audits, managing non-conformances, and implementing corrective and preventive actions.

8.10.3 Implementation of ISO 13485

Implementing ISO 13485 involves several steps to ensure that the quality management system is effectively established and maintained.

8.10.3.1 Gap Analysis

The first step is to conduct a **gap analysis** to compare the organization's current quality management practices with the requirements of ISO 13485. This analysis helps identify areas that need improvement and provides a roadmap for achieving compliance.

8.10.3.2 Documentation Development

Organizations must develop and maintain the necessary **documentation** to support the QMS. This includes creating a quality manual, standard operating procedures (SOPs), work instructions, and records. Documentation must be controlled and regularly updated to reflect changes in processes and regulatory requirements.

8.10.3.3 Training and Awareness

Training and awareness programs are essential to ensure that all employees understand their roles and responsibilities within the QMS. Regular training sessions help maintain competence and awareness of quality policies, procedures, and regulatory requirements.

8.10.3.4 Process Implementation

The next step is to **implement** the processes defined in the QMS. This involves establishing controls for design and development, production, service provision, and other critical activities. Organizations must ensure that all processes are consistently followed and that deviations are identified and addressed promptly.

8.10.3.5 Internal Audits and Management Reviews

Conducting regular **internal audits** and **management reviews** is crucial for maintaining the effectiveness of the QMS. Internal audits help identify non-conformances and areas for improvement, while management reviews ensure that the QMS remains aligned with organizational goals and regulatory requirements.

8.10.4 Benefits of ISO 13485 Certification

Achieving ISO 13485 certification offers several benefits to medical device manufacturers:

8.10.4.1 Regulatory Compliance

ISO 13485 certification demonstrates **regulatory compliance** with international standards, facilitating market access and approval by regulatory authorities. It helps organizations meet the quality and safety requirements of various markets, including the European Union, the United States, and other regions.

8.10.4.2 Improved Product Quality

Implementing a robust QMS based on ISO 13485 leads to **improved product quality**. By standardizing processes and implementing controls, organizations can consistently produce high-quality medical devices that meet customer and regulatory expectations.

8.10.4.3 Risk Management

ISO 13485 emphasizes **risk management** throughout the product lifecycle. By identifying and mitigating risks, organizations can enhance product safety, reduce the likelihood of recalls, and improve overall patient outcomes.

8.10.4.4 Enhanced Customer Satisfaction

By ensuring consistent quality and compliance, ISO 13485 helps organizations achieve **enhanced customer satisfaction**. Satisfied customers are more likely to trust the organization's products, leading to increased market share and business growth.

8.10.4.5 Competitive Advantage

ISO 13485 certification provides a **competitive advantage** in the medical device market. It demonstrates a commitment to quality and regulatory compliance, which can differentiate an organization from its competitors and build a strong reputation in the industry.

8.10.5 Continuous Improvement and ISO 13485

ISO 13485 is not a one-time achievement but a commitment to **continuous improvement**. Organizations must regularly review and update their QMS to adapt to changes in regulatory requirements, technological advancements, and market needs. Continuous improvement involves:

- **Regular Audits**: Conducting regular internal and external audits to assess the effectiveness of the QMS and identify opportunities for improvement.
- **Feedback Mechanisms**: Implementing mechanisms to collect and analyze feedback from customers, employees, and other stakeholders to drive improvements.
- **Corrective and Preventive Actions**: Addressing non-conformances through effective corrective and preventive actions to prevent recurrence and enhance processes.
- **Ongoing Training**: Providing ongoing training to employees to maintain competence and awareness of quality and regulatory requirements.

CHAPTER NINE

Inspections

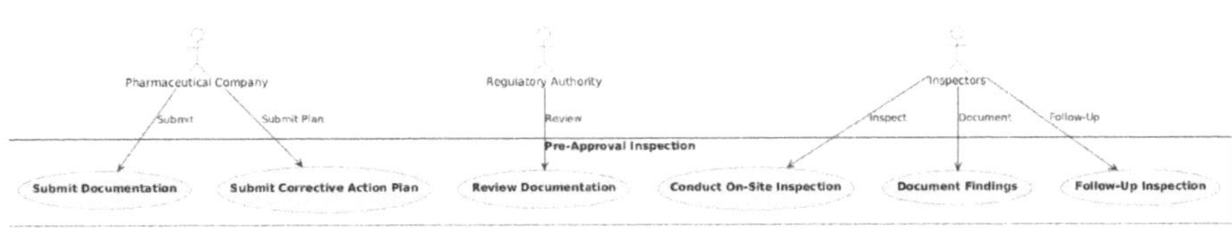

Fig: Pre-Approval Inspections

9.1 Pre-Approval Inspections

Pre-approval inspections are an integral part of the regulatory process for pharmaceutical products. These inspections are conducted to ensure that the facilities intending to manufacture new drugs comply with Good Manufacturing Practices (GMP) and are capable of producing products that meet the required quality standards. The primary objective of pre-approval inspections is to verify that the manufacturing processes, quality control systems, and facilities are adequate and aligned with the information submitted in the marketing application.

Pre-approval inspections typically begin with a thorough review of the documentation submitted by the manufacturer. This documentation includes detailed validation reports, batch records, stability data, and other critical quality attributes. Inspectors meticulously examine these documents to identify any discrepancies or potential issues that could affect product quality. This review helps inspectors understand the manufacturing processes and the controls in place, providing a foundation for the on-site inspection.

The next step in the pre-approval inspection process involves a comprehensive evaluation of the manufacturing facility. Inspectors visit the site to assess various aspects of the production environment. This includes examining the physical condition of the facility, the state of the equipment, and the adequacy of the infrastructure. Inspectors look for evidence of good housekeeping practices, proper maintenance of equipment, and the implementation of contamination control measures. They also verify that the facility layout supports efficient and safe manufacturing operations.

A critical component of the inspection is the evaluation of the manufacturing processes. Inspectors observe the production lines, focusing on key processes such as mixing, granulation, tablet compression, and packaging. They assess whether these processes are adequately controlled and whether there are proper in-process checks and balances. For example, during the tablet compression process, inspectors might check the uniformity of tablet weight, hardness, and thickness. They also ensure that there are systems in place to detect and address deviations from established parameters.

Personnel qualifications and training are also scrutinized during pre-approval inspections. Inspectors review training records to ensure that all employees involved in the manufacturing process are adequately trained and qualified for their roles. They assess whether there are ongoing training programs to keep staff updated on the latest GMP requirements and technological advancements. Inspectors may also interview employees to gauge their understanding of the processes and their ability to handle deviations or emergencies.

Another crucial aspect of pre-approval inspections is the verification of quality control systems. Inspectors evaluate the laboratory facilities and the procedures used for testing raw materials, in-process samples, and finished products. They review analytical methods to ensure they are validated and fit for purpose. For instance, if the product requires High-Performance Liquid Chromatography (HPLC) analysis, inspectors will check the validation of the HPLC method, including parameters such as precision, accuracy, specificity, and robustness. Inspectors also examine the calibration records of analytical instruments to ensure they are maintained and regularly checked.

Sampling and testing of products are often part of pre-approval inspections. Inspectors may take samples of raw materials, intermediates, and finished products for independent analysis. This step is crucial for verifying the quality of the product and ensuring that it meets the specifications outlined in the marketing application. The samples are tested for various quality attributes, such as potency, purity, and dissolution rate. Any deviations from the specifications can lead to further investigation and corrective actions.

The findings of the pre-approval inspection are documented in a detailed report. This report includes an executive summary that provides an overview of the inspection outcomes and a comprehensive account of the observations made during the inspection. The report categorizes the findings based on their severity, highlighting any critical, major, or minor deficiencies. Critical deficiencies are those that could directly impact product quality and patient safety, while major and minor deficiencies may relate to procedural lapses or documentation errors.

Based on the inspection report, the regulatory authority decides whether to approve the facility for manufacturing the new product. If deficiencies are identified, the manufacturer is required to implement corrective actions and may need to undergo a follow-up inspection to verify compliance. Pre-approval inspections are thus a vital mechanism for ensuring that pharmaceutical products entering the market are safe, effective, and of high quality, protecting public health and maintaining trust in the pharmaceutical industry.

9.2 Inspection of Pharmaceutical Manufacturers

Inspection of pharmaceutical manufacturers is a fundamental aspect of ensuring the continuous compliance of pharmaceutical companies with regulatory standards. These inspections are conducted regularly to ensure that manufacturers adhere to Good Manufacturing Practices (GMP), which are designed to guarantee the quality, safety, and efficacy of pharmaceutical products. Inspections are generally categorized into routine inspections and for-cause inspections, each serving a specific purpose in the regulatory framework.

Routine inspections are scheduled at regular intervals, typically every 2 to 3 years, depending on the regulatory authority's guidelines and the risk profile of the manufacturing site. The primary objective of routine inspections is to verify that the manufacturer maintains compliance with GMP over time. These inspections cover a wide range of areas, including quality control, production, personnel, and documentation.

In the **quality control** area, inspectors evaluate the laboratories where raw materials, intermediates, and finished products are tested. They review the procedures for sampling, testing, and validation of analytical methods. For example, inspectors may check the calibration records of instruments like High-Performance Liquid Chromatography (HPLC) and Gas Chromatography (GC) to ensure they are regularly maintained and calibrated. The stability testing program is also reviewed to verify that the products meet their shelf-life specifications under various storage conditions.

In the **production** area, inspectors examine the manufacturing processes to ensure they are consistently producing products of the required quality. This includes observing the equipment used, such as reactors, mixers, tablet presses, and packaging machines. Inspectors check for proper maintenance and cleaning procedures to prevent contamination. They also verify that there are adequate in-process controls to monitor critical parameters during manufacturing. For instance, during tablet production, inspectors may review the procedures for weight uniformity, hardness testing, and disintegration time.

Personnel qualifications and training are another crucial aspect of the inspection. Inspectors review the training records to ensure that all staff involved in the manufacturing process are adequately trained and competent. They assess whether the manufacturer has ongoing training programs to keep employees updated on GMP requirements and new technologies. Inspectors may interview key personnel to evaluate their understanding of the processes and their ability to handle deviations and emergencies.

Documentation is a cornerstone of GMP compliance. Inspectors review a wide range of documents, including standard operating procedures (SOPs), batch records, deviation reports, and corrective and preventive action (CAPA) reports. They ensure that all processes are adequately documented and that records are maintained accurately and promptly. For example, inspectors may check batch records for completeness and accuracy, ensuring that all critical steps are documented and any deviations are properly recorded and investigated.

For-cause inspections are conducted in response to specific issues or concerns, such as product recalls, complaints, or adverse events. These inspections are more focused and aim to identify the root cause of the issue and verify that appropriate corrective actions are taken. For example, if a manufacturer has a product recall due to contamination, inspectors will investigate the contamination's source and assess the effectiveness of the corrective actions implemented by the manufacturer.

A key component of these inspections is the **review of the manufacturer's quality management system**. Inspectors assess whether the manufacturer has a robust system in place to identify, investigate, and correct quality issues. This includes evaluating the CAPA system to ensure that it effectively addresses the root causes of problems and prevents their recurrence. Inspectors also review the internal audit program to verify that the manufacturer regularly audits its processes and systems to identify and rectify deficiencies.

At the end of the inspection, inspectors provide a detailed report that includes their findings and recommendations. The report categorizes observations based on their severity: critical, major, or minor. Critical observations indicate serious deficiencies that could impact product quality and patient safety, while major observations relate to significant non-compliances, and minor observations pertain to less serious issues.

The manufacturer must address the findings and submit a corrective action plan to the regulatory authority. Follow-up inspections may be conducted to verify the implementation and effectiveness of the corrective actions. By ensuring that manufacturers continuously comply with GMP, these inspections play a vital role in safeguarding public health and maintaining the integrity of the pharmaceutical supply chain.

9.3 Inspection of Drug Distribution Channels

The inspection of drug distribution channels is a critical component of the pharmaceutical regulatory framework, ensuring that drugs maintain their quality, safety, and efficacy as they move from the manufacturer to the end user. This process involves a detailed examination of various entities within the supply chain, including wholesalers, distributors, and retailers. The primary objective is to ensure that these entities comply with Good Distribution Practices (GDP) and other relevant regulations, thereby protecting public health.

Storage Conditions

One of the primary focus areas during the inspection of drug distribution channels is the **storage conditions**. Inspectors evaluate the facilities to ensure that drugs are stored under conditions that preserve their quality and stability. This includes verifying that temperature and humidity controls are in place and properly maintained. For instance, drugs requiring refrigeration must be stored in temperature-controlled units with continuous monitoring systems to ensure that the temperature remains within the specified range. Inspectors also check the calibration records of these monitoring devices to ensure their accuracy.

Proper storage conditions also involve ensuring that drugs are protected from contamination, degradation, and damage. Inspectors examine the cleanliness and organization of storage areas, looking for any signs of pests or environmental hazards. They verify that hazardous substances are stored separately from other drugs to prevent cross-contamination. Additionally, inspectors review the procedures for handling and storing returned or damaged goods to ensure they are managed appropriately and do not re-enter the supply chain.

Transportation

The **transportation** of drugs is another crucial aspect inspected within the distribution channel. Inspectors assess the transportation methods and conditions to ensure that drugs are not exposed to conditions that could compromise their quality. This includes verifying that vehicles used for transporting drugs are equipped with temperature control systems if required. For instance, refrigerated trucks must have validated systems to maintain the cold chain throughout the transportation process. Inspectors also review the procedures for loading and unloading drugs to ensure they are handled with care and protected from environmental factors.

Documentation and Traceability

Record-keeping and documentation are essential for maintaining the integrity and traceability of drugs within the distribution channel. Inspectors review a wide range of documents, including shipping records, invoices, and inventory logs. These documents must be accurate and complete, providing a clear traceability of each batch of drugs from the manufacturer to the final point of sale. Inspectors ensure that records are maintained in accordance with regulatory requirements and that they are readily available for review.

Traceability is crucial in the event of a product recall or investigation of a quality issue. Inspectors verify that distribution entities have robust systems in place to trace the movement of drugs through the supply chain. This includes ensuring that there are procedures for recalling products quickly and efficiently if necessary. Inspectors also review the records of past recalls to evaluate the effectiveness of the traceability and recall systems.

Good Distribution Practices (GDP)

Compliance with **Good Distribution Practices (GDP)** is a core requirement for all entities involved in the distribution of pharmaceutical products. Inspectors assess the overall quality management systems of distributors and wholesalers to ensure they adhere to GDP guidelines. This includes evaluating the procedures for handling, storing, and distributing drugs, as well as the training and qualification of personnel involved in these processes. Inspectors ensure that there are written procedures for all critical activities and that these procedures are followed consistently.

Counterfeit Drugs

One of the significant risks within the distribution channel is the infiltration of counterfeit drugs. Inspectors are vigilant in identifying and preventing the distribution of counterfeit or substandard drugs. They review the procedures for verifying the authenticity of drugs received from suppliers and ensure that there are systems in place to detect and report suspicious activities. Inspectors may also examine the packaging and labeling of drugs to ensure they are genuine and comply with regulatory requirements.

Security Measures

Ensuring the security of drugs within the distribution channel is vital to prevent theft, diversion, and tampering. Inspectors evaluate the physical security measures in place, such as surveillance systems, access controls, and secure storage areas. They also review the procedures for handling controlled substances and high-value drugs, ensuring that these products are given additional security to prevent unauthorized access and diversion.

9.4 Quality Systems Requirements for National GMP Inspectorates

The establishment and maintenance of robust quality systems are paramount for national Good Manufacturing Practice (GMP) inspectorates to effectively oversee pharmaceutical manufacturing practices. These quality systems ensure that inspectorates can perform their duties with a high level of consistency, reliability, and integrity, safeguarding public health by ensuring that pharmaceutical products meet regulatory standards.

Standard Operating Procedures (SOPs)

A cornerstone of any quality system within GMP inspectorates is the implementation of comprehensive **Standard Operating Procedures (SOPs)**. SOPs provide detailed instructions on how to carry out various inspection activities, ensuring consistency and accuracy in the inspection process. These procedures cover everything from the preparation and planning of inspections, conducting on-site evaluations, to the documentation and reporting of findings.

Inspectors follow SOPs to maintain uniformity in their approach, which includes specific protocols for inspecting different aspects of pharmaceutical manufacturing, such as production processes, quality control laboratories, and storage facilities. For example, an SOP for inspecting a sterile manufacturing facility would detail steps for evaluating cleanroom environments, aseptic techniques, and sterility testing procedures. This ensures that all inspectors evaluate the same criteria in the same manner, leading to reliable and reproducible inspection outcomes.

Training Programs

Effective **training programs** are essential to equip inspectors with the knowledge and skills necessary to conduct thorough and accurate inspections. These programs encompass initial training for new inspectors as well as ongoing training for experienced staff to keep them updated on the latest developments in GMP regulations and industry best practices.

Training covers a wide range of topics, including the fundamentals of GMP, advanced inspection techniques, and the use of specialized inspection tools and technologies. Inspectors are also trained in soft skills such as communication and negotiation, which are crucial for interacting with manufacturers and handling complex inspection scenarios. Regular training assessments and refresher courses ensure that inspectors maintain a high level of competency and are prepared to address emerging challenges in the pharmaceutical industry.

Audit and Review

A robust quality system includes regular **audits and reviews** to evaluate the performance and effectiveness of the inspectorate itself. Internal audits are conducted to assess compliance with established SOPs and to identify areas for improvement. These audits involve a systematic examination of inspection records, reports, and other documentation to ensure that inspections are being carried out as per the defined procedures.

External audits may also be conducted by independent bodies to provide an unbiased assessment of the inspectorate's operations. The findings from these audits are used to implement corrective and preventive actions (CAPA), enhancing the overall quality and reliability of the inspection process. Regular review meetings are held to discuss audit outcomes, share best practices, and develop strategies for continuous improvement.

Quality Control and Assurance

Quality control (QC) and **quality assurance (QA)** mechanisms are integral to maintaining the integrity of the inspection process. QC involves the systematic monitoring and evaluation of various aspects of the inspection activities to ensure they meet predefined standards. This includes reviewing inspection plans, verifying the accuracy of inspection findings, and ensuring the completeness of inspection reports.

QA, on the other hand, focuses on the overall system for ensuring quality. This includes the development and implementation of quality policies, the establishment of quality objectives, and the regular evaluation of the quality system's performance. QA activities ensure that the entire inspection process is aligned with regulatory requirements and industry standards, providing confidence in the reliability of inspection outcomes.

Information Management Systems

The use of advanced **information management systems** is crucial for effective inspection management. These systems facilitate the collection, storage, and analysis of inspection data, enabling inspectorates to manage their operations more efficiently. Information management systems support various functions, including scheduling inspections, tracking inspection findings, and generating reports.

By leveraging data analytics, inspectorates can identify trends and patterns in inspection findings, helping to prioritize high-risk areas and allocate resources more effectively. These systems also enable real-time communication and information sharing among inspectors, enhancing collaboration and ensuring that all team members are informed of the latest developments and inspection outcomes.

Stakeholder Engagement

Effective stakeholder engagement is essential for the success of national GMP inspectorates. This involves regular communication and collaboration with pharmaceutical manufacturers, regulatory authorities, and other stakeholders. Inspectorates engage with manufacturers to provide guidance on GMP compliance, address concerns, and facilitate a mutual understanding of regulatory expectations.

Inspectorates also participate in international regulatory forums and collaborations, sharing knowledge and best practices with their counterparts in other countries. This helps to harmonize inspection standards and practices globally, enhancing the overall quality of pharmaceutical products and ensuring consistent regulatory oversight.

Continuous Improvement

A fundamental principle of any quality system is **continuous improvement**. National GMP inspectorates are committed to continually enhancing their processes and procedures to adapt to changing regulatory landscapes and industry advancements. This involves regularly updating SOPs, enhancing training programs, and implementing new technologies and methodologies in the inspection process.

Feedback from inspections, audits, and stakeholder engagements is used to drive improvements. Inspectorates also conduct research and participate in professional development activities to stay abreast of the latest trends and innovations in GMP and pharmaceutical manufacturing. By fostering a culture of continuous improvement, inspectorates can ensure that their quality systems remain robust and effective in safeguarding public health.

9.5 Inspection Report and Model Certificate of GMP

The creation and issuance of inspection reports and Model Certificates of Good Manufacturing Practice (GMP) are crucial steps in the regulatory oversight process. These documents provide a detailed account of the findings from GMP inspections and serve as official certification that a manufacturing facility complies with the required standards. The inspection report and the Model Certificate of GMP are essential for ensuring transparency, accountability, and continuous improvement in pharmaceutical manufacturing.

Inspection Report

The inspection report is a comprehensive document that captures the entirety of the inspection process and its findings. It serves as a formal record of the inspection and provides a basis for regulatory decisions regarding the compliance status of the manufacturing facility.

Structure of the Inspection Report:

- **Executive Summary**: The executive summary provides a concise overview of the inspection, including the dates, scope, and key findings. It highlights the main issues identified and gives a brief conclusion about the facility's compliance status.
- **Introduction**: The introduction outlines the background and objectives of the inspection. It includes information about the regulatory framework, the reason for the inspection (routine, pre-approval, for-cause), and the products or processes being inspected.
- **Inspection Team**: This section lists the names, titles, and roles of the inspectors involved in the inspection. It may also include brief biographies to establish their qualifications and expertise.
- **Facility Overview**: A description of the manufacturing facility, including its location, size, and organizational structure. This section provides context about the facility's operations and the types of products manufactured.

- **Inspection Findings**: The core of the report, this section details the observations made during the inspection. Findings are categorized based on their severity:

  - **Critical Deficiencies**: Issues that pose a significant risk to product quality and patient safety. These require immediate corrective action.
  - **Major Deficiencies**: Significant non-compliances that could potentially affect product quality. These need to be addressed promptly.
  - **Minor Deficiencies**: Less severe issues that do not immediately impact product quality but should be corrected to maintain compliance.

- **Supporting Evidence**: This section includes documentation and data supporting the inspection findings. It may contain photographs, test results, and excerpts from records reviewed during the inspection.
- **Recommendations**: Based on the findings, inspectors provide recommendations for corrective actions. This section outlines the steps the manufacturer needs to take to address the deficiencies and improve compliance.
- **Conclusion**: The conclusion summarizes the overall assessment of the facility's compliance status. It indicates whether the facility is in compliance with GMP requirements and any conditions or timelines for implementing corrective actions.
- **Appendices**: Additional information, such as detailed checklists used during the inspection, copies of relevant documents, and supplementary data, is included in the appendices.

Model Certificate of GMP

The Model Certificate of GMP is an official document issued by the regulatory authority to certify that a manufacturing facility complies with GMP requirements. This certificate is crucial for the facility's ability to operate and for its products to be accepted in various markets.

Contents of the Model Certificate of GMP:

- **Certificate Title and Authority**: The certificate clearly states that it is a GMP certificate issued by the relevant regulatory authority.
- **Facility Information**: The certificate includes the name and address of the manufacturing facility, along with the name of the parent company if applicable.
- **Scope of Certification**: This section specifies the types of products and processes covered by the certification. It may include details about the dosage forms (e.g., tablets, injectables) and manufacturing processes (e.g., sterile manufacturing, packaging).
- **Certification Statement**: A formal statement declaring that the facility has been inspected and found to be in compliance with GMP standards. This statement is often signed by a senior official from the regulatory authority.
- **Dates**: The certificate includes the dates of the inspection and the date of issue of the certificate. It may also include the expiration date or the period for which the certificate is valid.
- **Conditions**: Any specific conditions or limitations associated with the certification are outlined in this section. For example, the certification might be contingent on the facility addressing certain deficiencies within a specified timeframe.

Issuance and Follow-Up

Once the inspection report and Model Certificate of GMP are prepared, they are reviewed and approved by senior regulatory officials. The manufacturer receives copies of both documents. The inspection report serves as a detailed feedback tool, while the Model Certificate of GMP is often required for regulatory submissions, product registrations, and market access.

Corrective Actions and Continuous Improvement

Manufacturers are expected to address any deficiencies identified in the inspection report through a Corrective and Preventive Action (CAPA) plan. This plan outlines the steps the facility will take to rectify the issues and prevent their recurrence. Regulatory authorities may conduct follow-up inspections to verify the implementation and effectiveness of these corrective actions.

Transparency and Public Trust

The transparency provided by the inspection report and Model Certificate of GMP helps build public trust in the regulatory system and the pharmaceutical industry. These documents demonstrate the rigorous oversight that ensures the safety, efficacy, and quality of pharmaceutical products.

9.6 Root Cause Analysis and Corrective and Preventive Action (CAPA)

Root Cause Analysis (RCA) and **Corrective and Preventive Action (CAPA)** are essential elements in the pharmaceutical industry to ensure continuous improvement and compliance with regulatory standards. These processes help identify the underlying causes of problems and implement effective solutions to prevent their recurrence, thereby maintaining the quality, safety, and efficacy of pharmaceutical products.

Root Cause Analysis (RCA)

Root Cause Analysis is a systematic approach used to identify the fundamental reasons for deviations, defects, or failures in the manufacturing process. The primary objective of RCA is to determine the root cause of an issue, rather than just addressing its symptoms, enabling the implementation of effective corrective and preventive actions.

Steps in Root Cause Analysis:

- **Problem Identification**: The first step in RCA is to clearly define the problem. This involves gathering data and evidence related to the issue, such as deviation reports, batch records, and test results. Accurate problem identification ensures that the RCA process is focused and effective.
- **Data Collection**: Collecting comprehensive data is crucial for a thorough RCA. This includes qualitative and quantitative data from various sources, such as production logs, laboratory reports, and interviews with personnel involved in the process. Detailed data helps in understanding the context and extent of the problem.
- **Causal Factor Charting**: This step involves mapping out the sequence of events leading to the problem. A causal factor chart visually represents the relationships between different events and conditions that contributed to the issue. This helps in identifying potential root causes.
- **Root Cause Identification**: Various tools and techniques are used to identify the root cause. Common methods include the **5 Whys**

technique, which involves asking "why" multiple times to drill down to the underlying cause, and **Fishbone Diagrams (Ishikawa Diagrams)**, which categorize potential causes into different groups such as people, processes, equipment, and materials.

- **Verification of Root Cause**: Once a potential root cause is identified, it needs to be verified. This involves testing hypotheses and validating findings through further analysis or experimentation. Verification ensures that the identified root cause is indeed the primary contributor to the problem.

Corrective and Preventive Action (CAPA)

Corrective and Preventive Action is a systematic process that follows RCA to address the root causes of identified problems and prevent their recurrence. CAPA ensures continuous improvement in the manufacturing process and compliance with regulatory requirements.

Corrective Actions:

- **Implementation of Solutions**: Once the root cause is identified, appropriate corrective actions are implemented to address it. These actions are aimed at eliminating the root cause and fixing the immediate problem. For example, if a deviation is caused by a malfunctioning piece of equipment, the corrective action may involve repairing or replacing the equipment.
- **Documentation**: All corrective actions must be thoroughly documented. This includes detailing the actions taken, the rationale behind them, and the expected outcomes. Proper documentation ensures traceability and accountability.
- **Effectiveness Check**: After implementing corrective actions, their effectiveness must be evaluated. This involves monitoring the process to ensure that the problem has been resolved and does not recur. Effectiveness checks may include additional testing, process monitoring, and review of subsequent batches.

Preventive Actions:

- **Risk Assessment**: Preventive actions are designed to address potential problems before they occur. This involves conducting a risk assessment to identify areas of the process that may be vulnerable to similar issues. Tools like Failure Modes and Effects Analysis (FMEA) can be used to assess and prioritize risks.
- **Proactive Measures**: Based on the risk assessment, proactive measures are implemented to mitigate potential risks. These measures may include process improvements, additional training for personnel, updating standard operating procedures (SOPs), and enhancing equipment maintenance schedules.
- **Continuous Monitoring**: Preventive actions require continuous monitoring to ensure their ongoing effectiveness. This involves regular reviews of process performance, trend analysis, and periodic audits. Continuous monitoring helps in early detection of potential issues and allows for timely intervention.

Integration into Quality Management System (QMS):

RCA and CAPA processes are integral parts of a pharmaceutical company's Quality Management System (QMS). They ensure that issues are systematically addressed and improvements are continuously made. Key elements of integrating RCA and CAPA into the QMS include:

- **Policy and Procedure Development**: Establishing comprehensive policies and procedures for RCA and CAPA is crucial. These documents provide guidelines for conducting RCA, implementing CAPA, and documenting the entire process.
- **Training and Awareness**: Ensuring that all employees are trained on RCA and CAPA processes is vital for effective implementation. Regular training sessions and awareness programs help in building a culture of quality and continuous improvement.
- **Management Review**: Senior management should regularly review the outcomes of RCA and CAPA activities. This includes assessing the effectiveness of implemented actions, allocating necessary resources, and supporting ongoing improvement initiatives.

Benefits of RCA and CAPA:

- **Improved Product Quality**: By addressing root causes and implementing effective corrective and preventive actions, the overall quality of pharmaceutical products is enhanced.
- **Regulatory Compliance**: Effective RCA and CAPA processes help companies comply with regulatory requirements, reducing the risk of non-compliance and associated penalties.
- **Cost Savings**: Identifying and resolving issues at their root prevents recurrence, reducing the costs associated with rework, recalls, and waste.
- **Enhanced Reputation**: Consistently delivering high-quality products builds trust and strengthens the company's reputation in the market.

Product Life Cycle Management

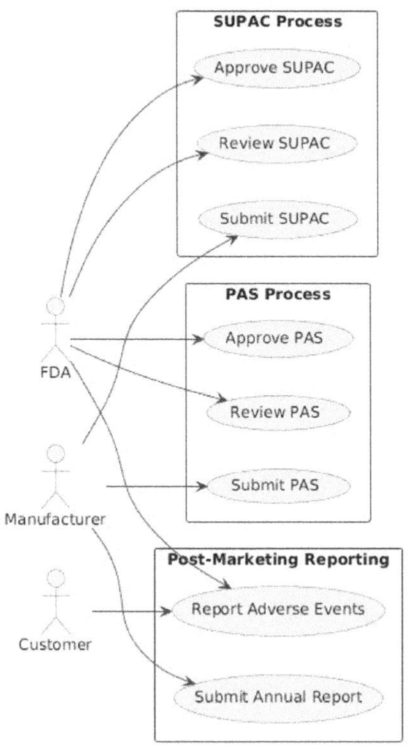

Fig: Pharmaceutical Regulatory Processes: PAS, SUPAC, and Post-Marketing Reporting

10.1 Prior Approval Supplement (PAS)

Introduction

The **Prior Approval Supplement (PAS)** is a critical component in the lifecycle management of pharmaceutical products. It refers to a submission that pharmaceutical manufacturers must file to the **Food and Drug Administration (FDA)** when they propose significant changes to an already approved drug product. These changes can affect the drug's formulation, production process, labeling, or packaging. The PAS ensures that any modification does not compromise the product's safety, efficacy, or quality.

When is PAS Required?

A **Prior Approval Supplement (PAS)** is required for changes that have a substantial potential to impact the drug's quality or performance. These changes can include:

1. **Formulation Changes:** Alterations in the composition of the drug, such as the addition or removal of an active ingredient or excipient.
2. **Manufacturing Process Changes:** Modifications in the manufacturing process that could affect the drug's purity, strength, or stability.
3. **Facility Changes:** Shifting the manufacturing site to a different location.
4. **Packaging Changes:** Significant changes to the drug's packaging that could affect its stability or delivery.
5. **Labeling Changes:** Major updates to the drug's labeling, such as new usage indications, contraindications, or warnings.

Submission Process

The **PAS** submission process involves several critical steps to ensure compliance and thorough evaluation by the **FDA**:

1. **Preparation of Supplement:** The manufacturer must compile comprehensive data and documentation supporting the proposed change. This includes detailed descriptions, justifications, and relevant

research or testing results.

2. **Filing with the FDA:** The prepared supplement is submitted to the **FDA** for review. It must adhere to specific formatting and content guidelines as stipulated by the **FDA**.

3. **Review and Assessment:** The **FDA** conducts a detailed review of the PAS. This involves evaluating the scientific and regulatory aspects to ensure the proposed change does not negatively impact the drug's quality, safety, or efficacy.

4. **Approval or Request for Additional Information:** Following the review, the **FDA** may approve the PAS, request additional information, or reject the proposed changes if they are deemed unacceptable.

Methodology and Procedures

The methodology for submitting a **PAS** involves rigorous documentation and adherence to regulatory requirements:

- **Comprehensive Testing:** Any proposed change must be backed by extensive testing to demonstrate that the modification does not adversely affect the drug. This can include stability studies, bioequivalence studies, and other relevant tests.
- **Risk Assessment:** A thorough risk assessment is conducted to identify potential risks associated with the change and to establish mitigation strategies.
- **Comparative Analysis:** The manufacturer must provide a comparative analysis between the original product and the modified version to highlight the differences and their potential impacts.
- **Quality Assurance:** The PAS must include detailed quality assurance measures to ensure that the modified product consistently meets all required standards.

Regulatory Compliance and Timelines

Adhering to regulatory timelines is crucial in the **PAS** process:

- **Submission Timelines:** The manufacturer must submit the PAS well in advance of the intended implementation date of the change. This allows sufficient time for the **FDA** review process.
- **Review Timelines:** The **FDA** typically reviews PAS submissions within a specified timeframe, often around 180 days, but this can vary depending on the complexity of the proposed change.
- **Post-Approval Monitoring:** Even after approval, the manufacturer must continue to monitor the modified product to ensure ongoing compliance and report any adverse findings to the **FDA**.

10.2 Post Approval Changes (SUPAC)

Introduction

Post Approval Changes (SUPAC) refers to a structured framework established by the **Food and Drug Administration (FDA)** to manage changes made to approved pharmaceutical products after they have been released to the market. SUPAC stands for **Scale-Up and Post-Approval Changes** and provides guidelines for manufacturers to follow when they need to make changes to the formulation, manufacturing process, equipment, or facilities of an already approved drug. The goal of SUPAC is to ensure that such changes do not adversely affect the drug's quality, safety, or efficacy.

Categories of SUPAC Changes

SUPAC changes are categorized into three main levels based on the potential impact on the drug product. These categories help determine the extent of regulatory submission and testing required:

1. **Level 1 Changes: Minor Changes**

    - **Definition:** These are changes that are unlikely to have any significant impact on the drug product's quality or performance.
    - **Examples:** Minor adjustments in the manufacturing process, small changes in batch size, or alterations in packaging components that do not affect the drug product.
    - **Documentation Required:** Minimal documentation is required, and often, a notification in the next Annual Report is sufficient.

2. **Level 2 Changes: Moderate Changes**

    - **Definition:** These changes may have a moderate impact on the drug product's quality and require more extensive documentation and testing.

- **Examples:** Changes in the manufacturing process, scale-up of batch size beyond certain limits, or changes in the formulation that do not affect the active ingredient.
- **Documentation Required:** A detailed report, including validation data, stability data, and a comparison of pre- and post-change product performance, must be submitted. This can be done through a Changes Being Effected (CBE-30) supplement.

3. **Level 3 Changes: Major Changes**

- **Definition:** These changes have the potential to significantly affect the drug product's quality, safety, or efficacy.
- **Examples:** Major changes in the manufacturing site, significant alterations in the formulation, or changes in the primary packaging that can affect drug stability.
- **Documentation Required:** Extensive documentation, including full validation, stability studies, bioequivalence studies (if applicable), and other relevant data. These changes typically require a Prior Approval Supplement (PAS) before implementation.

SUPAC Guidelines and Procedures

The SUPAC guidelines provide detailed instructions on how to document and report changes. The key components of SUPAC procedures include:

1. **Assessment of Change Impact:** The manufacturer must assess the potential impact of the proposed change on the drug product. This involves conducting risk assessments and identifying any critical quality attributes that might be affected.
2. **Testing and Validation:** Depending on the level of change, appropriate testing and validation must be performed. This can include stability testing, dissolution testing, and other quality control measures to ensure the product remains within specified limits.
3. **Documentation:** Comprehensive documentation must be prepared to support the change. This includes descriptions of the change, the rationale behind it, and detailed results from testing and validation studies.

4. **Submission to FDA:** The required documentation and reports must be submitted to the **FDA** for review. For minor changes, this can be included in the Annual Report, while moderate and major changes require specific supplements such as CBE-30 or PAS.

Regulatory Compliance and Timelines

Compliance with SUPAC guidelines ensures that changes to approved drug products are managed systematically and transparently:

- **Submission Timelines:** The manufacturer must adhere to the timelines for submitting documentation and awaiting approval before implementing the change. For example, PAS submissions typically require a 180-day review period.
- **Review and Approval:** The **FDA** reviews the submitted documentation to ensure that the change will not negatively impact the product. Approval must be obtained before the change is implemented, especially for major changes.
- **Post-Implementation Monitoring:** After implementing the change, ongoing monitoring and stability testing are required to ensure the product continues to meet quality standards.

10.3 Changes Being Effected in 30 Days (CBE-30)

Introduction

Changes Being Effected in 30 Days (CBE-30) is a regulatory mechanism established by the **Food and Drug Administration (FDA)** that allows pharmaceutical manufacturers to implement certain changes to approved drug products within 30 days of notifying the **FDA**. This process is designed to expedite the approval of changes that are necessary for maintaining or improving the quality, safety, or efficacy of a drug product without compromising public health.

Scope of CBE-30

The **CBE-30** process applies to moderate changes that have a potential, but not substantial, impact on the drug product. These changes are considered less critical than those requiring a Prior Approval Supplement (PAS) but still require FDA review and documentation. Typical changes that fall under CBE-30 include:

1. **Formulation Changes:** Minor modifications to the drug formulation, such as changes in excipients or non-active ingredients.
2. **Manufacturing Process Changes:** Adjustments in the manufacturing process that do not significantly alter the drug's characteristics.
3. **Packaging Changes:** Changes in packaging materials or configurations that do not affect the drug's stability or delivery.
4. **Labeling Changes:** Updates to the drug's labeling to include additional information, such as new usage instructions, warnings, or minor text revisions.

Submission Process

The **CBE-30** submission process involves several steps to ensure that the proposed changes are properly documented and reviewed by the **FDA**:

1. **Preparation of Supplement:** The manufacturer must prepare a comprehensive supplement that includes detailed descriptions of the proposed changes, justifications for the changes, and relevant supporting data. This data can include results from stability studies, validation studies, and comparative analyses.
2. **Filing with the FDA:** The prepared supplement is submitted to the **FDA** as a CBE-30 submission. The manufacturer must ensure that the submission adheres to the specific formatting and content requirements set forth by the **FDA**.
3. **Implementation Timeline:** Upon submission, the manufacturer can implement the proposed changes within 30 days, unless the **FDA** objects or requires additional information within that period.

Methodology and Procedures

The methodology for a **CBE-30** submission includes rigorous documentation and adherence to regulatory standards:

- **Comprehensive Testing:** Any proposed change must be supported by comprehensive testing to demonstrate that it does not adversely affect the drug's quality, safety, or efficacy. This can include stability testing, dissolution testing, and other relevant quality control measures.
- **Risk Assessment:** A thorough risk assessment is conducted to identify potential risks associated with the proposed change and to establish mitigation strategies.
- **Comparative Analysis:** The manufacturer must provide a comparative analysis between the original and modified product to highlight any differences and their potential impacts.
- **Quality Assurance:** The submission must include detailed quality assurance measures to ensure that the modified product consistently meets all required standards.

Regulatory Compliance and Timelines

Compliance with **CBE-30** guidelines ensures that changes are managed effectively and within the stipulated timelines:

- **Submission Timelines:** The manufacturer must submit the CBE-30 supplement to the **FDA** and await the 30-day period for any feedback or objections before fully implementing the changes.
- **Review and Feedback:** During the 30-day period, the **FDA** reviews the submission to ensure that the proposed changes do not negatively impact the drug product. If additional information is required or if the changes are deemed unacceptable, the **FDA** will notify the manufacturer.
- **Post-Implementation Monitoring:** After the changes are implemented, ongoing monitoring and stability testing are required to ensure the product continues to meet quality standards and to identify any potential issues promptly.

10.4 Annual Report and Post-Marketing Reporting Requirements

Introduction

Annual Report and Post-Marketing Reporting Requirements are essential regulatory mechanisms that ensure continuous monitoring of drug products after they have been approved by the **Food and Drug Administration (FDA)** and released to the market. These reports help maintain the quality, safety, and efficacy of the drug products by documenting any changes, adverse events, or new information that arises during the post-marketing phase. The process involves comprehensive documentation and submission of data to the **FDA** on a regular basis, typically annually.

Annual Report

The **Annual Report** is a mandatory submission that provides a detailed account of the changes and updates made to an approved drug product over the course of a year. The report includes information on various aspects of the drug product, including but not limited to:

1. **Manufacturing Changes:** Any changes to the manufacturing process, equipment, facilities, or personnel that could potentially impact the drug's quality.
2. **Labeling Changes:** Updates to the drug's labeling, including new usage instructions, contraindications, warnings, or changes in the design and layout.
3. **Formulation Changes:** Any alterations to the drug's formulation, including changes in excipients, preservatives, or other non-active ingredients.
4. **Packaging Changes:** Modifications to the packaging materials or configuration that could affect the drug's stability or delivery.
5. **Stability Data:** Updated stability data that demonstrates the drug's continued stability under specified storage conditions.

6. **Adverse Events:** A summary of adverse events reported during the year, including a detailed analysis of any serious or unexpected events.
7. **Clinical Data:** Any new clinical data or findings that have emerged since the last report.
8. **Marketing Data:** Information on the drug's market performance, including sales data, distribution, and usage patterns.

Submission Process for Annual Report

The process for preparing and submitting the **Annual Report** involves several key steps:

1. **Data Collection:** The manufacturer collects comprehensive data on all changes, updates, and findings related to the drug product over the past year.
2. **Documentation:** Detailed documentation is prepared, including descriptions of changes, justifications, and supporting data such as stability studies, clinical trial results, and adverse event reports.
3. **Compilation:** The collected data and documentation are compiled into a structured report following the guidelines provided by the **FDA**.
4. **Submission:** The completed **Annual Report** is submitted to the **FDA** within the specified timeframe, usually within 60 days of the anniversary date of the drug's approval.

Post-Marketing Reporting Requirements

Post-Marketing Reporting Requirements encompass a broader range of reporting obligations that manufacturers must fulfill to ensure ongoing surveillance of the drug product. These requirements include:

1. **Adverse Event Reporting:** Manufacturers must report any serious or unexpected adverse events to the **FDA** within a specified timeframe, typically within 15 days of becoming aware of the event. This includes events that could have a significant impact on patient safety.
2. **Periodic Safety Update Reports (PSURs):** These reports provide periodic updates on the safety profile of the drug, including a summary

of adverse events, risk assessments, and any new safety information that has emerged since the last report.

3. **Field Alerts:** Manufacturers must issue field alerts to the **FDA** in the event of significant quality issues, such as contamination, mislabeling, or defects in the drug product.

4. **Product Complaints:** A detailed record of product complaints received from consumers, healthcare professionals, or other stakeholders, along with an analysis of the nature and frequency of these complaints.

5. **Post-Marketing Studies:** Any post-marketing studies or surveillance programs conducted to further evaluate the drug's safety, efficacy, or optimal use must be reported to the **FDA**.

Regulatory Compliance and Timelines

Adherence to regulatory compliance and timelines is critical for effective post-marketing surveillance:

- **Timely Submissions:** The **Annual Report** and other post-marketing reports must be submitted to the **FDA** within the specified deadlines to ensure continuous monitoring and assessment.
- **Accurate Documentation:** All reports must be meticulously documented, with accurate and comprehensive data to support any findings, changes, or observations.
- **Ongoing Monitoring:** Manufacturers must establish robust systems for ongoing monitoring and reporting, including mechanisms for collecting, analyzing, and responding to post-marketing data.

10.5 Post-Approval Labeling Changes

Introduction

Post-Approval Labeling Changes refer to modifications made to the labeling of a pharmaceutical product after it has received approval from the **Food and Drug Administration (FDA)**. These changes can be essential for ensuring that the information provided to healthcare professionals and patients remains accurate, up-to-date, and reflective of the most current understanding of the drug's safety and efficacy. Labeling changes are vital for communicating new warnings, usage instructions, contraindications, or other important information that could impact patient care and drug utilization.

Types of Labeling Changes

Post-approval labeling changes can be categorized into several types based on their nature and potential impact:

1. **Safety-Related Changes:** Updates related to new safety information, including adverse reactions, warnings, precautions, and contraindications.
2. **Efficacy-Related Changes:** Modifications that provide new information about the drug's efficacy, such as new indications or changes in dosage recommendations.
3. **Administrative Changes:** Minor changes that correct typographical errors, update contact information, or make other non-substantive adjustments.
4. **Formatting Changes:** Alterations in the design or layout of the label to improve readability or compliance with regulatory guidelines.

Process for Implementing Labeling Changes

The process for implementing post-approval labeling changes involves several key steps to ensure regulatory compliance and effective communication:

1. **Identification of Need for Change:** The need for labeling changes may arise from various sources, such as new clinical data, post-marketing surveillance, pharmacovigilance reports, or regulatory requirements.
2. **Preparation of Revised Labeling:** The manufacturer prepares a revised version of the labeling that incorporates the proposed changes. This includes updating the prescribing information, patient information leaflets, and packaging labels as necessary.
3. **Submission to the FDA:** Depending on the nature of the changes, the revised labeling is submitted to the **FDA** for review. The type of submission required can vary:

   - **Prior Approval Supplement (PAS):** For major changes that significantly affect safety or efficacy.
   - **Changes Being Effected (CBE-0 or CBE-30):** For moderate changes that need to be implemented quickly. CBE-0 allows immediate implementation, while CBE-30 requires a 30-day notification period.
   - **Annual Report:** For minor changes that can be documented in the annual report without prior approval.

Safety-Related Labeling Changes

Safety-related labeling changes are critical for ensuring patient safety and must be communicated promptly:

- **Adverse Reaction Updates:** New adverse reactions identified through post-marketing surveillance must be added to the labeling to inform healthcare providers and patients.
- **Warnings and Precautions:** New warnings or changes to existing precautions must be included to mitigate risks associated with the drug.
- **Contraindications:** If new contraindications are identified, they must be clearly communicated to prevent use in populations at risk.

Efficacy-Related Labeling Changes

Efficacy-related changes provide updated information on the drug's use and effectiveness:

- **New Indications:** If the drug is approved for new therapeutic indications, this information must be added to the labeling.
- **Dosage Adjustments:** Changes in recommended dosages, including for specific populations (e.g., pediatric, geriatric), must be accurately reflected.
- **Clinical Trial Data:** New data from clinical trials that provide additional insights into the drug's efficacy must be included.

Administrative and Formatting Changes

Administrative and formatting changes ensure that the labeling remains accurate and user-friendly:

- **Contact Information:** Updates to the manufacturer's contact details, including phone numbers and addresses, must be made.
- **Typographical Corrections:** Correction of any typographical errors to maintain clarity and professionalism.
- **Design and Layout:** Improvements in the design or layout to enhance readability and compliance with **FDA** formatting guidelines.

Regulatory Compliance and Timelines

Compliance with regulatory guidelines and timelines is essential for effective implementation of labeling changes:

- **Timely Submissions:** All labeling changes must be submitted to the **FDA** within the specified timelines, particularly for safety-related changes that require expedited review.
- **Accurate Documentation:** The revised labeling must be meticulously documented, with clear justifications and supporting data for each change.

- **Post-Approval Monitoring:** Continuous monitoring and evaluation of the drug's safety and efficacy are necessary to identify the need for further labeling updates.

• 323 •

- **Post-Approval Monitoring:** Continuous monitoring and evaluation of the drug's safety and efficacy are necessary to identify the need for further labeling updates.

10.6 Lifecycle Management and FDA Inspection and Enforcement

Introduction

Lifecycle Management in the pharmaceutical industry involves a comprehensive strategy to manage a drug product from its development through to its post-market surveillance. It encompasses various stages, including research and development, regulatory approval, market launch, post-approval changes, and eventual discontinuation. Effective lifecycle management ensures the continuous quality, safety, and efficacy of drug products while maximizing their commercial value. **FDA Inspection and Enforcement** play a crucial role in this process by ensuring compliance with regulatory standards and safeguarding public health.

Lifecycle Management

Lifecycle Management involves several critical phases and activities to ensure the sustained success of a pharmaceutical product:

1. **Research and Development (R&D):** This phase involves the discovery and development of new drug candidates. Activities include preclinical studies, clinical trials, and formulation development.
2. **Regulatory Approval:** The drug undergoes rigorous evaluation by the **FDA** to ensure it meets safety and efficacy standards. This includes the submission of New Drug Applications (NDAs) or Biologics License Applications (BLAs).
3. **Market Launch:** Once approved, the drug is introduced to the market. This phase includes marketing strategies, distribution planning, and initial post-marketing surveillance.
4. **Post-Approval Changes:** After market launch, the drug may require modifications such as formulation adjustments, manufacturing process changes, or labeling updates. These changes must be managed according to regulatory requirements.

5. **Post-Market Surveillance:** Continuous monitoring of the drug's safety and efficacy through adverse event reporting, periodic safety update reports (PSURs), and other pharmacovigilance activities.
6. **Lifecycle Extension Strategies:** To extend the product's market life, manufacturers may explore new indications, dosage forms, or combination products. Patent strategies and market exclusivity also play a role.
7. **Discontinuation:** Eventually, the drug may be phased out due to market dynamics, patent expiration, or the introduction of more advanced therapies. A structured discontinuation plan ensures minimal impact on patients and the market.

FDA Inspection and Enforcement

FDA Inspection and Enforcement are critical components of ensuring compliance with regulatory standards throughout the lifecycle of a drug product. These activities involve regular inspections, compliance reviews, and enforcement actions when necessary.

Types of FDA Inspections

The **FDA** conducts various types of inspections to ensure compliance:

1. **Pre-Approval Inspections (PAIs):** Conducted before the approval of a new drug to verify data submitted in the NDA or BLA and ensure the manufacturing site meets Good Manufacturing Practices (GMP).
2. **Routine Inspections:** Regular inspections of manufacturing facilities to ensure ongoing compliance with GMP and other regulatory requirements.
3. **For-Cause Inspections:** Triggered by specific concerns such as adverse event reports, product complaints, or previous inspection findings.
4. **Post-Market Surveillance Inspections:** Focus on ensuring compliance with post-market requirements, including adverse event reporting and post-approval study commitments.

Inspection Process

The **FDA** inspection process involves several key steps:

1. **Preparation:** The **FDA** notifies the facility of the impending inspection and outlines the scope and objectives.
2. **On-Site Inspection:** FDA inspectors visit the facility to review processes, practices, and documentation. They may interview staff, observe operations, and collect samples.
3. **Inspection Report:** After the inspection, the **FDA** issues an Establishment Inspection Report (EIR) detailing findings and observations.
4. **Response and Corrective Actions:** The inspected facility must respond to any observations noted in the EIR, typically through a formal response outlining corrective actions and timelines for implementation.

Enforcement Actions

When non-compliance is identified, the **FDA** has several enforcement tools at its disposal:

1. **Warning Letters:** Issued to address significant violations, warning letters require the manufacturer to take corrective actions within a specified timeframe.
2. **Recalls:** The **FDA** may mandate the recall of a product if it poses a risk to public health. Recalls can be voluntary or enforced.
3. **Seizures:** The **FDA** can seize products that are adulterated, misbranded, or otherwise in violation of regulations.
4. **Injunctions:** Legal actions to halt operations at facilities that fail to comply with regulatory standards.
5. **Civil and Criminal Penalties:** In cases of severe or intentional violations, the **FDA** may pursue civil fines or criminal charges against the responsible parties.

Compliance and Best Practices

Maintaining compliance with **FDA** regulations throughout the drug lifecycle involves adopting best practices:

1. **Robust Quality Systems:** Implementing comprehensive quality management systems to ensure continuous compliance with GMP and other regulatory requirements.
2. **Regular Training:** Ongoing training for employees on regulatory requirements and best practices.
3. **Effective Documentation:** Maintaining accurate and detailed records of all processes, changes, and quality control measures.
4. **Proactive Monitoring:** Conducting regular internal audits and monitoring to identify and address potential compliance issues before they escalate.
5. **Timely Reporting:** Ensuring timely submission of all required reports and documentation to the **FDA**.

10.7 Establishment Inspection Report (EIR)

Introduction

The **Establishment Inspection Report (EIR)** is a detailed document generated by the **Food and Drug Administration (FDA)** following the inspection of a manufacturing facility, clinical trial site, or other regulated entity. The EIR provides a comprehensive account of the inspection process, findings, and any observations related to compliance with regulatory standards. This report plays a crucial role in ensuring that facilities adhere to Good Manufacturing Practices (GMP), Good Clinical Practices (GCP), and other regulatory requirements, thereby safeguarding the quality, safety, and efficacy of pharmaceutical products.

Purpose and Importance of the EIR

The primary purpose of the **EIR** is to document the inspection process and findings in a structured manner. It serves several important functions:

1. **Compliance Verification:** The EIR verifies whether the inspected facility complies with relevant regulatory requirements, including GMP, GCP, and Good Laboratory Practices (GLP).
2. **Regulatory Decision-Making:** The **FDA** uses the EIR to make informed decisions about regulatory actions, such as approvals, warning letters, or enforcement actions.
3. **Transparency and Accountability:** The EIR promotes transparency by providing a detailed record of the inspection process and findings. It holds facilities accountable for maintaining regulatory compliance.
4. **Continuous Improvement:** Facilities can use the EIR to identify areas for improvement and implement corrective actions to enhance their compliance and quality systems.

Components of the EIR

The **EIR** typically includes several key components that provide a thorough account of the inspection:

1. **Introduction:** The introduction section provides an overview of the inspection, including the purpose, scope, and dates of the inspection, as well as the names of the FDA inspectors involved.
2. **Facility Description:** This section describes the facility's operations, including the types of products manufactured, the production processes, and the organizational structure.
3. **Inspectional Findings:** The core of the EIR, this section details the observations made during the inspection. It includes both compliant practices and any deviations or non-compliances identified.

   ○ **Observations:** Specific observations are documented, highlighting areas where the facility failed to comply with regulatory requirements. Each observation is detailed with descriptions of the issue, its potential impact, and supporting evidence.
   ○ **Positive Findings:** In addition to observations, the EIR may also document areas where the facility demonstrated exemplary compliance or implemented best practices.

4. **Discussion and Analysis:** This section provides an analysis of the inspectional findings, discussing the significance of the observations and their potential impact on product quality and safety.
5. **Corrective Actions:** If applicable, the EIR includes information on the facility's proposed or implemented corrective actions to address the observed deficiencies.
6. **Conclusion:** The conclusion summarizes the overall findings of the inspection and provides recommendations for any further regulatory actions.

Process of Generating an EIR

The process of generating an **EIR** involves several critical steps to ensure thorough documentation and accuracy:

1. **Preparation for Inspection:** Prior to the inspection, FDA inspectors review the facility's history, previous inspection reports, and relevant regulatory requirements to prepare for the site visit.
2. **On-Site Inspection:** During the on-site inspection, FDA inspectors observe operations, review documents, interview staff, and collect samples as needed. They document their findings in real-time.
3. **Documentation of Findings:** Inspectors document their observations, both compliant and non-compliant, in detail. They gather evidence, such as photographs, documents, and sample results, to support their findings.
4. **Drafting the EIR:** After the inspection, inspectors compile their notes and observations into a structured report. They provide a detailed account of the inspection process, findings, and any necessary corrective actions.
5. **Review and Finalization:** The draft EIR undergoes internal review within the **FDA** to ensure accuracy and completeness. Once finalized, the EIR is shared with the inspected facility and relevant FDA offices.

Responding to an EIR

Facilities that receive an **EIR** with observations of non-compliance must respond promptly and effectively:

1. **Review and Assessment:** The facility's quality assurance team reviews the EIR in detail to understand the observations and their implications.
2. **Corrective Action Plan:** The facility develops a corrective action plan (CAP) to address each observation. The CAP should include specific actions, timelines, and responsibilities for implementing corrections.
3. **Implementation:** The facility implements the corrective actions, ensuring that all deficiencies are addressed and compliance is restored.
4. **Follow-Up Communication:** The facility communicates with the **FDA** to report on the progress and completion of corrective actions. This may involve submitting documentation and evidence of the implemented changes.
5. **Re-Inspection:** In some cases, the **FDA** may conduct a follow-up inspection to verify that the corrective actions have been effectively implemented and that the facility is in compliance.

10.8 Warning Letters, Recalls, Seizure, and Injunctions

Introduction

Warning Letters, Recalls, Seizure, and Injunctions are critical enforcement tools used by the **Food and Drug Administration (FDA)** to ensure compliance with regulatory standards and to protect public health. These measures are employed when there are significant violations or risks associated with pharmaceutical products. Each tool serves a specific purpose and is applied based on the severity and nature of the non-compliance.

Warning Letters

Warning Letters are formal notifications issued by the **FDA** to a company when significant violations of regulatory requirements are identified. These letters serve as a preliminary step in the enforcement process and require prompt corrective action from the recipient.

- **Purpose:** Warning letters inform the company of specific violations, such as non-compliance with Good Manufacturing Practices (GMP), misbranding, or failure to report adverse events. They provide the company with an opportunity to address and correct the issues before further enforcement actions are taken.
- **Content:** A warning letter details the violations observed during an inspection or review, the regulatory requirements that have been violated, and the potential risks posed by the non-compliance. It also outlines the necessary corrective actions and the timeframe within which the company must respond.
- **Response:** Companies must respond to warning letters within the specified timeframe, typically 15 days. The response should include a detailed corrective action plan addressing each violation, along with timelines for implementation.

Recalls

Recalls are actions taken to remove or correct products that are in violation of laws administered by the **FDA**. Recalls can be initiated voluntarily by the company or mandated by the **FDA**.

- **Purpose:** Recalls aim to protect public health by removing potentially harmful or defective products from the market. They are classified into three categories based on the severity of the risk:

  - **Class I Recall:** Involves a situation where there is a reasonable probability that the use of or exposure to a violative product will cause serious adverse health consequences or death.
  - **Class II Recall:** Involves a situation where the use of or exposure to a violative product may cause temporary or medically reversible adverse health consequences or where the probability of serious adverse health consequences is remote.
  - **Class III Recall:** Involves a situation where the use of or exposure to a violative product is not likely to cause adverse health consequences.

- **Process:** The recall process involves identifying the affected products, notifying customers and distributors, and implementing a strategy to remove the products from the market. The company must also provide the **FDA** with a recall strategy and regular updates on the recall's progress.

Seizure

Seizure is a legal action taken by the **FDA** to take possession of products that are found to be in violation of the law. Seizures are typically conducted through court orders.

- **Purpose:** The primary purpose of a seizure is to prevent the distribution of adulterated, misbranded, or otherwise violative products. Seizure actions are often taken when there is an immediate threat to public health or when previous enforcement actions, such as warning letters, have not been effective.

- **Process:** The **FDA** works with the Department of Justice (DOJ) to file a complaint in court seeking a seizure order. Once the court issues the order, federal marshals or other law enforcement officials carry out the seizure. The seized products are then held until the court determines their disposition, which may include destruction or correction.

Injunctions

Injunctions are court orders that compel a company to cease specific activities or to take specific actions to comply with regulatory requirements. They are one of the most severe enforcement actions used by the **FDA**.

- **Purpose:** Injunctions are used to prevent ongoing violations of the law, protect public health, and ensure that companies take necessary corrective actions. They are typically sought when there is a history of non-compliance or when other enforcement actions have been insufficient.
- **Process:** The **FDA** works with the DOJ to file a complaint in court seeking an injunction. If the court grants the injunction, the company is legally obligated to comply with the terms specified in the order. Non-compliance with an injunction can result in additional legal penalties, including fines or imprisonment.
- **Types of Injunctions:** Injunctions can be temporary, requiring immediate action to address an urgent issue, or permanent, imposing long-term requirements to ensure ongoing compliance.

10.9 ISO Risk Management Standard

Introduction

The **ISO Risk Management Standard** refers to the guidelines and requirements set forth by the International Organization for Standardization (ISO) to help organizations manage risk systematically and effectively. The most relevant standard for the pharmaceutical industry is **ISO 14971**, which focuses on the application of risk management to medical devices, and by extension, to pharmaceutical products and processes. This standard provides a framework for identifying, evaluating, controlling, and monitoring risks throughout the product lifecycle, ensuring the safety and efficacy of pharmaceutical products.

Overview of ISO 14971

ISO 14971 is designed to help organizations manage risks associated with the use of medical devices, including pharmaceuticals that are part of combination products. The standard outlines a comprehensive risk management process that includes the following key components:

1. **Risk Management Planning:** Establishing a risk management plan that defines the scope, activities, responsibilities, and criteria for risk acceptability. This plan serves as the foundation for all subsequent risk management activities.
2. **Risk Analysis:** Identifying potential hazards associated with the product and estimating the associated risks. This involves determining the probability of occurrence and the severity of harm.
3. **Risk Evaluation:** Comparing the estimated risks against predefined risk acceptance criteria to determine whether the risks are acceptable or require further mitigation.
4. **Risk Control:** Implementing measures to reduce or eliminate unacceptable risks. This may involve design changes, protective measures, or user instructions to mitigate identified risks.

5. **Residual Risk Evaluation:** Assessing the residual risks that remain after risk control measures have been implemented to ensure they are acceptable.
6. **Risk Management Review:** Periodically reviewing the risk management process and its outcomes to ensure its effectiveness and making improvements as necessary.
7. **Production and Post-Production Information:** Collecting and analyzing data from the production and post-production phases to identify new risks and ensure ongoing risk management.

Risk Management Process

The risk management process as outlined by **ISO 14971** involves several critical steps to ensure thorough and effective risk management:

1. **Risk Identification:** Systematically identifying potential hazards and hazardous situations related to the product. This includes considering all stages of the product lifecycle, from design and development to manufacturing, distribution, use, and disposal.
2. **Risk Estimation:** Quantifying the risks by assessing the likelihood of occurrence and the potential severity of harm. This step often involves qualitative and quantitative methods to provide a comprehensive understanding of the risks.
3. **Risk Evaluation:** Comparing the estimated risks with the organization's risk acceptance criteria to determine whether the risks are acceptable or require additional control measures.
4. **Risk Control:** Implementing strategies to mitigate identified risks. Risk control measures can include design modifications, protective barriers, safety features, warnings, and user training.
5. **Risk/Benefit Analysis:** Conducting a risk/benefit analysis to evaluate the overall benefit of the product against the identified risks. This analysis helps to justify the acceptance of residual risks based on the product's intended use and benefits to patients.
6. **Verification of Risk Control Measures:** Verifying that the implemented risk control measures effectively mitigate the risks and do not introduce new hazards.

7. **Documentation:** Thoroughly documenting all aspects of the risk management process, including risk analysis, evaluation, control measures, and residual risk assessment. Proper documentation ensures traceability and accountability.

Implementation in the Pharmaceutical Industry

Implementing the **ISO Risk Management Standard** in the pharmaceutical industry involves integrating risk management into all phases of the product lifecycle:

1. **Design and Development:** Incorporating risk management from the early stages of product design and development to identify and mitigate potential risks before they become critical issues.
2. **Manufacturing:** Applying risk management principles to the manufacturing process to ensure consistent product quality and safety. This includes controlling process variables, implementing quality control measures, and monitoring manufacturing environments.
3. **Regulatory Compliance:** Ensuring that risk management activities comply with regulatory requirements and guidelines set by agencies such as the **FDA** and the European Medicines Agency (EMA).
4. **Post-Market Surveillance:** Continuously monitoring product performance and safety in the market to identify and address new risks. This involves collecting and analyzing data from adverse event reports, customer feedback, and clinical studies.
5. **Quality Management Systems:** Integrating risk management into the organization's overall quality management system (QMS) to ensure a systematic approach to managing risks across all functions and processes.

Benefits of ISO Risk Management Standard

Adopting the **ISO Risk Management Standard** offers several significant benefits to pharmaceutical companies:

1. **Enhanced Safety:** Systematic risk management helps identify and mitigate potential hazards, ensuring the safety of pharmaceutical products for patients and users.
2. **Regulatory Compliance:** Compliance with **ISO 14971** demonstrates adherence to international standards and regulatory requirements, facilitating market approval and acceptance.
3. **Improved Quality:** Effective risk management contributes to consistent product quality and reliability, reducing the likelihood of recalls, defects, and customer complaints.
4. **Increased Confidence:** Implementing a robust risk management process builds confidence among stakeholders, including regulatory authorities, healthcare professionals, and patients.
5. **Proactive Risk Management:** Adopting a proactive approach to risk management helps prevent issues before they occur, reducing the overall cost and impact of risk-related problems.

Books

1. Willig, S. H., & Stoker, J. R. (2001). *Good Manufacturing Practices for Pharmaceuticals*. Marcel Dekker.
2. Potdar, M. A. (2001). *Pharmaceutical Quality Assurance*. Nirali Prakashan.
3. World Health Organization. (2007). *Quality Assurance of Pharmaceuticals: A Compendium of Guidelines and Related Materials*. World Health Organization.
4. Gad, S. C. (Ed.). (2008). *Pharmaceutical Manufacturing Handbook: Regulations and Quality*. John Wiley & Sons.
5. Weinberg, S. (1995). *Good Laboratory Practices: The Basis of Assurance of Laboratory Data*. Taylor & Francis.
6. Agalloco, J. P., & Carleton, F. J. (2008). *Validation of Pharmaceutical Processes*. Informa Healthcare.
7. Gupta, M. K. (2011). *Good Distribution Practice: A Handbook for Healthcare Manufacturers and Suppliers*. PharmaMed Press.
8. Sambamurthy, K., & Kar, A. (2006). *Pharmaceutical Regulatory Affairs: Open and Distance Learning (ODL) Education for Professionals*. Pharma Book Syndicate.
9. Lopez, J. (2008). *Fundamentals of Good Manufacturing Practices: Effective Applications*. CRC Press.
10. Wingate, G. (2014). *Pharmaceutical Computer Systems Validation: Quality Assurance, Risk Management, and Regulatory Compliance*. CRC Press.
11. International Society for Pharmaceutical Engineering (ISPE). (2008). *Good Automated Manufacturing Practice (GAMP-5): A Risk-Based Approach to Compliant GxP Computerized Systems*. ISPE.

Regulatory Guidelines and Standards

1. U.S. Food and Drug Administration. (2016). *Current Good Manufacturing Practices (cGMP) Regulations*. Title 21 CFR Parts 210 and 211. U.S. Government Publishing Office.
2. European Commission. (1991). *EU GMP Guidelines (EudraLex Volume 4)*. Directive 91/356/EEC.

3. World Health Organization. (2011). *WHO Good Manufacturing Practices for Pharmaceutical Products*. WHO Technical Report Series, No. 961.

4. International Society for Pharmaceutical Engineering (ISPE). (2008). *Good Automated Manufacturing Practice (GAMP-5) Guidelines*. ISPE.

5. Global Harmonization Task Force. (2012). *Medical Device and IVDs Global Harmonization Task Force (GHTF) Guidance Documents*. GHTF/SG1/N77:2012.

6. U.S. Food and Drug Administration. (2017). *USFDA GLP Regulations*. Title 21 CFR Part 58. U.S. Government Publishing Office.

7. International Organization for Standardization. (2017). *ISO/IEC 17025:2017 - General Requirements for the Competence of Testing and Calibration Laboratories*. ISO.

8. International Organization for Standardization. (2016). *ISO 13485:2016 - Medical Devices - Quality Management Systems - Requirements for Regulatory Purposes*. ISO.

9. International Council for Harmonisation of Technical Requirements for Pharmaceuticals for Human Use. (2019). *ICH Guidelines*. ICH.

10. U.S. Food and Drug Administration. (2003). *21 CFR Part 11 - Electronic Records; Electronic Signatures*. U.S. Government Publishing Office.

11. World Health Organization. (2010). *WHO Good Distribution Practices for Pharmaceutical Products*. WHO Technical Report Series, No. 957.

12. United States Pharmacopeial Convention. (2019). *USP General Chapter <1079> Good Storage and Distribution Practices for Drug Products*. USP.

Articles and Journals

1. Patel, A., & Sharma, R. (2019). "Implementation of Good Manufacturing Practices in Pharmaceutical Industry". *Journal of Pharmaceutical Innovation*, 14(2), 125-134.

2. Kumar, V., & Sinha, P. (2018). "Global Harmonization Task Force (GHTF) and its Impact on Regulatory Affairs". *Regulatory Affairs Journal*, 22(4), 207-218.

3. Smith, J., & Taylor, L. (2020). "Good Automated Laboratory Practices: Current Trends and Future Directions". *Journal of Laboratory Automation*, 25(3), 185-196.

4. Roberts, M., & Jones, D. (2017). "Documentation and Regulatory Writing in the Pharmaceutical Industry". *Regulatory Affairs Journal*, 21(1), 34-45.

5. Agarwal, S., & Gupta, P. (2018). "Good Distribution Practice: Challenges and Best Practices". *Pharmaceutical Commerce*, 29(5), 299-310.

6. Desai, R., & Patel, N. (2016). "Quality Management Systems in Pharmaceutical Industry". *Journal of Quality in Maintenance Engineering*, 22(3), 280-292.

7. Verma, A., & Singh, R. (2021). "The Future of Good Laboratory Practices (GLP) Regulations". *Regulatory Affairs Journal*, 25(2), 140-151.

Websites and Online Resources

1. U.S. Food and Drug Administration (FDA). (2024). *FDA Official Website.* Retrieved from www.fda.gov

2. European Medicines Agency (EMA). (2024). *EMA Official Website.* Retrieved from www.ema.europa.eu

3. World Health Organization (WHO). (2024). *WHO Official Website.* Retrieved from www.who.int

4. International Society for Pharmaceutical Engineering (ISPE). (2024). *ISPE Official Website.* Retrieved from www.ispe.org

5. International Council for Harmonisation of Technical Requirements for Pharmaceuticals for Human Use (ICH). (2024). *ICH Official Website.* Retrieved from www.ich.org

6. Global Harmonization Task Force (GHTF). (2024). *GHTF Official Website.* Retrieved from www.imdrf.org

7. United States Pharmacopeia (USP). (2024). *USP Official Website.* Retrieved from www.usp.org

8. International Organization for Standardization (ISO). (2024). *ISO Official Website.* Retrieved from www.iso.org

9. Pharmaceutical Inspection Co-operation Scheme (PIC/S). (2024). *PIC/S Official Website.* Retrieved from www.picscheme.org

10. Indian Pharmacopoeia Commission (IPC). (2024). *IPC Official Website.* Retrieved from www.ipc.gov.in

11. Central Drugs Standard Control Organization (CDSCO). (2024). *CDSCO Official Website.* Retrieved from www.cdsco.gov.in

Regulatory Agency Publications

1. U.S. Food and Drug Administration. (2011). *FDA Guidance for Industry: Process Validation: General Principles and Practices.* U.S. FDA.

2. European Medicines Agency. (2017). *EMA Guideline on the Requirements for Quality Documentation Concerning Biological Investigational Medicinal Products in Clinical Trials*. EMA.

3. World Health Organization. (2013). *WHO Technical Report Series on Good Manufacturing Practices*. WHO.

4. International Council for Harmonisation of Technical Requirements for Pharmaceuticals for Human Use. (2009). *ICH Q8(R2) - Pharmaceutical Development*. ICH.

5. International Council for Harmonisation of Technical Requirements for Pharmaceuticals for Human Use. (2005). *ICH Q9 - Quality Risk Management*. ICH.

6. International Council for Harmonisation of Technical Requirements for Pharmaceuticals for Human Use. (2008). *ICH Q10 - Pharmaceutical Quality System*. ICH.

Industry Reports and White Papers

1. International Society for Pharmaceutical Engineering. (2008). *ISPE GAMP Good Practice Guide: A Risk-Based Approach to Compliant GxP Computerized Systems*. ISPE.

2. Pharmaceutical Quality Group. (2012). *PQG Guides on Good Manufacturing Practices*. PQG.

3. Pharmaceutical Research and Manufacturers of America. (2016). *PhRMA Reports on Quality and Compliance*. PhRMA.